Sharpening the Focus
of the Church

Sharpening the Focus of the Church

By
Gene A. Getz

Foreword
by
George W. Peters

MOODY PRESS
CHICAGO

Library of Congress Catalog Card Number: 74-2934

ISBN: 0-8024-7902-2

Thirteenth Printing, 1981

Moody Press, a ministry of the Moody Bible Institute, is designed for education, evangelization and edification. If we may assist you in knowing more about Christ and the Christian life, please write us without obligation to: Moody Press, c/o MLM, Chicago, Illinois 60610.

Printed in the United States of America

This volume is affectionately dedicated to my good friends and fellow believers in Dallas, Texas who attend Faith Bible Church and Fellowship Bible Church. It was my great privilege to serve as the first pastor for both of these churches, and it was with these believers that I shared many of the biblical concepts in this volume. As new and growing churches, their response to my ministry in both word and deed has been a continual source of inspiration and motivation to prepare this material for publication.

But Lord,
   I've always bought brown sugar
   in square boxes
   with brown letters on the box.

I saw the plastic bags of sugar in the grocery store yesterday.
I could tell by looking that this was a better way.
   The strong, air-tight bags would keep the sugar soft and usable.
But I've always bought brown sugar in boxes.
   And I reached for the box.

Now, back at home, I wonder why.

Lord, why are we . . .
   why am I . . .
   so reluctant to change old ways?
   Some old ways are valid,
   but some need changing.
And I cling to square boxes with unthinking tenacity,
   just because I've always bought square boxes.

That is not reason enough.
Times have changed—and are changing
   so fast it makes my head swim.
I am obligated to face my days intentionally!
   The container that brown sugar comes in is no great thing.
But there are other, weightier matters
   that require rethinking—and perhaps revising.
If I am going to live significantly,
   I must make my big decisions purposefully,
                     intentionally,
                     comprehensively.

"New occasions teach new duties; Time makes ancient good uncouth.
They must upward still, and onward, who would keep abreast of Truth."

Forgive my square boxes.
                  Amen.

From *Bless This Mess and Other Prayers,* by Jo Carr and
Imogene Sorley. Copyright 1969 by Abingdon Press.
Used with permission.

CONTENTS

ILLUSTRATIONS

FOREWORD

There is no end to the making of books. But there are few books with distinct, relevant and directive messages. Such books are hard to produce. They demand an imaginative and creative mind. Such books do not die by criticism and crucifixion. They blaze new trails for the daring pioneer and explorer in the kingdom of God. Such a book, I believe, is *Sharpening the Focus of the Church* by Dr. Gene A. Getz.

According to the New Testament, the church of Jesus Christ is a glorious church. Christ loved the church and gave Himself for it. He builds it. He walks in the midst of the golden lampstands. It is His church and He will present it unto Himself without spot or wrinkle.

However, the glory of the church has not always and fully been reflected by the local churches in history. This tragic fact we must humbly admit. Because of this many churches are bitterly criticized, cruelly attacked, sadly neglected, and by many coldly rejected as irrelevant, antiquated and meaningless. In some places church buildings are not much more than historic monuments or even museums.

No doubt the judgment of the world is harsh and at times unfair. But is it altogether without reason? Have the churches been true to their divine calling? Have they faithfully served the total purpose God chartered for them? Must we not say even to the churches: You did run well: who did hinder you. . .? This then is our present situation.

But our Lord is not through with His church. He is walking in the midst of the lampstands right here and now. He is graciously leading some of His servants to apply their skills and knowledge to diagnose the ills of the churches and assist them in finding paths of renewal and reconstruction. I believe that Gene Getz has been led of the Lord in his diagnoses and in pointing a way out of a dilemma.

The threefold lens of Scripture, history and culture is effectively and consistently applied and is most searching and helpful. Such an approach points up the fact that the churches are not to live *in* the Bible but *by* the Bible and *in* history and *in* cutlural milieu. And while the former—the Bible—remains constant and is our absolute norm for church life, the latter—history and culture—constantly change and demand form and structural changes in order to remain related to the world in which they are to serve. The process of institutionalization can "freeze" churches into patterns that invite stagnation and death. The way out is the continuous metamorphosis of the churches without changing the changeless message and yielding the standards, ideals and purpose as stated in the Scriptures.

Dr. Getz's scriptural presentation of the New Testament churches is practical ecclesiology made alive and is well documented from the Bible. It puts local churches in the center of the Christian and evangelical movements—where the New Testament places them. It clearly defines their purpose, describes the function and functionaries in the churches and delineates between essential and incidental, the functional and the structural, the content and the form, the pneumena and the phenomena, the biblical dynamic organism and the culturally related organization.

There are details in word distinctions and definitions of preaching, teaching, evangelizing, and witnessing, and the description of offices and officers. The author divides between ministries to and in the local churches and the church universal where differences of opinion and interpretation are permissible without becoming disagreeable.

While in Part One the biblical treatment of the subject is fairly exhaustive, one could only wish the author would have expanded the sections on the historical and cultural aspects, experiences and relationships of the churches. Sufficient is said, however, to give direction to the thoughtful reader who can continue the search for fuller answers.

The book has a message for the churches today and we will do well to ponder it.

GEORGE W. PETERS
Professor of World Missions
Dallas Theological Seminary

ACKNOWLEDGMENTS

I am deeply indebted to a number of Christian men and women who have helped to make this volume a reality. Special appreciation is due my students and brothers in Christ at Dallas Theological Seminary, who, over a period of several years, have continued to prod my thinking regarding the needs and problems of the twentieth century church. Their forthright questions, their comments, and particularly their positive responses to the concepts in this volume have been a perpetual source of stimulation and encouragement.

I am also indebted to a number of my fellow faculty members at Dallas Theological Seminary. Professor Jim Westgate in the Christian Education Department and Dr. Phil Hook, Professor of Systematic Theology, both served as constant stimulators, interpreters and critics of this material in a team-teaching situation.

I am very grateful to Dr. George Peters, Professor of World Missions, who has written the foreword to this work. He also served as a guest lecturer in this team-taught course, and his perceptive world view has made a significant contribution to my own thinking.

Zane Hodges, Professor of New Testament Literature and Exegesis, has also made a unique contribution to this book—especially as he also served as a guest lecturer and interacter along with Dr. Peters. However, he will not agree with all of my conclusions regarding what is pattern and what is principle. A special word of appreciation goes to Mal Couch, president of the Evangelical Communications Research Foundation. Mal and I first field-tested some of these principles together in home Bible classes and later in a "house church."

To my close friend and colleague, Dr. Howard Hendricks, goes special thanks for assigning me the responsibility of coordinating this team effort. I'm deeply appreciative of the freedom he has given me to explore, reconstruct and rethink this foundational course in the light of Scripture, history and contemporary culture.

An additional word of thanks needs to be given to a number of pastors, laymen, authors, and other friends who have helped greatly in their evaluation of this material. As it has been shared across the country in various churches and professional conferences, their response has been highly motivating in helping me to complete this writing assignment.

A final word of appreciation goes to Dr. Phil Williams, Professor of New Testament Literature and Exegesis at Dallas Theological Seminary, who evaluated certain technical aspects of the manuscript.

HOW TO GET THE MOST
FROM THIS BOOK

First, understand its objective. It is designed to help you develop a philosophy of the ministry and a contemporary strategy that is built foursquare on the Word of God. It will *not* give you specific ideas for church form and structure, but rather supracultural principles that can be applied to your specific problems. Furthermore, it will show you *how* to translate these principles into purposes, objectives and goals for your particular church—wherever it may be. And perhaps of utmost importance, it will assist you in involving every member of the body of Christ in the process of creative thinking and constant renewal under the leadership of the Holy Spirit.

Second, understand its form and structure. Several visuals will enable you to get the "big picture" quickly:

The three lenses in figure 1 represent the overall framework for this book.

Figure 2 sets the stage for PART I.

Figure 8 sets the stage for PART II.

Figure 9 sets the stage for PART III.

Figure 13 sets the stage for PART IV.

Figures 14-18 illustrate the process from which the principles were gleaned from the Scriptures and also summarizes the principles.

Figure 19 illustrates the process from which lessons were gleaned from history and summarizes five of these lessons.

Figure 20 illustrates the process from which implications were gleaned from a study of contemporary culture and summarizes some of these implications.

Figure 21 illustrates for you the contemporary strategy in total perspective. It is this tool and the concepts in this book that can help you solve your local church problems.

Third, learn how to use this contemporary strategy. To do this, read the chapters consecutively. As you read, you will find the process greatly enhanced if you follow the suggestions to do your own inductive studies, which are explained in Appendixes A and B.

Once you have read and digested the material, you are now ready to sit down with the spiritual leaders in your church and begin the process with them.

Once they too have the "big picture," use chapter 21 as a "workbook" and together, under the leadership of the Holy Spirit, determine objectives, goals, and standards for your church.

It is the author's prayer that this process will cause the people in your church to change, reshape, and develop functional forms and structures, and to become a dynamic New Testament church in the twentieth century.

1

TOWARD A PROPER PERSPECTIVE

Today we hear much . . . we read much . . . about the church. Some say the church is outmoded—out of date—and will soon be a reflection on the pages of history.

Others say the church is good . . . and necessary . . . but it's not relevant. "The church *must* change!" cry the renewal writers. "It must change or it may die"—at least in its present form.

Then, too, Christians-at-large seem to reflect a general concern and uneasiness about the church—yes, the evangelical church!

Some Christians are downright critical. They feel that regular services and meetings of the church are lifeless and void of real purpose and meaning. Some have taken notes in their Bibles for years as they have listened to good Bible expositions in good Bible teaching churches . . . but they are still asking the question—"What's wrong in my church?" or, more specifically, "What's wrong in my own life?"

TUNNEL VISION

Among evangelical Christians there are probably three major classes when it comes to discussing church renewal. First, there are those who are ready to change almost everything but the doctrinal statement (and some are not so sure about that). The key word in their vocabulary is *change!* The world is changing, and therefore the church, too, must change. "These are those" who having their thinking rooted pretty much in contemporary culture.

Then there are those Christians who are *afraid* of change. Change is threatening. Change is a bad word. In their minds, it is frequently classified as synonymous with theological liberalism.

These people are those whose thinking, attitudes and life style are firmly entrenched in the past. They have developed security in doing

15

things in a certain way. Because of their fears and uncertainties, they have even come to equate tradition with biblical absolutes. Going to church at 11:00 on Sunday morning and at 7:00 on Sunday evening, and 7:30 on Wednesday night is almost as sacred to them as the "virgin birth" and the "second coming of Christ."

Then there is another group—what we might call the "biblical purists." They study the Bible carefully, with little regard for either the past or the present. To them culture and current needs are irrelevant, and studying history is a waste of time. The Bible is enough! "Expose people to the Bible," they say, "and God will do the rest."

In one sense all of these groups are speaking *some* truth—important truth! But in a broad sense, all are wrong—dead wrong! They've all missed the mark. They have all fallen short of formulating a philosophy of the ministry that is truly biblical.

The "Big Picture"

Christians must have the "big picture" if we are to carry out the Great Commission of our Lord. We *must not* develop tunnel vision. We need to develop a contemporary strategy that grows out of at least three sources. Put another way, we must carry out our task today and develop our strategy by looking through three lenses—the lens of Scripture (the eternal), the lens of history (the past), and the lens of contemporary culture (the present). (See fig. 1.) To do less will result in a severe case of ecclesiastical myopia and blurred vision regarding many aspects of the ministry.

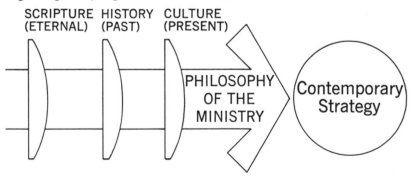

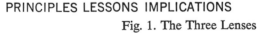

Fig. 1. The Three Lenses

THE LENS OF SCRIPTURE

This concept is treated first for a purpose—because it's basic and foundational to developing a philosophy of the ministry that is truly Christian. Without apology I align myself here with the "biblical purists" in their absolute dependence on the authority of Scripture and their faith in the Word of God to do the work of God.

In a day when everything is changing—from natural surroundings to life styles—thank God for something to believe in that doesn't change; thank God for something that provides absolutes in a day when, in the minds of many, there is no such thing.

At no other time in history than now, in a time of great change, is it so essential to go back to the Scriptures to get our theological bearings. If not, even as evangelical Christians, we're in danger of being swept along with contemporary currents that will lead us in wrong directions.

THE LENS OF HISTORY

To avoid tunnel vision we need to view the church today through a second lens—the lens of the past—the lens of history.

Most important to Christians is "God-breathed" history—the Word of God, itself. Great portions of the Bible contain historical accounts of the way God has dealt with His people. Paul wrote to the New Testament church at Corinth and said, "Now these things happened to them as an example, and they were written for our instruction, upon whom the ends of the ages have come" (1 Co 10:11). Today, both Old Testament and New Testament history can assist Christians to refocus their thinking. Today, we need to take a fresh look at this biblical history to see what lessons we can learn in order to become a thriving New Testament church in a changing world.

But there is also the whole area of history generally, and in particular church history. The pages of the past are replete with the accounts of the church's successes as well as its failures. And these accounts are rich in lessons that can be learned by the church today. The people of God need to study history with a new perspective, for it is in knowing history that we can make more intelligent decisions in this present world.

THE LENS OF CONTEMPORARY CULTURE

There is a third lens that must not be bypassed—the lens that gives us a sharp and clear look at the world around us. The world *is* changing, and so are the minds of men. People think differently today than they did even five or ten years ago. We are living in a new era—some call it the post-Christian era.

There are many currents flowing today that are affecting people generally. We need not have 20-20 vision to recognize the effects of secularism, materialism, sensualism, existentialism, mysticism and institutionalism. Our moral climate has changed, and is changing even more. The technological revolution is making an impact that is staggering.

The church must not close its eyes to contemporary culture. We must understand it, penetrate it, and by God's grace, use it as a bridge to reach people for Jesus Christ. We must also equip Christians to live *in* the world without becoming "a part of it."

DEVELOPING A CONTEMPORARY STRATEGY

Once we develop a proper perspective biblically, historically and culturally, we must develop a contemporary strategy based particularly on New Testament principles. We must determine current needs in our own local church, formulate relevant objectives and goals, devise contemporary forms and structures, and use every legitimate resource to be a New Testament church in contemporary culture.

SUMMING UP

This series is devoted to this task. Part I is a New Testament study particularly, and focuses New Testament *principles*. Part II is a study of a very relevant aspect of history—the history of institutionalism in the church, which yields some important *lessons*. Part III is a look at contemporary culture—particularly, the American culture—and provides us with some significant *implications* for the twentieth century church. Part IV is devoted to a step-by-step strategy illustrating how a church can renew itself, building on biblical principles, historical lessons and implications from contemporary culture.

PART I
THE LENS OF SCRIPTURE

Part I is designed to help you view the church today through the lens of Scripture. By design, it is the largest section because it is felt to be the most significant section. It's a biblical study, and these chapters have been prepared to raise and answer some bedrock questions regarding the church in the New Testament, and in turn to look for principles which will serve as guidelines for the twentieth century church.

What were its activities, and what were the results of those activities? What were its directives and objectives? How did the church relate to the first century culture and community? What were the significant experiences of New Testament believers as they gathered for edification? Who were their leaders? How were they chosen, and what were their qualifications? How did members of the New Testament church communicate with one another and with the world? What were their structures and forms?

This study, of course, is not exhaustive, for who alone can plumb the depths of the eternal Word of God. But it is hoped that it is comprehensive enough to confront you in a new and vital way with that dynamic group of people who changed the course of history—the first century church.

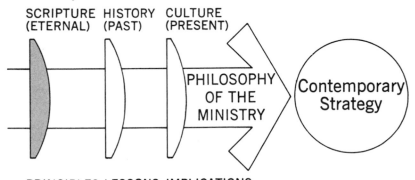

Fig. 2. The Lens of Scripture

2

WHY THE CHURCH EXISTS

Anyone who attempts to formulate a biblical philosophy of the ministry and develop a contemporary strategy, a methodology that stands foursquare on scriptural foundations *must* ask and answer a very fundamental question. Why does the church exist? Put in another way, what is its ultimate purpose? Why has God left it in the world in the first place?

The Bible has not left us without the answer. Jesus Christ, before ascending to the Father, spoke directly to this question. One day on a mountain in Galilee He spoke in clear and simple language. "Go therefore and make disciples of all the nations, baptizing them in the name of the Father and the Son and the Holy Spirit, teaching them to observe all that I commanded you; and lo, I am with you always, even to the end of the age" (Mt 28:19-20).

Earlier He had said in the presence of the disciples, and more specifically to Peter, "I will build My church; and the gates of Hades (the power of death) shall not overpower it" (Mt 16:18).

Now prior to leaving them to carry on His work and to fulfill His prophetic words, He tells them what they must do. MAKE DISCIPLES OF ALL THE NATIONS! The command is clear, concise, comprehensive! First they must wait in Jerusalem for the Holy Spirit (Ac 1:4-5). Then they would "receive power" and become His witnesses—"both in Jerusalem and in all Judea and Samaria and even to the remotest part of the earth" (Ac 1:8).

The disciples understood! The book of Acts demonstrates this beyond doubt. Luke's document is a precise record of the disciples' activities and accomplishments as they seriously and systematically carried out Jesus Christ's marching orders.

Look more carefully at the content of this enormous command.

21

They were to *make disciples*—an imperative. In verse 19 the word "go" in the original text is a participle, along with two additional participles in verse 20, "baptizing" and "teaching." But all of these verbal forms imply *action* and spell out in greater detail what Christ wanted them to do. In essence Jesus is saying, "As you *go, make disciples, baptize* these disciples, and *teach* them to do what I have taught you." Stating it still more simply, the disciples of Christ heard Jesus say that day, "Go everywhere and win men to Christ (that is, make Christians), and then baptize them and teach these Christians the truth that I have taught you."

People who became followers of Christ were immediately identified as "disciples." They were not called Christians until the church was founded in Antioch (Ac 11:26). A clear illustration of the fulfill-ment of Jesus' instructions to *make disciples* as well as *to teach* them is seen in Acts 14:21-22a: "And after they had preached the gospel to that city (Derbe) and had made many disciples, they returned to Lystra and to Iconium and to Antioch, strengthening the souls of the disciples, encouraging them to continue in the faith.[1]

In other words, on Paul's first missionary journey, he and Barna-bas preached the gospel and won many to Christ (made many disci-ples). Later, on the same journey, they returned to Lystra, to Iconium and to Antioch, and strengthened the new Christians (the disciples)— a direct fulfillment of Christ's commission in Matthew 28:19-20.

The church therefore exists to carry out two functions—evangelism (to make disciples) and edification (to teach them). These two functions in turn answer two questions: First, Why does the church exist in the world? and second, Why does the church exist as a gathered community?

When you ask, "Why does the church exist in the world?" you are asking what God expects to do through His people as they come in contact with the unbelieving world! When you ask, "Why does the church exist as a gathered community?", you are asking what God in-tends to happen to believers as they meet together as members of the body of Christ.[2]

---

1. Note that the words "make disciples" in Mt 28:19 and "made . . . disciples" in Ac 14:21 represent the same verb form in the Greek New Testament.
2. It will be shown later that the "church gathered" exists to carry on *more* than a teaching function. Teaching, however, is the first step in developing a body of mature believers. This is demonstrated clearly in the book of Acts.

For the most part, these are separate functions in the New Testament. Both types of activity are very clear and observable, but not always mutually exclusive. The church as a "gathered community" is shown as having distinctive activities and objectives. The church as it ministers to the world likewise has distinctive activities and objectives.

This can best be illustrated with the table "Why Does the Church Exist?" Though space prohibits an exhaustive presentation of all of the New Testament content which illustrates how the early church carried out the Great Commission of our Lord, most of the basic Scripture references and passages are categorized so you can make your own study.

You will note that the two tasks of *evangelism* and *edification* have been classified into two columns. Scripture texts are included which illustrate both the *activity* and *directives* (that is, how these tasks are carried out), as well as the *results* and *objectives* which were achieved. In some instances *evangelistic activity* and *edification activity* are so interrelated in Luke's records they are indistinguishable. In these cases the Scripture texts appear in the middle of the table.

As you study through the New Testament with these two basic questions in mind (that is, "why the church exists in the world" and "why the church exists as a gathered community"), you will discover, of course, that the correspondence which makes up a large segment of the New Testament was written by James, Paul, Peter, John and Jude for the primary purpose of edification. These letters were to be read and studied by the churches for the purpose of spiritual growth and development. Therefore, all of this biblical content should be included in column two in the table. Consequently, each epistle is identified (in name only) somewhere on the table.

However also note that many of the epistles include biographical material and other information and instructions which are particularly illustrative of and pertinent to the tasks of *evangelism* and *edification*. Therefore in addition to including the name of each letter per se in the edification column, selected references from the epistles are also included in both columns.[3]

---

3. An unusual example of this is found in 1 Thessalonians, particularly in chapters 1 and 2 where Paul reflects upon his ministry in Thessalonica where the church was first founded. (See Ac 17.) Paul states ideas and concepts in 1 Thessalonians that are very illustrative of both his evangelistic work among them (1 Th 1), as well as his ministry among the new converts in carrying out the process of edification (1 Th 2).

SUMMING UP

This, then, is where tó begin a study of the New Testament church. Christ's commission states in general terms why He left the church on earth. The book of Acts and the Epistles demonstrate, first, that His disciples took Christ's instructions seriously, and, second, the *way* in which they carried out His command. Put in another way, Matthew 28:19-20 outlines the basic tasks, and the rest of the New Testament fills in that outline with dynamic examples and additional instructions, which help us understand in a more comprehensive way what Christ had in mind for the church on earth.[4]

WHY DOES THE CHURCH EXIST?

Why Does the Church Exist in the World?		Why Does the Church Exist as a "Gathered Community"?	
GOING—MAKE DISCIPLES		BAPTIZING—TEACHING THEM	
EVANGELISM		EDIFICATION	
Activities and Directives	Results and Objectives	Activities and Directives	Results and Objectives
Acts 1:8 Acts 2:14		Acts 2:41-42	
Acts 2:46-47			
Acts 4:1, 2, 4 Acts 4:31 Acts 5:12-14 Acts 5:19-21a Acts 5:25		Acts 4:32	

The list of the epistles in the "edification" column is not meant to be completely chronological and sequential. In some instances they are; in other instances, they are included so as to be ᵢn close proximity to the record of the founding of that particular church in the book of Acts. The general chronologies, however, are based upon Merrill C. Tenney's *New Testament Survey*, rev. ed. (Grand Rapids: Eerdmans, 1968).

4. To assist you with your own inductive study, Appendix A includes a written compilation of the Scriptures outlined in the chart in this chapter. Specific instructions are also given regarding how this study can be done, as well as a visual "model" for recording your findings.

Acts 5:27-28
Acts 5:42
Acts 6:4, 7
Acts 8:1b-4
Acts 8:5   Acts 8:12
Acts 8:25
Acts 8:35   Acts 8:36, 38
Acts 9:20
              Acts 9:31
Acts 10:42-43
Acts 11:19-21   Acts 11:22-26
           Acts 12:24
Acts 13:5a
Acts 13:13-16, 42-44
Acts 13:45-49

                              THE EPISTLE OF JAMES
                                 James 3:1-2

Acts 14:1
Acts 14:5-7
Acts 14:19-21a   Acts 14:21b-23
Acts 14:25   Acts 14:26-28
                                     Acts 15:2-4
Acts 16:31-32   Acts 16:33-34, 40
Acts 17:2-4

                              THE THESSALONIAN LETTERS
                                (written from Corinth)
1 Thessalonians 1:5-10   1 Thessalonians 2:7-12
                                  1 Thessalonians 3:1-5
                                  1 Thessalonians 3:10-13
                                  1 Thessalonians 5:11
                                  1 Thessalonians 5:14-15

2 Thessalonians 3:1

Acts 17:10-12
Acts 17:16-17
Acts 17:22, 34
Acts 18:4-5
           Acts 18:8-11

                              THE CORINTHIAN LETTERS
                               (written from Ephesus and
                                    Macedonia)

1 Corinthians 1:17	1 Corinthians 1:10
1 Corinthians 1:21-24	1 Corinthians 4:17
1 Corinthians 2:1-5	
1 Corinthians 5:9-10	
1 Corinthians 9:16	
1 Corinthians 11:26	
1 Corinthians 14:23-25	

1 Corinthians 15:58

2 Corinthians 1:29	
2 Corinthians 4:5	
2 Corinthians 5:18-20	
Acts 18:19-21	Acts 18:22-23
	Acts 18:24-28
	Acts 19:1-7
	Acts 19:9
Acts 19:8	Acts 19:23; 20:1-2

Acts 19:10, 20

THE ROMAN LETTER

Romans 1:8	Romans 1:9-13

Romans 1:14-16

Romans 13:8-10	

Romans 16:25-27

	Acts 20:6-7
	Acts 20:17-21
Acts 20:22-24	Acts 20:25-35
Acts 22-26 (Paul's	
testimony in Jerusalem,	
before Felix,	
Festus and Agrippa)	
Acts 28:23-24	
Acts 28:30-31	

THE PRISON EPISTLES
Philemon

Ephesians 3:8-9	Ephesians 1:15-19a;
	3:14-19
	Ephesians 2:19-22
	Ephesians 4:11-16
	Ephesians 6:1-4
Colossians 1:25-28a	Colossians 1:9-12
Colossians 4:5-6	Colossians 1:28b-29

	Colossians 2:2-5
	Colossians 3:16
	Colossians 3:18-23
Philippians 1:12-14	
Philippians 1:27-28	
	Philippians 2:1-4
	Philippians 2:19-24
	Philippians 4:9

THE PASTORAL EPISTLES

1 Timothy 2:1-7	1 Timothy 1:3-7
	1 Timothy 4:11-16
	1 Timothy 5:17
1 Timothy 6:1	1 Timothy 6:2
	2 Timothy 1:6-11
	2 Timothy 2:2
	2 Timothy 3:14-17
	2 Timothy 4:1-2
2 Timothy 4:4-5	
	Titus 1:5
	Titus 2:1-15

ADDITIONAL CORRESPONDENCE

	Hebrews 3:12-14
	Hebrews 5:12-14
	Hebrews 6:1
	Hebrews 10:24-25
1 Peter 2:12	1 Peter 2:1-5
1 Peter 2:18	1 Peter 4:10-11
1 Peter 3:1-2	1 Peter 5:1-3
1 Peter 3:15	
	2 Peter
1 John 1:1-2	1 John 1:2-4
	2 John
	3 John
	Jude 3
	Jude 20-21
	Jude 24
	Revelation 1-3

3

MAKING DISCIPLES

Before you read this chapter, complete the inductive study in Appendix A, then study Appendix B. These will provide you with a biblical foundation for the following material.

A PANORAMIC VIEW

Jesus Christ spent three and one-half years ministering on this earth. He went everywhere preaching the kingdom of God to the multitudes, teaching men who He was, and demonstrating His deity by working miracles (Jn 20:30-31).

But He also spent much of His time with twelve men whom He had carefully selected and trained, not in a formal educational setting, but rather in a "field-type" real-life learning situation. They associated with Him in His ministry and they saw Him demonstrate with His own life how to work among men. He eventually sent them out on their own and then carefully helped them to learn from their successes and failures.[1]

Finally after these three and one-half years, Jesus had basically accomplished two major goals in terms of strategy: He had *saturated the minds of the multitudes* with His teachings, and *prepared a small group of men* in depth to enter into His labors and bring in the harvest (Jn 4:35-38). After His death and resurrection (His primary purpose in coming into this world), He gave His followers a great evangelistic commission—"Make disciples"!

They did! They built immediately upon the foundations which Jesus had laid. They began in Jerusalem where He had taught, died, and rose again. Anywhere and everywhere they went—in the temple,

---

1. For an excellent study of how Jesus worked with the twelve, see Robert E. Coleman, *The Master Plan of Evangelism* (Old Tappan, N. J.: Fleming Revell, 1963).

from house to house, before the Jewish council, in the synagogues and on the streets.[2]

Hearts were prepared. The Holy Spirit worked in power! The harvest was great!—*so great* the Jewish leaders were threatened and responded with hatred and counteraction.

But this response only served to fulfill the ultimate plan of God, for believers were scattered everywhere throughout Judea and Samaria and to the uttermost parts of the then known world. Everywhere they carried the message of Christ's death and resurrection and that He truly *was the promised Messiah*—not only for the Jews but also the One spoken of to Abraham so many years before—the One in whom "all the families of the earth" would "be blessed" (Gen 12:3). "And I have other sheep," Jesus said, "which are not of this fold; I must bring them also, and they shall hear My voice; and they shall become one flock with one Shepherd" (Jn 10:16).

Both Jews and Gentiles entered the family of God, after the church expanded its outreach and its impact upon the world.

As a result a new phenomenon came into being—something which had not existed while Christ was on earth. It began in Jerusalem after the ascension and then spread throughout the New Testament world. Wherever the apostles and evangelists *made disciples,* local churches came into being. People who lived in various communities were now brought together in a new relationship as brothers and sisters in Christ—now members of the family of God. A new force was established, not as a "travelling group" but as a people "settled in a community," where they lived, worked and carried on the other routine responsibilities in life.

And as they were taught and edified they soon discovered that they had two basic responsibilities—one "to the world" and the other "to each other."

Interestingly, the epistles contain few instructions regarding direct evangelism as it was practiced by those who "travelled" in the book of Acts. Great emphasis is now placed on "corporate" responsibility. Emphasis on "verbal presentation" of the gospel seems to be subordinated to "maintaining a dynamic relationship within the church" and

---

2. Appendix B includes a compilation of the biblical activities and results, and directives and objectives which grow out of an inductive study of the scriptural materials outlined in chapter 2 and compiled in Appendix A.

"maintaining a loving, exemplary relationship" with those in the world.

Opportunities to present the gospel of Christ were to grow naturally out of the saturation that took place in the community, saturation that reflected "love and concern for all men." Life styles were to be so different and dramatically changed by Christ that unbelievers could not help but notice and inquire what made the difference.

Above all, the love and unity that existed among the local groups of believers were to be so forceful that people outside of Christ would be convinced that they were unusual people—people who were disciples of Jesus Christ. Further, they would become convinced that Jesus truly *was* who He said He *was*.

As Christ was approaching the time of His crucifixion, He remarked to His disciples one day, "A new commandment I give to you, that you love one another, even as I have loved you, that you also love one another." Notice the objective which follows this directive from the Lord Jesus: "By this all men will know that you are My disciples, if you have love for one another" (Jn 13:34-35).

Community evangelism was to be preceded by a corporate example of "love" among believers. It would be "proof positive" that the disciples of Christ reside there. For no other sect, religion, or group was ever capable of rising to the level of love that is potentially possible in the true family of God. And without its existence, evangelistic efforts are thwarted.

But there is another factor here that is basic to community evangelism. It is what Francis Schaeffer has called "the final apologetic."[3] Jesus spoke of it in John 17:21, 23 while He was praying for His disciples. He asked the Father "that they may all be one; even as Thou, Father, art in Me, and I in Thee, that they also may be in Us; that the world may believe that Thou didst send Me. . . . I in them, and Thou in Me, that they may be perfected in unity, that the world may know that Thou didst send Me, and didst love them, even as Thou didst love Me."

Here Christ speaks of the results of love—that is, unity and oneness. By seeing love, non-Christians would come to know and understand that people are Christians, followers of Jesus Christ. But by

---

3. Francis A. Schaeffer, *The Church at the End of the Twentieth Century* (Downers Grove, Ill.: Inter-Varsity, 1970), p. 138.

observing *unity* and *oneness* they would become convinced of who Christ really was—that He came from God—that He was truly the Son of God, the Saviour of the world.

In the book of Acts this phenomena was demonstrated forcefully. It was the love and unity among Christians in Jerusalem that provided the base for effective witness. And this idea, as demonstrated earlier, is reinforced again and again throughout the epistles. But it will be demonstrated even more as we look later at the edification process as it is illustrated in the churches in the New Testament.

A CLOSER LOOK

EVANGELISTIC COMMUNICATION IN THE BOOK OF ACTS

Though a number of words are used to recount the evangelistic activity of these first century believers, Luke uses several basic words to describe the process of communication with non-Christians. Those which follow appear most frequently, and although similar in meaning, each, as used in context, contributes to our understanding of *how* the unsaved world was reached with the gospel of Christ in the first century.

They spoke. One of the most common words is the one translated "speaking" or "spoke." The word *laleo* simply means to talk or to tell. We read that Peter and John were in the temple "speaking to the people" (Ac 4:1). Later as the congregation of the disciples was filled with the Holy Spirit, they all "began to speak the word of God with boldness" (4:31).[4]

Though this word is the most common one used in describing the way the message of Christianity was presented, we can learn several lessons about the process from the context in which the word was used. Frequently we are told they "spoke the word" (their message); they spoke "in the name of Jesus" (their authority); and they spoke with "boldness" (their manner). They were to speak "the whole message of this Life"; and they spoke "in such a manner that a great multitude believed."

They evangelized. This word is frequently translated that the followers of Christ "preached the gospel" or "told the good news." Unlike the word "to speak," this word (*euangelidzo*) is a "content" word

---

4. See also Ac 5:20, 40; 11:19-20; 14:1, 25; 16:13, 32.

in itself. It refers to the message that was being spoken *as well* as the *process* of communication. In Acts 5:42 we read that "every day, in the temple and from house to house, they kept right on . . . preaching Jesus as the Christ"; that is, "they kept right on . . . telling the good news: Jesus is the Promised Saviour" (Beck).[5]

As you look at this word, note carefully that it was a process carried on with both groups and individuals; it was carried out by *all* believers; it took place in the temple, from house to house, from village to village, from city to city, on a desert road, and constantly expanded its outreach to regions beyond. They went everywhere to everyone telling the good news.

They taught. Though *didasko* (meaning to teach) is one of the most common words in the New Testament used to describe the communication process among Christians, it is also used to describe this communication process with non-Christians. In this latter sense, the word appears most frequently in the opening chapters of the book of Acts, and on several occasions is used in a context of displeasure and unhappiness on the part of the Jews. They were "greatly disturbed because they [Peter and John] were teaching the people" (4:2).[6]

Following the apostles' secret release from jail, they all entered the "temple about daybreak, and began to teach" (5:21). Surprised by their appearance, someone rushed off to tell the chief priest that the men they had locked in prison the day before were "standing in the temple and teaching the people" (5:25). The apostles were immediately taken into custody again and in consternation the high priest said, "We gave you strict orders not to continue teaching in this name, and behold, you have filled Jerusalem with your teaching"[7] (5:28).

Perhaps the most significant observation regarding the teaching process with non-Christians as it appears in the book of Acts is that it was used primarily by the apostles. This may imply that it is a more sophisticated process than just "speaking" or "evangelizing," and calling for greater skill and knowledge. Obviously it involved more than just presenting the gospel of Christ, but rather included the presentation of the total message of the Scriptures (see 5:21-22). The

5. See also Ac 8:4, 25, 35; 11:20; 14:6-7, 21; 16:10.
6. See also Ac 5:41, 42; 28:30-31.
7. Frequently translated "doctrine."

apostles, of course, were in a unique position to communicate this message, having spent three and one-half years being trained by the greatest Teacher who ever lived. It is significant that prior to the apostles' imprisonment, the rulers and elders and scribes "observed the confidence of Peter and John, and understood that they were uneducated and untrained men. . ." Consequently, "they were marveling, and began to recognize them as having been with Jesus" (Ac 4:13).

Note too that the apostles' teaching among non-Christians brought both positive and negative results. The positive results were conversions, first among the Jewish laymen. Consequently the negative results came from their religious leaders. Here was one group of religious leaders against another group of religious leaders, false teachers reacting to true teachers. The apostles were presenting the truth, which laid bare the sins and false views of the priests and leaders of Israel. They became jealous and angry and fought back.

But, interestingly, we read in the chapter following this persecution that when the apostles resolved the material problems in Acts 6 and were able to maintain their priorities in teaching the Scriptures, "many of the priests" responded to the gospel (6:7).

Here we see the true test of effective teaching among non-Christians. The apostles not only won laymen to Christ, but eventually won many religious leaders as well.

They proclaimed or preached. The word *kerusso* means to cry or proclaim as a herald. Of all the words used in the book of Acts to describe the communication process with non-Christians, this word is used the most infrequently. It is, however, a very significant word.

We read that "Philip went down to the city of Samaria and began proclaiming Christ to them. And the multitudes with one accord were giving attention to what was said by Philip" (8:5-6).[8]

Significantly this word "proclaim" is used primarily in conjunction with the activities of certain key people in the book of Acts, specifically, Philip the evangelist, the apostle Peter and the apostle Paul. Again, like teaching, this activity among non-Christians seemed to be the responsibility of certain gifted individuals who had been chosen by God to proclaim in a special way the gospel of Christ. (See Ac 10:40-42). All Christians, of course, spoke about Christ and witnessed for Him, but not all proclaimed Christ in a formal way.

---

8. See also Ac 9:20; 10:39, 42; 20:25; 28:30-31.

They announced. A word closely related to *kerusso* is the word *katangello* meaning to announce publicly, or to proclaim and tell thoroughly. Like *kerusso* it is used in Acts in describing the communication of apostolic leaders, particularly the ministry of Paul.[9]

In most cases this word is used to describe communication in the various synagogues of the Jews. Here in these religious centers of learning and worship Paul "thoroughly announced" and "proclaimed" the Word of God.

They solemnly testified. A common word for testify is *martureo,* meaning to bear witness (Ac 1:8). However, throughout the book of Acts some form of the verb *diamarturomai* is used to describe communication with non-Christians and is frequently translated that they "solemnly testified." It means to "earnestly charge and attest." In describing the process of communication, it has both strong intellectual and emotional overtones. The Word of God was being presented seriously, carefully, and with determination. If *martureo* means "to bear witness," *diamarturomai* means "to bear a thorough witness."

This concept first appears in Acts in Peter's sermon on the day of Pentecost, when "with many other words he solemnly testified and kept on exhorting them, saying, 'Be saved from this perverse generation!' " (2:40).

And it appears finally in the last chapter of Acts where we find Paul in Rome. When he arrived he was allowed to "stay by himself, with the soldier who was guarding him" (28:16). Paul called together the Jewish leaders and rehearsed the events from Jerusalem onward. The Jews appointed a day for Paul to present his total case. And on that day, "they came to him at his lodging in large numbers; and he was explaining to them by solemnly testifying about the kingdom of God, and trying to persuade them concerning Jesus, from both the Law of Moses and from the Prophets, from morning until evening" (28:23).[10]

As you trace this word through the book of Acts it is obvious that in context it takes on a strong "apologetic" syndrome. Both Peter and Paul, the two apostles whose communication is described by this word, were attempting to convince their hearers that Jesus Christ was truly the Messiah promised in the Old Testament. They were not

---

9. See Ac 4:2; 13:5, 38; 15:36; 17:3.
10. See also Ac 10:42; 18:5; 20:20-24; 23:11.

simply presenting the gospel but were attesting and giving evidence from the Old Testament as well as from their own personal experience that Jesus was the Christ.

They reasoned. Interestingly the word *dialegomai,* meaning "to reason, to discourse with, or to discuss," is used *only* of Paul's communication with the non-Christian world. And, also, the word does not appear in Acts until Paul arrived in Thessalonica. Here we find him going into the synagogue and "for three Sabbaths reasoned with them from the Scriptures, explaining and giving evidence that the Christ had to suffer and rise again from the dead" (17:2-3).[11]

As you look at the communication process that took place in this new dimension involving extensive dialogue and interaction, it is significant to note that Paul's ministry was increasingly taking him into a pagan environment impregnated with Greek and Roman thought and culture. Both Jews and Greeks were no doubt almost totally ignorant of what had really transpired in the land of Palestine over the last several years. To the Jews the coming Messiah was not a new concept, but the geographic location probably served as a barrier to their hearing much about Jesus of Nazareth. What they *had* heard was no doubt colored with prejudicial meanings and interpretations. The Greeks, of course, would have known little if anything, their only source of information being the Jewish community.

Notice, too, that Luke began recording time factors in the context where this word is used. For example he stayed on in Corinth for a year and one-half (18:11) and in Ephesus for two years (19:10).

Taking into consideration the mentality of these people, their cultural backgrounds, their total ignorance regarding Christianity as well as the method of communication they were used to, the implication seems to be obvious. Paul evidently adopted a methodology in communication that could more effectively reach these people. Furthermore he knew he had no foundation from which to build, and consequently he settled into these strategic communities, got to know the thinking of these people, and taught the Scriptures in depth on their wave length.

EVANGELISTIC COMMUNICATION IN THE EPISTLES

As you trace through the communication process in the book of

---

11. See also Ac 17:17; 18:4, 19; 19:8-10; 24:24-25.

Acts, the emphasis is naturally upon the activities of first century Christians as they *spoke* about Christ, *told* the good news, *taught, proclaimed, testified* and *reasoned* with unbelievers. But as you move to a study of the epistles, activities become directives. This, of course, is what we would expect. Luke's purpose was to record the "acts" of the followers of Christ, and the epistles were written to teach and nurture those who responded to the gospel.

This leads also to a decided shift in emphasis as far as what can be learned about communication in the unsaved world. The epistles add a new dimension to the way this process was carried out by the established churches.

You cannot study these directives and objectives without concluding that the evangelistic thrust launched in Acts was to continue in communities where local churches had been established. Paul was particularly pleased with the impact of the churches in Thessalonica and Rome (1 Th 1:9; Ro 1:8.) Everywhere he went, he seemed to get positive feedback regarding the testimony of these Christians.

But as you read through the epistles with "evangelism" in mind, you soon discover that to be settled in a community calls for more than verbalization. In fact, communication must be solidly aligned with a Christian life style—both at the individual and corporate level. This Christian life style must be demonstrated in the various contexts of living—the Christian's business life, his social life, his home life, his church life, and his life in general.

Business life. Paul admonished the Thessalonians particularly to conduct their business affairs in a proper manner. Some of them were no doubt using the doctrine of the second coming of Christ as an excuse for being lazy. "Attend to your own business and work with your hands," Paul exhorted (1 Th 4:11) and then gave the reason why—"so that you may behave properly toward outsiders and not be in any need" (1 Th 4:12). Paul taught that for a Christian to have material needs because of laziness was to bring the gospel and the church of Jesus Christ into ill repute. If they were to effectively evangelize their unsaved neighbors, they certainly would not be able to communicate the gospel effectively by living irresponsible lives.

Both Paul and Peter were concerned about the fact that Christians should maintain a good testimony before unsaved masters. They were to "regard their (unsaved) masters as worthy of all honor so that the name of God and our doctrine may not be spoken against" (1 Th 6:1). "Be submissive to your masters," said Peter (1 Pe 2:18).

What a way to attack the evils of slavery! In many instances, no doubt, they won their unsaved masters to Christ as well *as their freedom*. To do the opposite in those days may have brought instant persecution and perhaps even death. But most of all, it would have interfered with the cause of Christ.

Regarding Paul's approach to the problem of slavery, Merrill Tenney succinctly observes:

> Nowhere in its pages is the institution attacked or is it defended. According to Paul's letters to the Asian churches, there were both slaves and slave holders who were Christians. Slaves were enjoined to obey their masters, and the masters were commanded not to be cruel to them. Such was the power of Christian fellowship, however, that the institution of slavery gradually weakened under its impact and finally disappeared.[12]

Social life. To live in a community day after day, week after week, and, in short, to be a human being necessitates maintaining human relationships. Many of the believers of the New Testament were converted out of a society that involved a life style unbecoming to a Christian. With their unsaved friends in view, Paul admonished Christians to "give no offense either to Jews or to Greeks" in their social life. "Whether, then, you eat or drink or whatever you do, do all to the glory of God" in order, said Paul, "that they may be saved" (1 Co 10:31-33).

With the pagan Corinthian culture in view these words are not hard to understand. The way to win men to Christ was *not* to tell them about Jesus Christ and then to participate in their immoral and anti-Christian activities either within the church or outside in the community. To do so would only offend the unbeliever and create disillusionment with the true message of Christianity.

"Keep your behavior excellent among the Gentiles," wrote Peter, "so that . . . they may . . . glorify God in the day of visitation" (1 Pe 2:12). Also, he said, "Keep a good conscience so that . . . those who revile your good behavior in Christ may be put to shame" (1 Pe 3:16).

---

12. Merrill C. Tenney, *New Testament Survey,* rev. ed. (Grand Rapids: Eerdmans, 1968), p. 50.

Not all will respond in making a decision for Christ, but when the Holy Spirit begins His work in the heart of a man, he needs the backdrop of a Christian lifestyle to be able to evaluate objectively the claims of Christianity. Furthermore Peter is telling us that those who do not respond will be "put to shame" or silenced.

Home life. There were those in New Testament days who were married to unbelievers. Their marital partners had not yet come to Christ, particularly husbands.

Were these Christian wives to bombard their unsaved husbands with the verbalization of the gospel? Were they to hound them to come out to church and hear the pastor or visiting evangelist? Were they to talk about the virtues of other Christian men, particularly the leaders of the church?

Not at all! "Be submissive to your own husbands," wrote Peter, "so that even if any of them are disobedient to the word they may be won without a word by the behavior of their wives" (1 Pe 3:1).

The apostle is stating a profound truth! It is not the piling up of verbalizations that convinces unsaved spouses that they need Christ, but rather the impact of a continuous life style that reflects the reality of the indwelling Holy Spirit (1 Pe 3:2-7).

Church life. Very little is said in the New Testament about evangelism *in* the church; that is, where believers gather to be edified. This is of course a New Testament norm. Generally speaking, unsaved people are to be reached *by* the church, not *in* the church.

But there will be those who do come in, and if the atmosphere is warm and inviting, reflecting love among Christians, it will be an impressive atmosphere! But Paul tells us it must also reflect something else—order!

This was a major criticism against the Corinthians. Their church meetings were chaotic. People spoke in tongues—one after the other—with no interpreter. No doubt more than one spoke at the same time, and women were obviously doing much of the talking. "If . . . unbelievers enter, will they not say you are mad?" queried Paul.

This is why he put an emphasis on prophesying in church meetings and speaking the Word of God clearly and in an orderly manner. Unbelievers must understand the Word in order to be saved (1 Co 14:25).

The church was also to engage in another very important evangelistic ministry—that of prayer. They were to pray for all men that they may be saved (1 Ti 2:1-4). They were also to pray for those who were called especially to preach the gospel to regions beyond their own community. On several occasions Paul requested prayers for his own evangelistic ministry, "that the word of the Lord may spread rapidly and be glorified" (2 Th 3:1; Eph 6:19).

Life in general. Though the epistles pinpoint special situations and environments in which Christians were to maintain a good testimony, they also speak to life in general. "You are our letter . . . known and read by all men," Paul said to the Corinthians (2 Co 3:2) "Love your neighbor as yourself," he wrote to the Romans (Ro 13:9). "Conduct yourself with wisdom toward outsiders, making the most of the opportunity," he admonished the Colossians. "Let your speech always be with grace, seasoned, as it were, with salt, so that you may know how you should respond to each person" (Col 4:5, 6). To this Peter adds: "Being ready to make a defense to every one who asks you to give an account for the hope that is in you" (I Pe 3:15). The Philippians were told to conduct themselves "in a manner worthy of the gospel" (Phil 1:27).

SUMMING UP

The book of Acts and the New Testament correspondence leave no doubt that the great evangelistic impact of a group of believers in a given community is based first of all upon an individual and corporate testimony before the unsaved world, reflecting love, unity and godly living. This was to become the backdrop against which a vital verbal witness was to be shared with those who were influenced daily, as Christians carried on their business in the community, associated with the unsaved through social contacts, demonstrated a dynamic homelife in each particular community, reflected love, unity, and maturity as a local body of believers, and in general lived a Christian life, both in what was said and what was done.

4

PRINCIPLES OF NEW TESTAMENT EVANGELISM

What does a study of first century evangelism say to the twentieth century church, wherever it may be? What overarching principles can we glean from the study, which in turn can be established as objectives for the church today, in any culture or subculture?

Following are seven key principles which grow naturally out of the study of the evangelistic activities recorded in the book of Acts, and the directives which are stated in the epistles.

First, *every local body of believers must be responsible for its own community*. It is responsible to saturate that community with *love* and to demonstrate a *unity* and *oneness* that provide the basis for verbal communication; to demonstrate a Christian life style in all human relationships, so as to create a basis on which to discuss the life-changing Christ.

This principle is very clear from the activities of the New Testament and the directives given to local groups of believers in the epistles. They began in Jerusalem, and then, as churches were established in other communities and countries, Christians were instructed to live like Jesus Christ in every human relationship so as to be able to share the gospel forcefully.

Frequently local churches neglect their own communities. A virile foreign missions program becomes a substitute for local outreach. Missionary budgets replace on-the-spot evangelistic activity. Overseas missionaries supported by the church become a substitute for engaging in local evangelism.

This ought not to be! There is no excuse for a local church neglecting its own "Jerusalem." The field is the world—of course—but the world begins in our own backyard, or across the street. This was

40

the story of New Testament believers. They set the example for foreign missions—true—but they had a proper world view. It included "Jerusalem," "Judea," "Samaria," and then "the remotest part of the earth" (Ac 1:8).

True, one of the greatest accomplishments of evangelical Christianity has been its foreign missionary thrust. It is commendable! And it should be continued and expanded. But the words of Jesus apply at this juncture, "These are the things you should have done without neglecting the others" (Mt 23:23).

It is important to underscore again that when Jesus Christ was on earth, people saw and heard *Him*. His miracles and life style became the means by which unbelievers could evaluate His claims (Jn 20:20-31). But when He returned to heaven, His body, the church, became the means by which people could evaluate the message of Christ. (Read again Jn 13:13-35; 17:19-23.)

And this leads us to a second New Testament principle.

Second, *corporate evangelism is basic to personal evangelism.* In the New Testament the functioning body of Christ set the stage for individual witness. This is why Jesus said, "Love one another" so that "all men will know that you are My disciples." This is why Paul said, "Love your neighbor as yourself" (Ro 13:9), and why Peter exhorted believers to keep their "behavior excellent among the Gentiles" (1 Pe 2:12). Personal evangelism takes on unusual significance against the backdrop of a mature body of local believers—Christians who are making an impact in their communities because of their integrity (1 Th 4:11-12), their unselfish behavior (Ro 13:7); their orderly conduct (1 Co 10:31-33); their wisdom (Col 4:6); their diligence (1 Co 6:1); their humility (1 Pe 2:18); and yet, their forthright testimony for Jesus Christ (1 Pe 3:15).

It is difficult to witness in isolation. It is often necessary, but God's general plan is that community evangelism be carried out in the context of dynamic Christianity, and vigorous body life.

United and functioning in all of its parts, the local church can make a powerful impact upon a pagan community. Then it is not so much the extrovertish individuals who are often glamorized as the "most spiritual" because they witness, but it becomes a ministry of the total body of Christ, in which all share the joy and reward of those who have the privilege of "drawing the net" for Christ.

Third, *presenting the gospel to the unsaved is to take place primarily "in the world"—not "in the church."*

The Scriptures do not suggest that non-Christians should be excluded from the "church gathered." Rather Paul referred to unbelievers who might enter a meeting of believers and misinterpret what is happening because of the lack of orderliness, but he also speaks of non-Christians who might enter and fall under conviction and come to Christ (1 Co 14:23-25).[1]

Notice in this passage that the unbeliever will be "convicted by all," he will be "called to account by all" (1 Co 14:24). Here is a clear-cut reference to "body evangelism." It is the whole church functioning that is used by the Holy Spirit to win this person to Christ.

Note too that he does not come to Christ because of a special evangelistic message preached from the pulpit by a pastor, geared to the unsaved in the audience. Rather he is impressed by the believers themselves, their behavior, and the process of mutual edification.[2]

I am reminded of a non-Christian businessman who was attending a new church I was pastoring in its initial days. He asked if he might talk to me about his spiritual condition.

Later when he walked into my office, he proceeded to inform me how impressed he was with the love and concern expressed among the members of this new church. "I have been in many churches," he said, "and served on a number of boards—but have never experienced the kind of Christianity I have seen in this new church."

He then stated openly that he was sure he didn't know Christ personally.

Interestingly, he did not tell me how impressed he was with my sermons, although I know he appreciated the messages. Rather he was impressed with the "body." Yes, I had the privilege of leading him to Christ, but it was the local body of functioning believers that were used by God to bring conviction to this man's soul.

The New Testament then presents the "church gathered" as a context in which non-Christians, if present, can view and experience the

---

1. Note that this is the only illustration in the New Testament of evangelism "in the church."

2. This does not mean it is "wrong" to preach an evangelistic message in a church service. God has used and continues to use this approach. It *does* mean, however, that the New Testament does not present this as the divine plan for carrying out local church evangelism.

realities of Christianity—love, unity, and Christlike living. And within this context, the Holy Spirit is able to bring conviction and a desire to worship the same God and to know the same Saviour.

But generally, evangelism in the New Testament took place, not as the "church gathered" but as the church was "scattered" into the world—at work, in the communities where the believers lived, in their homes, etc.—it was here that non-Christians were confronted with the gospel of Jesus Christ.

Fourth, *the primary target for evangelism should be adults and consequently whole households.*

Nowhere in the New Testament are examples given of "child evangelism" as we frequently practice it today; that is, to win children to Christ out in the community apart from the family setting.

Don't misunderstand! This does not mean there is no emphasis on the importance of child life and child conversion. Jesus Christ Himself set the supreme example in His attitude toward children. Also Paul wrote to Timothy reminding him of his religious heritage, "From childhood you have known the sacred writings which are able to give you the wisdom that leads to salvation through faith which is in Christ Jesus" (2 Ti 3:15).

New Testament evidence is also buttressed by the tremendous Old Testament examples of child nurture. In fact, when the family is discussed in Scripture, more seems to be said about children—their needs and their importance—than any other aspects of family life.[3]

The New Testament pattern is clear! The target for conversion was adults. Jesus chose twelve grown men—not children. He spoke to the multitudes (children were no doubt included in the crowds), but His remarks were directed at the adults.

Similarly, in the book of Acts, the apostles won adults to Christ first of all. They did not go after children as their primary target, hoping to use this as a means to get to parents, nor did they go after children because they were more pliable or easier to reach for Christ.

No, they reversed the process. They went after adults—knowing that parental conversion meant reaching the whole household. Dr. George Peters goes so far as to say in his excellent book *Saturation Evangelism* that "Household evangelism and household salvation are

3. See Gene A. Getz, *The Christian Home in a Changing World* (Chicago: Moody, 1972).

the biblical ideal and norm in evangelism and salvation."[4] By this he does not mean that children become Christians because of their parents' decision. Nor does he mean a "covenant idea" which teaches that children of believing parents experience regeneration through "infant baptism," or that through this rite the child is related to God in some unique way that makes him a potential and actual candidate for conversion later in life.[5]

Conversion is not automatic for any human being. It is an individual matter based upon an intelligent and responsible decision—receiving Christ as personal Saviour.

Household salvation, however, refers to first reaching parents and consequently reaching the whole family for Christ. The New Testament gives several outstanding illustrations of this process. In Philippi, Paul first spoke to Lydia at the riverside. She was converted, and consequently her whole household came to Christ (Ac 16:15). Later in the same city the Philippian jailer believed in Christ, and as a result his whole household was converted (Ac 16:31-34).

Other examples in the New Testament include Zaccheus, and the nobleman in the gospels (Lk 19:9; Jn 4:53). In the Acts and the epistles we see Cornelius (Acts 10), Crispus (Ac 18:8), Stephanas (1 Co 1:16), Onesiphorus (2 Ti 1:16), and Philemon (Phile 1). In fact the household churches referred to frequently both in the book of Acts and in the epistles were no doubt the results of the conversion of whole families.

There are some very practical advantages in reaching adults for Christ and consequently the whole family. Firstly, it is often psychologically very frustrating for a small child to become a Christian apart from the understanding and blessing of his father and mother and other members of the family. In fact, the basic need of a child is "acceptance" and "love" within the family setting, and to experience rejection is not only spiritually devastating but frequently psychologically harmful. A child is ordinarily emotionally incapable of tolerating this kind of "family persecution."

Secondly, parents who are also Christians become the primary means for the child's spiritual growth following conversion. If adults

---

4. George W. Peters, *Saturation Evangelism* (Grand Rapids: Zondervan, 1970), p. 160. Dr. Peters, Professor of World Missions at Dallas Theological Seminary, discusses this idea in depth in his book on pages 147-67.
5. Ibid., pp. 148-49.

need nuture and help following conversion (and they do,) so much more do children. The family is a natural spiritual womb for spiritual growth and development.

Thirdly, a total family reached for Christ can create a tremendous impact in a community. Each member of the household in turn becomes an influence for Christ in winning other households.

Fourthly, "family units" are the building blocks for a healthy church. Again Dr. Peters reminds us:

> Only churches that are built out of basic social units have the true health and the potential of rapid growth and steady expansion. The decisive question in founding a church is not how many people are interested in the project, but rather how many families form the foundation of the church. Churches founded by families have the potential to flourish.[6]

Let me say in conclusion, however, that this does not mean that children should not be reached for Christ before parents are reached. Though biblical examples do not support the sequence, it certainly does not eliminate this approach. The Lord *is concerned* about children and that they come to know Him personally.

But what the biblical examples *do* say is that when the child is reached for Christ through an individual Christian or through an agency of the church, every attempt should be made to reach the parents for Christ as well, and in the process, to seek to keep from interferring with the family's unity and harmony. It may also mean that the church must provide in some way a "father or mother substitute" in cases where non-Christian parents are unresponsive and particularly if they are antagonistic. The very nature of the child makes this almost imperative in order to keep the personality of the child intact, and to keep the traumatic experience of parental rejection from creating psychological problems that may even carry over into adult life, and perhaps cause the individual to eventually turn against Christianity.

And finally it means that Christians must not allow the difficulty of reaching adults and the fear of rejection themselves to cause them to put all of their efforts in winning children because they are more responsive and it is easier to "secure decisions."

---

6. Ibid., p. 155.

One reason statistics show that more children come to Christ is that we are *not winning adults.* Statistics simply reflect our failure, not what *could* be done. If whole families could be reached for Christ in the first century pagan community, we can reach whole families in the twentieth century. The task before us is to develop the right strategy and approach that will work in pagan America.

Fifth, *the church is responsible to identify those who feel especially called by God to carry the good news in a special way out into the community and beyond the immediate community—even to "the remotest part of the earth."*

As emphasized earlier, the unique nature of the church, with its potential for mutual love and unity, gives it unlimited opportunities for an "apologetic" ministry among the unsaved. But within the body are certain people who sense a special burden for evangelistic work. These people must be encouraged to use their talents and represent the local body in a special ministry of evangelism.

Don't misunderstand! They must not become substitutes for the other members of the body, but rather function as those who are able in a special way to present Christ to various individuals and groups. We see this principle demonstrated clearly in the book of Acts. Many believers "spoke" the message of Christ and all believers seemed to have a part in "telling the good news," but it was the apostles especially who engaged in evangelistic *teaching* and *preaching.* It was Peter and particularly Paul who engaged in an evangelistic ministry that was characterized by "solemnly testifying" and "reasoning" with unbelievers.

The church is further responsible to pray God's blessing upon these individuals and in some cases to support them financially as they engage in a part-time or full-time ministry of evangelism and missionary work. This principle is illustrated by the church at Antioch when it set apart Barnabas and Saul and commissioned them for an evangelistic ministry (Ac 13:1-2).

But the church must be careful at this point! Its tendency is to look beyond its immediate community and to overlook those within the whole group of believers who are *not* led to leave the community and sail the seven seas. There are those who should be encouraged, trained, and used in a special way to reach out into the community surrounding the church and to lead people to Christ. But it should not be done as a work involving "a few individuals" alone, but in a way that the whole body assists by saturating the community with the realities of Christianity and the message of the gospel. Not all may be able to "draw the net" with ease, but all have the capacity to love people and to "sow the seed" and to prepare the way for those who can.

Sixth, *new believers as soon as possible should be integrated into the life of the local church.*

What it means to be a part of a New Testament church will be discussed in more detail later, but at this juncture it is important to emphasize—and to emphasize emphatically—that outside of the context of the church and the experience of drawing upon other members of the body, a new babe in Christ will not grow into a mature responsible disciple of Jesus Christ. He cannot, for he is not involved in basic experiences which God has designed as absolutely essential for spiritual growth.

There are some who will interpret these ideas as criticisms of extra-church organizations and agencies. Let me clarify! I believe God has raised up many organizations, firstly to supplement the work of the local church, and secondly to do what, in many cases, the churches have failed to do. But I firmly believe that these organizations must not ignore biblical examples and principles; for if they do, God's richest blessings will not rest upon them ultimately. The most obvious example and principle is that God ordained the local church as the primary place where believers are to be nurtured and edified. Each new Christian needs the body of Christ in order to be built up in the Christian life.

Every Christian organization that operates with New Testament principles in view should seriously consider its relationship to the local church. It must teach this biblical doctrine, promote it as basic to Christian nurture and strive in a loving and tactful way to correct both the church's theological and functional errors. It must not become a substitute for the local church nor antagonistic to the local church. It must in every way cooperate in furthering the ministry and outreach of this God-ordained plan.

Seventh, *the twentieth century church must develop its own contemporary strategies and approaches to evangelism, utilizing the principles just stated as biblical guidelines.*

One thing becomes very clear from the study of the activities of the New Testament church. *What* they said is consistent; the *way* they said it and *how* they went about evangelizing varies from situation to situation. They considered the directives as *absolute,* but their methods were *relative*—they merely served as means to accomplish divine ends.

This is the genius of the Scriptures. They set men free to create unique approaches and devise methods that are workable in any culture and at any time in history.

Whether you study the structure of Peter's sermons, or follow Paul as he moved out from the Jewish community into the Gentile world, one thing is certain! These men were not locked into *one* approach or a single way of presenting the divine message. They varied their methodology, depending on the circumstances. As a result, as we have noted, as Paul entered the pagan world and moved farther and farther away from the environment that had been previously saturated with the teachings of Jesus Christ, he changed his methods of communication. What had been previously a "proclaiming" type approach became one that was characterized by dialogue and interaction. In Paul's initial work he could at least assume a basic belief in God and divine revelation, but in the pagan world he could assume neither. It called for a distinct, apologetic approach to evangelism.

Thus the new culture, the new mentality, the difference in awareness—all of these things—served to help Paul determine what method he should use to reach these people with the gospel of Christ. True, he always communicated the "simple gospel" and did so "with humility," but this has to do with message and attitude, not methods.

One of the key problems with the evangelical church in the twentieth century is that we have allowed non-absolutes to become absolute. We have permitted "ways of doing things" to become normative.

On the one hand we have taken biblical patterns (which vary considerably throughout the Bible) and fixate on the one we feel is the right one; perhaps the one with which we feel the most comfortable. Rather than viewing *all biblical* examples as divine resources which yield absolute principles and guidelines, we develop tunnel vision and allow ourselves to get locked into a single method.

Furthermore, we have allowed purely human patterns and forms which have been developed in the last fifty to one hundred years to become absolute. We actually believe some of the ways we do things now are biblical norms.

A typical example of allowing a purely human approach to become absolute is our thinking regarding the Sunday night evangelistic service (or for that matter any other evangelistic service in the church). Many believers actually believe this is the way the church in the New Testament functioned, whereas we don't have a single example of this approach, nor is it alluded to. In fact, as already pointed out, all church meetings illustrated in the New Testament were designed for believers, not unbelievers.

Is it wrong, then, to have a Sunday night evangelistic service? Of course not. The New Testament certainly allows this freedom. But let's remember that this approach was developed in America around the turn of the century and it worked effectively because of a completely different cultural situation and religious mentality. In many places in America today the Sunday night evangelistic service is a total failure, for unbelievers no longer come out to church. And yet some pastors keep preaching their Sunday night evangelistic sermons to a crowd of "ho-hum" believers, and actually feel guilty if they even consider changing the format and thrust of the service.

The evangelical church *cannot* and *must not* allow itself to get locked into forms and patterns, either first century or twentieth century, that have been designed as a means to biblical ends. Every church in every culture and subculture needs to develop its own unique approaches to community evangelism. Under the creative leadership of the Holy Spirit, and using all of the human resources available, we need to develop dynamic twentieth century churches that are creating contemporary evangelistic strategies that are built upon New Testament principles and guidelines.

Summing Up

Why the church exists in the world is clear! Ultimately God is calling out a people to be His very own. Someday Christ will return to take the church to be with Himself.

But *why* has He not returned? This question was asked even by the skeptics in the first century (2 Pe 3:4). Notice Peter's answer! "The Lord is not slow about His promise, as some count slowness, but is patient toward you, not wishing for any to perish but for all to come to repentance" (2 Pe 3:9).

How well is your church reaching people for Jesus Christ—*first* in your "own Jerusalem" and *then* in "all Judea and Samaria, and even to the remotest part of the earth"?

The following New Testament principles will guide you in carrying out this aspect of the Great Commission:

1. Every body of believers must be responsible to its own community first.
2. Corporate evangelism is basic to personal evangelism.
3. Presenting the gospel to the unsaved is to take place primarily "in the world" not "in the church."
4. The primary target for evangelism should be adults and consequently whole households.
5. The church is responsible to identify those who are especially endowed by God as people who can carry the good news in a special way out into the community and beyond the immediate community, even to "the remotest part of the earth."
6. New believers as soon as possible should be integrated into the life of the church.
7. The twentieth century church must develop its own contemporary structures and approaches to evangelism utilizing the principles and purposes just stated as biblical guidelines.

5

BUILDING THE CHURCH

Disciples were to be taught! This is the second great task spelled out in Christ's commission. Believers were to meet as a "gathered community" in order to become a mature organism.

Just as there are a variety of words used to describe the activities of the disciples as they went about "evangelizing," there are also a number of different words used to recount their ministry of "edification." They of course *baptized* and *taught* the new believers as Jesus had commanded in the Great Commission. But this process of growth and development also involved *fellowshipping* with one another, *breaking bread*, uniting their hearts in *prayer*, and *praising God*. They were *encouraged, strengthened, implored, exhorted, admonished*, and *established* in the faith.

They also received oral reports which *described* the results of evangelistic effort in other parts of the world. They, of course, received a number of letters (the epistles) instructing them *how* to live the Christian life.

On occasion, too, there was *dissension* and *debate* as the apostles and leaders confronted other Christians who were guilty of causing confusion among the brethren through false and incorrect teaching. The results of this activity are described in the book of Acts as causing disciples to "be of one mind," to "be of one heart and soul," and to "be built up." We read that "the churches were being strengthened in the faith," and "the word of the Lord was growing mightily and prevailing." They also experienced "gladness," and "sincerity of heart," and "great joy." For example, when the disciples in Antioch received the letter from Jerusalem, "they rejoiced because it was encouraging" (Ac 15:31).

51

Interestingly, as you move from the study of the *activities* and *results* among believers in the book of Acts to an analysis of the epistles, once again *activities* often become *directives,* and *results* often become *objectives.* "Encourage one another," build up one another," "admonish the unruly," "encourage the fainthearted," "help the weak," "seek after that which is good for one another," are all examples of Pauline directives to the body as a whole (1 Th 5:11-15). All believers are to be involved in the edification process, ministering to each other. They are to "always abound in the work of the Lord" and to "teach and admonish one another with psalms and hymns and spiritual songs."

Timothy as a young pastor was also given specific directives: "prescribe and teach these things," "give attention to public reading of the Scriptures, to exhortation, to teaching." He is told to "preach the word," "be ready in season and out of season," "and to reprove, rebuke," and "exhort." In turn, Titus is also told to "set in order what remains," "appoint elders," and "speak the things which are fitting for sound doctrine."

Elders were to "shepherd the flock of God," and all believers were to "contend earnestly for the faith which was once for all delivered to the saints." Husbands are told to "love their wives" and wives are told "to submit to their husbands." Fathers are instructed not to "provoke their children to wrath," and not to "exasperate" them lest "they lose heart." Rather they are told to bring up their children "in the discipline and instruction of the Lord."

Frequently *directives* regarding edification in the epistles are followed *immediately* with a statement of "expected results" or *objectives,* just as in the area of evangelism. Paul wrote to the Corinthians that he, along with Timothy and Silas, had exhorted and encouraged and implored them so that they might "walk in a manner worthy of the God" who had called them. Later he said that they constantly prayed that they might see the Thessalonians again so as to "complete" what was lacking in their faith. Paul urged the Roman Christians to present themselves to God so as to be able to "prove what the will of God is." He prayed for the Ephesians that they might be "filled up to all the fullness of God." He instructed the Colossians to "bear fruit in every good work." "Let us press on to maturity," said the writer to the Hebrews.

Why then does the church exist as a gathered community? The answer to this question is clear-cut in the New Testament. *The church is to become a mature organism through the process of edification* so that it will become a dynamic witness to the world and so that it will honor and glorify God.

Luke tells us that "the church throughout all Judea and Galilee and Samaria enjoyed peace, being built up [that is edified]" (Ac 9:31). Paul informs us that gifted leaders were given to the church to equip all Christians for service so that the body of Christ would be built up [edified] (Eph 4:11-12, 16). "Build up one another," he exhorted the Thessalonians (1 Th 5:11).

Some form of the word "edification" appears more times in Paul's letter to the Corinthians (particularly in his first epistle) than in any other New Testament book (1 Co 8:1; 10:23; 14:4-5, 12, 17, 26; 2 Co 12:19). This of course is not surprising, for, of all the churches in the New Testament world, this church was the most carnal and immature and in need of spiritual growth and development (1 Co 3:1-3).

Edification should lead to *maturity* or *completeness* in Christ. "And we proclaim Him," wrote Paul to the Colossians, "admonishing every man and teaching every man with all wisdom, that we may present every man complete [mature] in Christ" (Col 1:28). The apostle's primary concern for the body of Christ was that we "all attain to the unity of the faith, and a knowledge of the Son of God, to a mature man, to the measure of the stature which belongs to the fullness of Christ" (Eph 4:13).

A MATURE CHURCH—WHAT IS IT?

How can you recognize a mature church? By what criteria can we measure ourselves as a body to see if we have arrived at a degree of completeness? Again the New Testament is explicit. "But now abide faith, hope, love, these three; but the greatest of these is love" (1 Co 13:13). Maturity in the body of Christ can be identified by the enduring virtues. The degree of completeness can be measured by the degree to which the church manifests faith, hope, and love. This is quite clear from Paul's writings, since he frequently used these three virtues to measure the maturity level of the New Testament churches. Notice these introductory paragraphs in his letters to various churches.

THE FIRST THESSALONIAN LETTER

We give thanks to God always for all of you, making mention of you in our prayers; constantly bearing in mind your work of (faith) and labor of (love) and steadfastness of (hope) in our Lord Jesus Christ in the presence of our God and Father (1 Th 1:2-3).

THE SECOND THESSALONIAN LETTER

We ought always to give thanks to God for you, brethren, as is only fitting because your (faith) is greatly enlarged, and the (love) of each of you all toward one another grows even greater; therefore, we ourselves speak proudly of you among the churches of God for your perseverance and (faith) in the midst of all your persecutions and afflictions which you endure (2 Th 1:3-4).

THE COLOSSIAN LETTER

We give thanks to God, the Father of our Lord Jesus Christ, praying always for you, since we heard of your (faith) in Christ Jesus and the (love) which you have for all the saints; because of the (hope) laid up for you in heaven, of which you previously heard in the word of truth, the gospel (Col 1:3-5).

THE EPHESIAN LETTER

For this reason I too, having heard of the (faith) in the Lord Jesus which exists among you, and your (love) for all the saints, do not cease giving thanks for you, while making mention of you in my prayers; that the God of our Lord Jesus Christ, the Father of glory, may give to you a spirit of wisdom and of revelation in the knowledge of Him. I pray that the eyes of your heart may be enlightened, so that you may know what is the (hope) of His calling, what are the riches of the glory of His inheritance in the saints (Eph 1:15-18).

THE FIRST LETTER TO TIMOTHY

But the goal of our instruction is (love) from a pure heart and a good conscience and a sincere (faith) (1 Ti 1:5).

Peter too makes reference to this trilogy:

For He was foreknown before the foundation of the world, but has appeared in these last times for the sake of you who through Him are believers in God, who raised Him from the dead and gave Him glory, so that your (faith) and (hope) are in God. Since you have in obedience to the truth purified your souls for a sincere (love) of the brethren, fervently love one another from the heart (1 Pe 1:20-22).

Obviously it is transparent what the New Testament criteria is for determining the maturity level of a local body of believers. First of all, is there *love* manifested toward other members of the body of Christ? Second, is there a strong and vital *faith*? Third, is there a demonstration of *hope*? But these words can be merely theological symbols. What do they mean? It is only as we reinforce these words with meaning and content that we get the complete picture. Once again the New Testament speaks articulately.

LOVE

"The greatest of these is love," concludes Paul (1 Co 13:13). The apostle consistently drives home this truth in his correspondence with the churches.

THE COLOSSIAN LETTER

And so, as those who have been chosen of God, holy and beloved, put on a heart of compassion, kindness, humility, gentleness and patience; bearing with one another, and forgiving each other, whoever has a complaint against any one; just as the Lord forgave you, so also should you. And beyond all these things put on love, which is the perfect bond of unity (Col 3:12-14).

THE FIRST THESSALONIAN LETTER

Now may our God and Father Himself and Jesus our Lord direct our way to you; and may the Lord cause you to increase and abound in love for one another, and for all men, just as we also do for you (1 Th 3:11-12).

THE PHILIPPIAN LETTER

And this I pray, that your love may abound still more and more in real knowledge and all discernment, so that you may approve the things that are excellent, in order to be sincere and blameless until the day of Christ (Phil 1:9-10).

THE EPHESIAN LETTER

As a result, we are no longer to be children, tossed here and there by waves, and carried about by every wind of doctrine, by the trickery of men, by craftiness in deceitful scheming; but speaking the truth in love we are to grow up in all aspects into Him, who is the head, even Christ, from whom the whole body, being fitted and held together by that which every joint supplies, according to the proper working of each individual part, causes the growth of the body for the building up of itself in ⟨love⟩ (Eph 4:14-16).

The apostle Peter also elevates love to the "greatest level" when he says, "Above all, keep fervent in your ⟨love⟩ for one another, because love covers a multitude of sins" (1 Pe 4:8). And there is no question as to John's concern, for in his first epistle alone he states four times that believers are to "love one another" (1 Jn 3:11; 3:23; 4:7; 4:11).

But what is *love?* How is it manifested? How can it be recognized in the body of Christ? The most prominent passage portraying the particular aspects of love is, of course, 1 Corinthians 13. Here Paul spells out for the *immature* Corinthian church exactly *what love is*—how it is to be manifested by the body of Christ. Unfortunately this "great love chapter" is often lifted out of context and used in isolation. To get the full meaning and impact of Paul's words, you must see his description of love in the light of the whole Corinthian epistle and you must interpret his definitions in the light of the Corinthian carnality. Then, too, we must observe Paul's words in 1 Corinthians 13 in relationship to the *body* of Christ, not just to individual Christians.

First, note that the Corinthians were "not lacking in any gift" (1 Co 1:7). Yet, they were an immature church. Paul classified them as "babes in Christ" (3:1), carnal and fleshly (3:3). Obviously the manifestation of spiritual gifts in a local church is not synonymous with spirituality and maturity. It certainly was not true with the Corinthians.

This is Paul's major assertion in 1 Corinthians 13. No doubt there were more individuals in the Corinthian church who spoke in tongues than in any other New Testament church; yet there was a lack of love and, consequently, they had become as a "noisy gong or a clanging cymbal" (13:1).

These Corinthians also had the gifts of prophecy, wisdom, knowledge and faith, but they did not have love and, therefore, Paul implies, they are "nothing" (13:2).

Some of these believers at Corinth no doubt had the gift of "giving" and were even willing to physically sacrifice their lives in acts of martyrdom, but said Paul, without love this type of behavior is totally unprofitable (13:3).

The apostle then describes how to recognize love in the body of Christ. If it is not the manifestation of spiritual gifts, then what is it?

Love is patient (13:4). In other words, it is the opposite of what the Corinthians were demonstrating. They were *impatient* with one another, and there were disagreements and divisions among them (1:10).

Love is kind, and is not jealous (13:4). Earlier in his letter Paul had written about the "jealousy and strife" among the Corinthians (3:3).

Love does not brag and is not arrogant (13:4). Paul had to warn the Corinthians against false boasting (1:29). "If any man among you thinks that he is wise in this age, let him become foolish that he may become wise. . . . Let no one boast in men. . . . What do you have that you did not receive? But if you did receive it, why do you boast as if you had not received it?" (3:18, 21; 4:7).

Love . . . does not act unbecomingly (13:5). There was immorality in the church at Corinth and, said Paul, "immorality of such a kind as does not exist even among the Gentiles" (5:1; 6:15-20). Furthermore, they were acting in a most unbecoming manner at the Lord's table—some even overeating and overdrinking—even to the point of drunkenness (11:20-21).

Love . . . does not seek its own, is not provoked, does not take into account a wrong suffered (13:5). Here were believers who were taking each other to court (6:1-7). They were wronging and defrauding each other (6:8). They were also insensitive to the weaker members of the body of Christ and some allowed their liberty in Christ to become a "stumbling block to the weak" (8:9). Some in fact were actually participating in idolatry (10:14).

Love . . . does not rejoice in unrighteousness, but rejoices with the truth (13:6). It is hard to conceive of gifted Christians bragging about the immorality in the church, but Paul states emphatically, "You have become arrogant [about this immorality], and have not mourned instead" (5:2).

After defining love, and contrasting its ingredients with what the Corinthians so glaringly lacked, Paul gives some positive statements about love (13:7). It "bears all things" (that is, it suffers and bears up under pressure.) It "believes all things" (that is, it is "always eager to believe the best," Moffatt). It "hopes all things" (that is, it demonstrates a forward look, not hopeless pessimism). It "endures all things" (that is, it is steadfast and enables a Christian to continue on in the thick of battle).

The Corinthians, of course, were guilty of failure on every count. They were not bearing with one another; they were eager to believe falsehoods, even about the apostle Paul (4:3-5; 9:1-3); they were negative in their attitudes; and they were succumbing to the pressures of the world and its system.

Now as we approach verses 8-12 in 1 Corinthians 13, some aspects of Paul's statements are somewhat difficult to understand. But in context, certain truths become very obvious. Paul naturally and logically concludes that "love never fails" (13:8). Certain gifts will cease, specifically, the gifts of "prophecy," "tongues," and "knowledge" (13:8).

"For," says Paul, "we know in part, and we prophesy in part; but when the perfect comes, the partial will be done away" (13:9-10).

What is Paul referring to? Notice the contrasting words and phrases he uses in these verses just quoted and the ones to follow (that is, in verses 9-12):

PART OR PARTIAL	←——→	PERFECT OR COMPLETE
child	←——→	man
childish	←——→	manly
we see in a mirror dimly	←——→	we see face to face
I know in part	←——→	I shall know fully

Looking at the whole of 1 Corinthians and comparing it with the epistles Paul wrote to other churches, several conclusions stand out. These believers had not reached the degree of maturity and completeness or perfection that other New Testament churches had reached. They were still *babes* or *infants*. They were *childish* in their behavior. They had made very little progress in becoming conformed to the image of Jesus Christ.[1] They had not yet reached the place in

---

1. Note that Paul utilizes the same literary technique throughout this chapter. He uses the personal pronouns and applies these statements to himself: "If I speak . . . I have become . . . If I have the gift . . . I am nothing . . . . And if I give . . . it profits me nothing. . . . When I was a child, I used to speak as a child. . . . When I became a man, I did away with childish things. . . . Now I know in part, but then I shall know fully." In the light of the context it is obvious he is speaking of the deep spiritual needs of the Corinthians, but he illustrates these truths by referring to his own life. The Corinthians had no problem in getting the point.

their spiritual development where Paul could write to them, as he did to the Thessalonians, the Colossians, the Ephesians, and the Philippians, and thank God for their *faith, hope,* and *love.* Rather, it seems, they were almost void of these virtues as a local body of believers. They were living in a state of "partiality," "childishness," and "dimness" in their spiritual life, and in order to correct the situation Paul admonished them to refocus their priorities. First he told them to strive for the "more excellent way"; they were to "pursue love" (12: 31; 14:1); and then, "earnestly desire" for the body "the greater gifts" (12:31).[2]

FAITH AND HOPE

Faith and *hope,* the other two virtues which Paul sets forth as standards by which we can measure the maturity level of the local church, are also uniquely described in the New Testament. Though there is no central passage describing these virtues such as 1 Corinthians 13 does for love, there are a number of descriptive words and phrases used by the New Testament writers to add significant meaning and content to these words. Some of these phrases are listed below:

FAITH

Work of faith (1 Th 1:3)
Breastplate of faith (1 Th 5:8)
Faith in Jesus Christ (Col 1:4)
Faith in the Lord Jesus (Eph 1:15)
Faith in God (1 Pe 1:21)
Faith greatly enlarged (2 Th 1:3)
Faith without hypocrisy (1 Ti 1:5)
Faith toward the Lord Jesus and toward all the saints (Phile 5)
Full assurance of faith (Heb 10:22)

HOPE

Steadfastness of hope (1 Th 1:3)
Hope of salvation (1 Th 5:8)
Hope laid up for you (Col 1:5)
That you may know what is the hope of His calling (Eph 1:18)
Hope in God (1 Pe 1:21)
Hold fast the confession of our hope without wavering (Heb 10:23)
Christ Jesus who is our hope (1 Ti 1:1)
We fixed our hope on the living God (1 Ti 4:10)
Not to fix our hope on the uncertainty of riches but on God (1 Ti 6:17)
Hope of eternal life (Titus 1:2)

---

2. The concept of the "greater gifts" is developed at length in chapter 8.

> Looking for the blessed hope
> (Titus 2:13)
> Born again to a living hope (1 Pe
> 1:3)
> Fix your hope completely on the
> grace to be brought to you at
> the revelation of Jesus Christ
> (1 Pe 1:3).

Even a casual reading of this list reveals that *faith* and *hope* are closely aligned in meaning and significance. The writer of Hebrews clarifies this relationship when he says, "Faith is the assurance of things hoped for, the conviction of things not seen" (Heb 11:1). Faith has to do with Christians themselves—their personalities—that is, their minds, their attitudes, their wills. It involves inner convictions and assurance. The primary object of our faith is God the Father and His Son Jesus Christ, but it also includes faith in our fellow Christians (1 Co 13:7; Phile 5).

Hope on the other hand, though linked to faith, has to do with the object and content of faith. It is most frequently used to refer to salvation and ultimate deliverance from this world into the presence of Jesus Christ when He comes again.

The word hope is also used to describe the state of Christians. It is used in conjunction with such words and phrases as "steadfastness" (1 Th 1:3), "without wavering" (Heb 10:23), and "fixed" (1 Ti 4:10; 6:17; 1 Pe 1:13). It is used to describe "certainty" and "stability."

In conclusion it is obvious why Paul refers to *faith, hope* and *love* as the primary virtues by which we may measure the maturity level of the church. *Love* has to do with Christlike relationships among members of the body and toward all men—an attitude that creates unity and one mindedness.

Faith has to do with the confidence that the body of Christ has in its Head—the Lord Jesus Christ. There is that unified conviction and assurance that God is, and that He answers prayer and that He is their divine source of life and existence.

The presence of *hope* is manifested in stability, steadfastness and certainty, and particularly looks beyond the present to that day when Jesus Christ shall come again for the church, and in turn, to set up His eternal kingdom.

SUMMING UP

Why then does the church exist as a gathered community? The church is to become a mature organism through the process of edification, and this maturity is reflected, first of all by the degree of love that exists in the body of Christ, and second by the degree of corporate faith and hope that is manifested.

"Be careful how you build!" warned Paul. A church can be weak and immature—constructed of wood, hay and stubble. Or it can be strong and mature—composed of gold, silver and precious stones (1 Co 3:10-15). If it is immature, it reflects impatience, jealousy, strife, divisions, pride, arrogance and unbecoming behavior. If it is mature, it reflects a growing love, a unity of faith, and a steadfast hope.

6

VITAL NEW TESTAMENT EXPERIENCES

When attempting to formulate guidelines for the twentieth century church and to establish purposes and principles that grow out of the New Testament, it is important to look at the experiences of first century Christians. Though there are a variety of such experiences recorded in the book of Acts, and additional instructions given in the epistles regarding these experiences, they seem to fall into three basic categories: vital learning experiences with the Word of God; vital relational experiences with God and with one another; and vital witnessing experience with the non-Christian world.

VITAL LEARNING EXPERIENCES

The Great Commission of our Lord is quite emphatic about the importance of teaching new believers the Word of God. "Make disciples," exhorted Jesus, and then "teach" these disciples.

And this the apostles did, for the new believers in Jerusalem were "continually devoting themselves to the apostles' teaching. . . ." (Ac 2:42). There was the immediate intake of biblical truth and doctrine. "Like newborn babes," wrote Peter, "long for the pure milk of the word, that by it you may grow in respect to salvation" (1 Pe 2:2).

Though there are a number of words used for "teaching" in the Greek New Testament, the form used in Matthew 28:20 is the most common. There are about one hundred occurrences of the verb *didasko,* and its use is about evenly distributed in each gospel, the book of Acts, and in the epistles. Interestingly, the word is used about half the time in Acts to describe the teaching-learning process among non-Christians, and about half the time with Christians.[1]

---

1. For an excellent treatment of the Greek words for "teach," see Roy B. Zuck, "Greek Words for Teach," *Bibliotheca Sacra* 122 (April-June 1965): 158-68.

No one can deny the importance of "data input" in the process of edification. A church that does not provide good Bible teaching cannot be classified as a New Testament church. It is important to note, however, that the form that this teaching took varied greatly. There are no absolute guidelines or stereotype patterns. The methods and approaches—whether used by Jesus, the apostles, or other members of the body of Christ—varied according to the situation. Sometimes the group was large; sometimes it was small. Sometimes teaching was done by one person; other times it was done by two or more. Sometimes the presentation was lengthy; sometimes it was brief. Sometimes it took place spontaneously; at other times it was planned. Sometimes it was basically a lecture; sometimes it involved the people in interaction and discussion. Sometimes it was verbalized; sometimes it was visualized. Sometimes it involved mostly transmission of truth; sometimes it involved a process. But all with one objective in view (when it took place among Christians), their edification. Methods and approaches were means to this dynamic end.

VITAL RELATIONAL EXPERIENCES

The New Testament is filled with illustrations and instructions regarding relational type experiences that believers had with one another and with God. Furthermore, these two relationships are so closely interwoven and linked together, it is difficult to separate the two even when writing about them.

For example, the new believers in Jerusalem, in addition to being instructed in doctrine, were "continually devoting themselves to fellowship [*koinonia*], to the breaking of bread and to prayer." As they ate together and prayed together, they experienced dynamic fellowship with one another and with God. In this peculiar set of circumstances, they were no doubt literally sharing their food with each other—and at the same time remembering the Lord's broken body and shed blood. As they prayed for one another, they no doubt worshiped God in praise and thanksgiving.

John recognized the interrelatedness of these two experiences when he wrote: "What we have seen and heard we proclaim to you also, that you also may have *fellowship with us;* and indeed our *fellowship is with the Father, and with His Son Jesus Christ*" [Italics mine] (1 Jn 1:3).

CORPORATE PRAYER

At the time the church was born, one of the most predominant experiences of those who were waiting in the upper room was corporate prayer. In the spirit of unity and "one mindedness," the one hundred and twenty believers "were continually devoting themselves to prayer" (Ac 1:14) as they waited for the Holy Spirit to come as Jesus had promised.

When the Holy Spirit came on the day of Pentecost, Peter, hereafter a frequent spokesman for the believers in Jerusalem, interpreted this marvelous manifestation to the multitudes. And as he preached the gospel with power and conviction, immediately the one hundred and twenty believers swelled to over three thousand (Ac 2:41). We then are told that these new Christians, within the context of teaching and fellowship, were "continually devoting themselves. . . *to prayer*" (Ac 2:42).

In many of the epistles, the church was instructed to engage in corporate prayer.[2] Paul told the Christians in Rome and Colosse to devote themselves to prayer (Ro 12:12; Col 4:2). He told the believers at Ephesus and Thessalonica to "pray at all times" and "without ceasing" (Eph 6:18; 1 Th 5:17). To the Philippians he wrote, "Be anxious for nothing, but in everything by prayer and supplication with thanksgiving let your requests be made known to God" (Phil 4:6). James admonished believers to "pray for one another" (Ja 5:16), and Paul told Timothy to "urge that entreaties and prayers, petitions and thanksgivings, be made on behalf of all men" (1 Ti 2:1).

Interestingly, many of these references to prayer appear in a context that seems to imply "body life" and *koinonia*. For example, note the *context* of prayer in each of the passages which follow, giving special attention to the term "one another."

> Be devoted to <u>one another</u> in brotherly love; give preference to <u>one</u> <u>another</u> in honor; not lagging behind in diligence, fervent in <u>spirit,</u> <u>serving</u> the Lord; rejoicing in hope, persevering in tribulation, <u>devoted</u> <u>to prayer,</u> contributing to the needs of the saints, practicing hospitality (Ro 12:10-13).

---

2. Not all of these references would be limited to corporate prayer. It would also apply to the believer's personal prayer life. However, the context in which most of these injunctions to prayer are given strongly suggest the idea of corporate prayer.

And we urge you, brethren, admonish the unruly, encourage the fainthearted, help the weak, be patient with all men. See that no one repays another with evil for evil, but always seek after that which is good for one another and for all men. Rejoice always; pray without ceasing; in everything give thanks; for this is God's will for you in Christ Jesus (1 Th 5:14-18).

Is anyone among you suffering? Let him pray. Is anyone cheerful? Let him sing praises. Is anyone among you sick? Let him call for the elders of the church, and let them pray over him, anointing him with oil in the name of the Lord; and the prayer offered in faith will restore the one who is sick, and the Lord will raise him up, and if he has committed sins, they will be forgiven him. Therefore, confess your sins to one another, and pray for one another, so that you may be healed. The effective prayer of a righteous man can accomplish much (Ja 5:13-16).

The end of all things is at hand; therefore, be of sound judgment and sober spirit for the purpose of prayer. Above all, keep fervent in your love for one another, because love covers a multitude of sins. Be hospitable to one another without complaint. As each one has received a special gift, employ it in serving one another, as good stewards of the manifold grace of God (1 Pe 4:7-10).

Notice also how frequently corporate prayer is put in the context of being thankful (Eph 5:20; Phil 4:6; Col 4:2; 1 Th 5:17-18; 1 Ti 2:1). Prayer, though it was to include petition and request for personal needs, was not to be oriented toward "selfish behavior" but to flow out of hearts overflowing with "thanksgiving to God."

On several occasions Paul requested prayer for himself (2 Th 3:1; Eph 6:19), particularly that the Word of the Lord would spread rapidly and be glorified (2 Th 3:1) and that he might be able to speak out boldly in presenting the "mystery of the gospel" (Eph 6:19). In turn, Paul frequently reminded believers of his personal prayer for them (Ro 1:8; Eph 1:16; 3:14; Phil 1:9-10).

These were the characteristics of a New Testament "prayer meeting." These prayer experiences did not seem to be only "periods of prayer," or a "time," or an "evening," or a "day" set aside for prayer, though it certainly included this. On special occasions they met for prayer, particularly when there were special needs (Ac 12:12). More frequently, however, prayer seemed to be interwoven into a variety of experiences believers participated in as they met together to be edified. And as they prayed, they prayed for each other's needs. They prayed for those carrying the gospel to others, and they prayed for *all* men.

CORPORATE SINGING

Music has always been a part of the life of the people of God. The Old Testament is filled with illustrations of various types of musical expression, particularly singing. David, of course, is the outstanding example of a man who used his voice both for song and as an instrument to praise God.

In the New Testament Jesus exemplified the place of singing, for after He had eaten the last supper with His disciples, and just before "they went out to the Mount of Olives" they sang a hymn (Mk 14:26).

Paul particularly made reference to singing, "Speaking to one another in psalms and hymns and spiritual songs," he wrote in the Ephesian letter, "singing and making melody with your heart to the Lord" (Eph 5:19).

To the Colossians, he said, "Let the word of Christ richly dwell within you; with all wisdom teaching and admonishing one another with psalms and hymns and . . . singing with thankfulness in your hearts to God" (Col 3:16).

Notice again the context of "corporate singing" and especially its purpose. They were to minister to *one another*—to "teach" and "admonish" *one another*. It was to edify the body of Christ. It was also to flow out of a heart of "thankfulness" to God. Just as with corporate prayer, corporate singing was to be a natural and spontaneous expression and a specific experience that was vitally related to the basic experience of body life and *koinonia*.

Notice, too, that Paul relates corporate singing to the basic experience of *learning biblical truth*. In fact, singing actually is to be a means whereby believers "teach" and "admonish" one another and whereby the "word of Christ" can "richly dwell" within them (Col 3:16).

Regarding this concept, Herbert Carson suggests the following:

> Their experience of the Word is not merely an individual one, for it is in the context of a fellowship of the Church that they are to learn its truths. Thus there must be a mutual sharing of the Word. It is

from the indwelling Word that they will learn the wisdom of God, and that wisdom will then become the atmosphere in which they move as they seek to build one another up in knowledge. The worship of the Church is here viewed from the standpoint of the edification of the believers. . . such singing will not be of mere form of release, but will be a means of instruction.[3]

This is a direct correlation between the purpose of corporate singing and the content Paul refers to, both in Ephesians and Colossians. These believers were to teach and admonish one another with "psalms, and hymns, and spiritual songs" (Col 3:16; Eph 5:19).

Some believe the apostle may have been referring to the Old Testament psalter when he used the word "psalms." If this be true, no further comment is necessary to emphasize the quality of this content. Nothing can surpass the very "words of God" as a basis for edification.

The term "hymn" no doubt refers to "praise psalms"—poetic composition, uninspired from the standpoint of biblical revelation, but very much "inspired" in terms of the human spirit. Though of human origin, these hymns were to be used to teach one another and to glorify God.

"Spiritual songs" may be called "spiritual odes." The term *ode* used by itself is broad in meaning and refers to any poetry, sacred or secular. Believers, however, were to make melody in their hearts with *spiritual* odes—songs that expressed their attitudes and feelings toward the Lord and each other.

Be careful, however, that you do not interpret Paul's words here through a traditional grid of various Christian approaches to "musical expression" over the years. Paul is not speaking here of musical *forms*—that is, tempo, rhythm, melody, or harmony. The "words" or the "poetic expression" become the focal point. The words used are to be, says Paul, first, the very words of God (as the psalms); second, words of praise to God (those written by believers); and third, words that express true Christian experiences.

The *way* the New Testament church expressed itself "musically" would be hardly identifiable if compared with the typical hymnbook used in the evangelical church today.

---

3. Herbert M. Carson, *The Epistles of Paul to the Colossians and to Philemon* (Grand Rapids: Eerdmans, 1960), p. 90.

But the *way* that it was expressed is not the important matter—
what was expressed *is!* As will be developed at length later, the Bible
allows a great deal of freedom when it comes to form, but it is very
specific when it comes to content and purpose. Here Paul is speaking
of one aspect of church form—music. Tempo, rhythm, melody—
these are all relative factors in musical expression. They are culturally
related. But the purpose of Christian music—edification—is absolute.
And the Bible is clear that Christians need to "sing together" in order
to build up one another. The kinds of musical expressions really don't
matter provided they create dynamic relational Christianity and help
believers to learn the Word of God.

CORPORATE GIVING

The story of the church in the New Testament is a story of a group
of people who "cared about others," particularly other believers.
"Let us do good to all men," but, Paul added, "especially to those
who are of the household of the faith" (Gal 6:10; 1 Th 5). Writing
to the Christians at Rome, he exhorted them to contribute to the
needs of the saints, and to practice hospitality (Ro 12:13).

Corporate sharing and giving is exemplified by believers right
from the very beginning of the church in Jerusalem. Because of the
socio-economic factors at that time, they "had all things in common."
The Christians sold their "property and possessions . . . sharing them
with all, as anyone might have need" (Ac 2:44-45).

But as the disciples were scattered and as the Word was proclaimed
and taught throughout Judea and Samaria and all over the New Testament world, the concept of corporate giving and sharing was never
lost. Even though socio-economic conditions were different—people
had their own homes, their own particular jobs, and they made their
own livings—they still demonstrated care for other believers in need.

When Paul wrote to the church at Philippi he thanked God for
their "participation [*koinonia*] in the gospel from the first day until
now" (Phil 1:5). No doubt, he was referring to the fact that these
Christians had "more than once" sent material gifts to care for his
material needs (Phil 4:14-16).

Writing to the Corinthians, and urging them to get involved in the
"gracious work" of corporate giving, Paul used the church in Macedonia as an example. "For I testify," he said, "that according to their
ability, and beyond their ability they gave of their own accord, beg-

ging us with much entreaty for the favor of participation in the support of the saints" (2 Co 8:3-4).

Paul believed and taught that corporate giving was an essential experience for all believers. "You will be enriched in everything for all liberality," he wrote to the Corinthians (2 Co 9:11). But he went on to explain that corporate giving will be an experience bringing mutual edification. "For the ministry of this service is not only fully supplying the needs of the saints, but is also overflowing through many thanksgivings to God. Because of the proof given by this ministry they [the recipients of the gifts] will glorify God for your obedience to your confession of the gospel of Christ, and for the liberality of your contribution to them and to all, while they also, by prayer on your behalf, yearn for you because of the surpassing grace of God in you" (2 Co 9:12-14).

This Corinthian passage (2 Co:8-9) in itself provides a fascinating study in relational Christianity. It demonstrates the importance of caring for the needs of other members of the body of Christ; it emphasizes the spiritual growth that results in the life of those who share; it refers to not only the physical benefits to those who receive the gifts, but also the spiritual benefits; it illustrates the development of mutual care, not only in giving but in praying for each other (2 Co 9:14).

Furthermore, the implication is clear (as it was in Jerusalem in the early days of the church), non-believers took cognizance of the body of Christ at work caring for itself, not only in local geographical settings, but all over the New Testament world. This in itself became a backdrop against which the gospel of Christ, as it was preached to the pagan world, took on meaning and true theological significance. No activity like sharing material blessings can demonstrate so well the concepts of "true Christian love," "unity," and "the reality of the Christian faith." Verbal appreciation and concern are inexpensive and relatively easy acts of kindness. But tangibly sharing what is "yours" with others "costs," and it is an experience all mankind (saved and unsaved) can identify with. How easy it is to "love ourselves"—but how difficult it is to "love" our neighbors as ourselves.

Unbelievers who saw these sacrificial acts of kindness could not but be impressed with the supernatural qualities of life in Christ. This was against nature! This was the opposite of what man *wants* to do!

This was a demonstration of unusual qualities that came from a super-natural source—the indwelling Christ—the One who was being proclaimed as the Son of God.

CORPORATE EATING

It is impossible to read the New Testament carefully without concluding that "corporate eating" *was* a significant experience for first-century Christians. It was, of course, a *regular* experience for the disciples of Jesus—particularly the twelve—as they traveled with Him during His ministry on earth. But their meal together, just prior to the time Christ was taken captive, took on special significance. It was during this meal that "Jesus took some bread, and after a blessing, He broke it and gave it to the disciples, and said, 'Take, eat; this is My body' " (Mt 26:26).

Next, the Lord "took a cup and gave thanks, and gave it to them, saying, 'Drink from it, all of you; for this is My blood of the covenant, which is to be shed on behalf of many for forgiveness of sins' " (Mt 26:27-28).

No doubt the new Christians in Jerusalem in the early days of the church emulated this experience the twelve had with Christ. Luke records that "they were continually devoting themselves . . . to the breaking of bread and prayer. . . . And day by day continuing with one mind in the temple, and breaking bread from house to house, they were taking their meals together with gladness and sincerity of heart, praising God, and having favor with all the people" (Ac 2:42, 46-47b).

These meals were not just ordinary meals for these new believers. No doubt they often broke bread and partook of the cup, and in so doing proclaimed the death of Christ. Some feel that in these early days they remembered the Lord in this way on a daily basis.

Religious meals were not an uncommon practice in these days even among the pagans and other religious sects. The Jews, of course, had historically kept the Passover. It was, therefore, not a totally new experience for these Jewish Christians to participate in a religious meal. What *was* new, however, was that a part of the meal now became a special means to remember the sacrificial death of Jesus Christ.

When Paul wrote to the Christians in Corinth, he had to correct the misuse of this religious meal (1 Co 11:28-34). Some were coming and eating early; some were not getting any food and were still hungry; some were actually overeating and overdrinking. In general, they were selfishly using this meal for their own benefit and not for its original purpose.

Paul had to remind them of the Lord's example, how that during the last supper He had broken the bread as a reminder of His broken body, and after supper He had shared the cup with His disciples as "the new covenant" in His blood. The Corinthians were partaking of these elements in an "unworthy manner" (11:27). They were ignoring the original purpose and meaning of this sacred experience.

The most important aspect of this meal, of course, was the breaking of bread and the sharing of the cup. Thus these two elements have been shared by Christians down through the years as a token meal and has been designated as holy communion.

There is no biblical reason, however, to reject the concept of the religious meal as being "out of order" or improper in the church of the twentieth century. In fact, Zane Hodges, Professor of New Testament Literature and Exegesis at Dallas Theological Seminary, believes that the religious meal should be a definite part of Christian worship and experience today. He argues his position by referring to the Lord's example with the disciples, plus the obvious practice of the Corinthians and Paul's instructions in Corinthians 11:20-24. He feels to reject the "religious meal" concept on the basis of its misuse by the Corinthians is not adequate grounds for abandoning this total experience and replacing it with a token meal.

The crucial aspect, he believes, is the breaking of bread and partaking of the cup. He believes, however, that these elements are only part of the Lord's Supper, and that the meal proper provides opportunity for Christian fellowship and mutual edification as the Word of God is informally discussed. He believes further that this experience helps to create a family environment for the body of Christ, and if done with reverence and respect, adds a great deal to the process of mutual Christian growth.

It cannot be denied that "corporate eating" is a concept in the New Testament. Whether it should be practiced in the same way as in the early days of the church is, in my opinion, a matter of interpretation. No one who reads the Scriptures objectively can deny the necessity of remembering the Lord by means of holy communion. Paul said, "For as often as you eat this bread and drink the cup, you proclaim the Lord's death until He comes." Obviously, Paul believed and taught that this aspect of the meal should continue until Jesus Christ returns again.

Many factors in the twentieth century culture are naturally different today than in the first century, particularly in Jerusalem where the communal life in those early days of the church made the Lord's Supper a frequent and natural experience. However, even if the religious meal is not a normative pattern for the church today, is there not inherent in these biblical examples a principle—that of utilizing "corporate eating" as a vital experience for Christians? Leon Morris reminds us in his commentary on 1 Corinthians that "there is a marked stress throughout this whole passage on the corporate nature of the rite and on the responsibility to all."[4]

Much was stated earlier regarding relational Christianity. What better environment can be used to create this kind of experience when a group of dedicated Christians gather about a table eating together. Whether it is related to communion or not, it should and can always be a spiritual experience with "one another" and "with God." For, said Paul on another occasion, "whether, then, you eat or drink or whatever you do, do all to the glory of God" (1 Co 10:31).

All close-knit families will testify that there is no experience that equals the intimate fellowship of gathering about a table and eating together. Are not all Christians brothers and sisters in Christ? Are not believers members of the family of God? Are not we *one* body? Is the church today utilizing the experience of "corporate eating" in its most vital way to contribute to the building up of the body of Christ?

VITAL WITNESSING EXPERIENCES

There is another dimension to the edification process which can be easily overlooked—and is in many churches—especially among those who attempt to duplicate the New Testament pattern. A church can become so intent on fulfilling its purpose as a "gathered community" that, without actually being aware of what is happening, it is becom-

---

4. Leon Morris, *The First Epistle of Paul to the Corinthians* (Grand Rapids: Eerdmans, 1958) p. 164.

ing an "inward-oriented group" rather than an "outward-oriented group."

The church exists for two basic purposes—remember?—"to make disciples" and "to teach them." An "inward-oriented" church becomes an end in itself. It grows "stale" and "self-centered" and "lifeless." The basic experiences of learning biblical truth can become purely academic, and relational experiences can become very superficial.

Only as a church, both as a body and as individual members within that body, reaches out and touches the lost world will it maintain the fresh flow of life and power that keeps "learning biblical truth" and "relational Christianity" dynamic and fresh.

The churches founded in the book of Acts are excellent examples of this! Following the persecution which was initiated in Jerusalem, the believers "enjoyed peace." But we read that they were "being built up" (edified); and, going on in the fear of the Lord and in the comfort of the Holy Spirit, it (the church) continued to increase (to grow numerically) (Ac 9:31).[5]

The record in Acts and the epistles of the total impact of the church on the world is clear. Extrabiblical history also records the continuing influence the church had upon the world. Christians helped to change the total culture. They affected and infected the total community. In addition to the scriptural record, history reports "that in the Greek and Roman world the cry went out, 'behold, how they love one another.' "[6]

The Thessalonians are probably one of the most outstanding examples of a witnessing church, "For," said Paul, "the word of the Lord has sounded forth from you, not only in Macedonia and Achaia, but also in every place your faith toward God has gone forth, so that we have no need to say anything" (1 Th 1:8). To the Roman Christians he also wrote, "First, I thank my God through Jesus Christ for you all, because your faith is being proclaimed throughout the whole world" (Ro 1:8).

Note, too, that Christian witness in the New Testament church was

---

5. In this verse the term for church is seemingly used to refer to the universal church; however, the total context implies that there were many local congregations scattered throughout Judea, Galilee, and Samaria. This general growth was reflected through the growth of individual local assemblies.
6. Francis A. Schaeffer, *The Church at the End of the Twentieth Century*, p. 71.

both "corporate" and "individual." The functioning body became the backdrop against which effective personal witness took place.

At this juncture, it is important to remind ourselves again of Jesus' words to His disciples and of His words to the Father in His high priestly prayer. "By this," said Jesus, "all men will know that you are My disciples, if you have love for one another" (Jn 13:35). And to His Father He prayed that His disciples might "be one . . . that they may be perfected in unity," in order "that the world may know that Thou didst send Me" (Jn 17:21, 23).

SUMMING UP

What then is edification in the New Testament sense of the word? It seems to be that ongoing experience, where biblical truth (doctrine) is learned within the context of "relational Christianity" and "dynamic Christian witness." All three experiences are needed to create a mature body of believers. To neglect any one of these facets of New Testament life is to interfere with the God-ordained plan for edification in the local church.

7

PRINCIPLES OF NEW TESTAMENT EDIFICATION

In order for a local church to become a mature body of believers reflecting *faith, hope* and *love,* there are certain New Testament principles that must be applied. These principles grow naturally out of our study of the activities of New Testament Christians and the directives that were given to them in the epistles.

First, *the local church must be kept in focus as the primary means by which edification is to take place.* Paul's ultimate concern was that the *whole* body—the universal church—become a mature organism (Eph 4:11-13), but he demonstrated unequivocably in his own ministry that the way to achieve this goal was to establish local churches and then to help these "microcosms" of the universal church to become mature entities and independent units. He with his co-workers made disciples, taught and encouraged them, and helped each group to become a dynamic *koinonia.*

Part of his teaching, of course, was to help them recognize their relationship to the universal church—that they were part of the whole. This was even more difficult to achieve in New Testament times, since these local groups were much more geographically cut off from one another. Their primary means of relationship with other local bodies of believers was through oral reports from traveling representatives and through correspondence. But even with a limited means for communication, it is obvious that strong ties and relationships developed between local groups, even when they had never met personally (2 Co 8:1-6).

At this juncture no attempt will be made to exhaust the various ideas regarding what must be present to have a local church. There is a variety of opinions. I personally tend toward a simple view, and that is a body of *believers* can be classified as a church whenever and wherever that group meets on a regular basis for the purpose of mutual edification. *Why* a group meets is more significant, it seems, than coming up with a list of norms or specifics which must be present to have, in actuality, a church. Having said this, it must be hurriedly added that any group as just described may be an *infant church*. It must grow and develop taking on certain norms and practices to be a full-grown, mature and dynamic church. The most basic of these norms are quite clear in Scripture. The most foundational of these has already been stated: that the church is a body of *believers*— born-again people; second, they must meet *regularly*. Also the Bible clearly states that there should eventually be *qualified leaders*,[1] and a form of *discipline* for those who claim to be believers but violate scriptural teachings regarding living the Christian life. Certainly there must also be *teaching* of the Word, *prayer*, practice of *baptism*, and sharing of the *Lord's Supper*. All of these factors point to a church that has the potential for maturity. But it must be emphatically emphasized that many of these practices can be present, and still there may be a dead, sterile, immature church. It takes true life and vitality to give meaning to these norms. It is God's plan that as these norms are established, they contribute to edification.

In conclusion, then, this first New Testament principle for edification must be reemphasized and amplified. It is simply this! Any of us who wishes to have good spiritual success in our ministry, and have the full blessing of God upon our efforts, must work toward either the establishment of local churches as new converts are won to Christ; or, if we are serving with an extra-church agency, we must channel new Christians into an already established church. It is there that they can be nurtured into full-grown Christians, as they become a part of a local body of believers, drawing strength from other members of the body, as well as contributing to the growth of the church.

But how do we actually produce a mature local church? This leads us to the second New Testament principle of edification.

Second, *believers must be provided with a basic knowledge of the Word of God*. This is why Paul spent an "entire year" in Antioch

---

1. Note in Ac 14:21-23 that the text seems to indicate that elders were appointed in Lystra, Iconium and Antioch *after* the groups of believers were designated as churches. In other words, it was not necessary to have elders before a group of believers were called a church.

teaching the disciples and why Paul and Barnabas returned to Lystra and Iconium and Antioch "strengthening the souls of the disciples, encouraging them to continue in the faith." This is why Paul said on another occasion, "Let us return and visit the brethren in every city in which we proclaimed the word of the Lord and see how they are. . . ." This is why Paul also spent "a year and six months" in Corinth (Ac 8:11) and "for a period of three years" he did not "cease to admonish each one with tears" in Ephesus.

Paul also went beyond a personal ministry among his converts. While in Athens he sent Timothy back to Thessalonica "to strengthen and encourage" the believers in their faith (1 Th 3:2). Likewise Paul sent Timothy back to Corinth to teach them the doctrines that he was teaching "everywhere in every church" (1 Co 4:17). Titus was left in Crete to "speak the things which are fitting for sound doctrine" (Titus 2:1). Beyond doubt, Paul was vitally concerned that believers be instructed in basic doctrine.

It is the Word of God that is basic to spiritual growth, "Like newborn babes," said Peter, "long for the pure milk of the word, that by it you may grow in respect to salvation" (1 Pe 2:2). Unfortunately, there are individuals in the twentieth century church who have been Christians for years, but who have never been taught even the most elementary Bible doctrines. It is here we must begin in the edification process, whether we are ministering to "new babes" or "old ones."

Third, *believers must be provided with an in-depth knowledge of the Word of God*. Teaching his new converts face to face and sending others to instruct and lead them was not sufficient follow-up in Paul's opinion. His next step involved correspondence—letters to the Thessalonians, to the Corinthians, the Galatians, the Ephesians and the Philippians. All of these epistles were written to provide these believers, not just with a basic knowledge of the Word of God, but with a deeper knowledge of God's truth. And of no little significance, he put this instruction in permanent form, so that it could be rehearsed again and again, studied and circulated among other churches. On occasions they wrote back to him about what he meant, and he in turn wrote another letter to elaborate on his previous correspondence. (For example, 1 and 2 Corinthians). Ultimately, of course, he was providing us with the Word of God, which we have at our disposal today to use in the very same way it was intended to be used in the first century—to provide Christians with a knowledge in depth of God's Word to man.

Fourth, *believers must be provided with opportunities to develop capacities that go beyond knowledge*—to include wisdom, an enlightenment, appreciation, and an awareness and sensitivity to the Spirit of God. That is why Paul prayed for the Ephesians the way he did! Probably no Christians had no more opportunity to be exposed to Paul's teachings than those in Ephesus. They had the wonderful privilege of listening to him teach month after month; and remember, too, that it was in Ephesus that Paul lectured daily for two years in the school of Tyrannus. This helps to explain the "in-depth-ness" of the Ephesian letter. These people were beyond the "infant" stage!

But notice what Paul prays for these well-fed Christians: that they may gain a "spirit of wisdom," that the eyes "of your heart may be enlightened," that they may truly *know* what it means to be called, that they may really know how *rich* they are, and how much power was demonstrated toward them in saving their souls. Paul further prays that they might be strengthened with power through the Spirit in the *inner man,* so that they may "be able to comprehend with all the saints what is the breadth and length and height and depth, and to know the love of Christ which surpasses knowledge," in order that they "may be filled up to all the fulness of God" (Eph 1:16-19; 3:14-19).

Note carefully: Paul wanted them to know the love of Christ which *goes beyond* knowledge! The greatest danger today in the edification process is that Christians learn the deep truths of the Word of God, but never move to the level of behavior that demonstrates wisdom, appreciation, deep awareness and sensitivity to their position in Christ.

We must lead Christians beyond the realm of knowing in the superficial sense of the word. Experience has demonstrated beyond doubt that knowing does not automatically lead to doing. "Association psychology" is a dead theory. It simply does not work. A Christian can know many things about God without sensing His greatness, His power, His riches, and His grace, without being moved by the marvel and wonder of it all. It is possible to know every jot and tittle in the Scriptures and still to lack the conviction and motivatoin to live out one iota of its truth. In short, it is possible to have doctrine and truth "coming out of our ears" without being mature disciples of Jesus Christ.[2]

We have established that knowledge, however, is *basic* to arriving at maturity. What, then, is the means by which Christians go beyond the knowledge level? The answer lies in another New Testament principle.

Fifth, *believers must be provided with the sum total of experiences which will help them to get beyond the knowledge level.* This begins with teaching-learning experiences, but it is far more inclusive than a transmissive-receiving type process. It must go beyond mere dissemination of scriptural content and even beyond interaction with that content by those who are being taught.

This learning process must be in the context of relational Christianity—fellowshipping with God and with one another. It must also be in the context of dynamic Christian witness and outreach. If believers are merely recipients of truth without the opportunity to truly worship God, minister to one another and to win others to Christ, they will not get beyond the knowledge level.

The great problem in many evangelical churches has been in maintaining a balance in all three vital New Testament experiences. In fact, churches can almost be classified by these emphases.

There is the church that has a strong emphasis on Christian witness. Most of the time the believers hear evangelistic messages from the pulpit, and what Bible teaching they get is often superficial. For those who are sensitive to the Lord, their cry is for solid Bible teaching and good exposition. Many who get dissatisfied eventually leave and find a good Bible-teaching church. Here the Word is faithfully taught every Sunday morning and every Sunday night and several times during the week. For a while their hearts are thrilled and their souls are fed. But eventually the excitement of hearing the Word taught begins to disappear. Taking notes and underscoring scriptural

---

2. Association psychology was a prominent theory in the nineteenth Century which advocated that knowing something automatically resulted in feeling and willing and doing. The totality of ideas constituted the will. Ideas once in the mind keep seeking to return and similar ideas tend to reinforce each other. On the other hand, dissimilar ideas tend to repel each other.

Even a brief reflection upon our own personal experience is ample reason as to why this theory has been discredited. Yet there are many Christians who seem to believe that if you store the mind with Bible truth and doctrine, it will automatically become a part of life.

truth in their Bibles becomes purely an academic routine. Again, those who are sensitive to the Lord begin asking the question, "what's wrong with my Christian life?"

Then there are those who are starved for fellowship and long for intimate relationships within the body of Christ. They seek out a church where there is sharing and discussion and informality. They have small-group involvement and an emphasis on "honesty" and "openness." There is body life. Individual members of the church function. For a while the vacuum is filled in their lives. They are excited and thrilled with their new relationships. But gradually these experiences seem to become mechanical and routine, and even superficial. In some cases relationships are spawned that degenerate into behavior that is questionable and have led at times even to immoral activities.

What is the problem? Believers need *all three vital experiences* to grow into mature Christians. They need good Bible teaching that will give them theological and spiritual stability; they need deep and satisfying relationships both, with each other and with Jesus Christ; and they need to experience seeing people come to Jesus Christ as a result of corporate and individual witness to the non-Christian world.

And they need *all* three! Not just one or two will do. Any combination other than the three in proper balance will not produce New Testament results. It is therefore the task of every church leader to determine and plan a structure for the twentieth century church that will allow Christians to have these vital experiences, which were also the experiences of first century Christians.

Sixth, *all believers must be equipped for Christian service*. Note again: this involves *all believers*.

This is the primary thrust of Ephesians 4: "And He gave some as apostles, and some as prophets, and some as evangelists, and some as pastors and teachers, for the equipping of the saints for the work of service, to the building up of the body of Christ . . . but speaking the truth in love, we are to grow up in all aspects into Him, who is the head, even Christ, from whom the whole body, being fitted and held together by that which every joint supplies, according to the proper working of each individual part, causes the growth of the body for the building up of itself in love" (Eph 4:11-12, 15-16).

The church is a unique organism. It is edified and becomes mature as every member functions. God never intended for the members of the body of Christ to become dependent on one leader to do "the work of the ministry." As will be shown in more detail later, God did not even intend for *several leaders* to do the work of the ministry. Rather, He intended for the *whole* church to do this work. It is a responsibility of church leaders to "equip the saints" to serve. Then— and only then—can a local body of believers grow and develop into a mature church.

Seventh, *believers must be helped to develop qualitative family life.* Husbands and wives must grow in their own relationship even as the church grows in its relationship to Christ (Eph 5:24-33). Fathers and mothers must be assisted in rearing their children in the discipline and instruction of the Lord (Eph 6:1-4).

The family unit has a central place in the Bible. It antedates the church, being a basic unit throughout the Old Testament. And in the New Testament it is to form the "building blocks" of the church. Strong Christian families make strong churches, both in terms of evangelism and edification.

Deuteronomy 6:6-9 is a classic biblical example of how a home should function according to God's pattern. This message was delivered to the children of Israel before they entered the promised land. They had been wandering in the wilderness as a result of their disobedience. Now as they are ready to take the final step securing for themselves the land God had promised, they were given these instructions: "And these words, which I am commanding you today, shall be on your heart; and you shall teach them diligently to your sons and shall talk of them when you sit in your house and when you walk by the way and when you lie down and when you rise up" (Deu 6:6-7).

These instructions were followed by a warning. Be careful, Moses said, for when you get into the land your tendency will be to "forget the Lord." When you inherit "houses full of all good things" and "cisterns" and "vineyards and olive trees," then "watch yourself, lest you forget the Lord who brought you from the land of Egypt, out of the house of slavery" (Deu 6:11-12).

Unfortunately when they arrived in the land they *did* forget God. When they had "eaten" and were "satisfied," when their "herds" and their "flocks" and their "silver and gold" multiplied (Deu 8:12-13), they said in their hearts "My power and the strength of my hand made me this wealth" (Deu 8:17).

Most tragic of all, they forgot to instruct and teach their children by precept and example. The instructions in Deuteronomy 6 became only a memory, so far removed from their consciousness, that they were no doubt unaware of their existence. The result was pitiful! Consequently, "there arose another generation after them who did not know the Lord, nor yet the work which He had done for Israel" (Judg 2:10). The rest of the story can be simply told. The family unit failed and so did the nation, for it has always been true that a strong nation is no stronger than its family units. Because of this breakdown in Israel, they are a scattered people still under judgment. The same is true of the Christian community or the church. If the family unit fails to function, if husbands and wives do not experience true *koinonia,* if members of the family as a whole cannot relate to each other, how can we expect dynamic fellowship at the church level? It is virtually impossible!

Then we must—I repeat—assist husbands and wives to develop in their marital life, and help fathers and mothers to rear their children in the discipline and instruction of the Lord. We must help them to develop qualitative Christian families that will serve as solid building blocks within the local church and also serve as dynamic examples in their individual communities. This is particularly true at a time in our own nation when we are beginning to experience disintegration. Interestingly, many sociologists agree that disintegration is distinctly related to the breakdown at the family level. Thus the church can have a dual role in bolstering the family: it can help to build dynamic and thriving churches and also help to preserve the strength of the nation.

Eighth, *the twentieth century church must develop its own contemporary forms and structures for applying the biblical principles just outlined.*

One thing is very clear from a careful study of the New Testament. Forms and structures in the Scriptures are presented as a means to biblical ends. In themselves they are not absolute. This is a danger area for evangelicals because we think in terms of absolutes. We believe in a God who has spoken through the inscripturated Word and who has given us propositional truth that is *absolute* and "never changing." We believe in a God who is *eternal* and a Saviour who is the same "yesterday, today, and forever." Consequently it is easy for us to allow forms and patterns and ways of doing things to become just as sacred as our theology.

The twentieth century church *must* be creative in the areas where God intended it to be free. For example, the Bible does not dictate how *frequently* believers should meet together, nor does it dictate *when*. We are not told what *kinds* of meetings to have, nor are we locked into certain *formats* or *patterns* which should characterize these meetings. Furthermore the Bible doesn't dictate *where* we should meet. All of these are areas of freedom. The important factor is that whatever structures we develop, we must make sure they are helping us to become a mature body of believers, and that they are not causing us to violate the biblical principles for edification just outlined. And above all, whatever structures the twentieth century church develops, they must never be allowed to become absolute or an end in themselves. If we do, we will fall into the same subtle trap that the church has fallen into again and again throughout church history.

Summing Up

1. The local church must be kept in focus as the primary means by which edification is to take place.
2. Believers must be provided with a basic knowledge of the Word of God.
3. Believers must be provided with an in-depth knowledge of the Word of God.
4. Believers must be provided with opportunities to develop capacities that go beyond knowledge.
5. Believers must be provided with the sum total of experiences learning experiences with the Word, vital relational experiences which will help them get beyond the knowledge level—vital with one another and with God, and vital witnessing experiences, both individually and corporately.
6. All believers must be equipped for Christian service.
7. Believers must be helped to develop qualitative family life.
8. The twentieth century church must develop its own contemporary forms and structures for applying the biblical principles just outlined.

8

LEADERSHIP IN THE NEW TESTAMENT CHURCH—PHASE 1

The study of leadership in the New Testament church must be classified into two phases. They are overlapping phases, and yet each one is distinctive.

The first one has to do with the very early days of the church, and particularly the *church in general*. Phase two grows naturally out of phase one, and has to do with leadership in each *local church*.

HISTORICAL BACKGROUND

In order to understand the need for the two phases in God's plan for church leadership, it is necessary to gain some historical perspective.

As the followers of Christ began to carry out the Great Commission and to "make disciples," keep in mind that the only Bible was the Old Testament, which was used primarily to convince people that Jesus Christ was the promised Messiah.[1] But, they had no body of New Testament literature from which to instruct these new Christians. After Pentecost, this literature as we know it today did not even begin to come into existence for approximately another fifteen or twenty years.[2]

As churches were founded, the Epistles were gradually written— particularly the Pauline letters to the churches. They were composed during the decade leading up to A.D. 60, nearly thirty years after Pentecost.[3] The Pastoral epistles were written still later, during the

---

1. It is a very enlightening study to trace in the book of Acts the way the apostles used the Old Testament in winning people to Christ.

2. James and Galatians represent some of the earliest New Testament Epistles, probably written between A.D. 45 and A.D. 50.

3. Approximate dates: 1 and 2 Thessalonians and 1 Corinthians (A.D. 52); 2 Corinthians (A.D. 54); Romans (A.D. 55); Colossians, Ephesians, and Philemon (A.D. 56); Philippians (A.D. 60).

early part of the sixties, and John did not complete his Epistles until sometime in the eighties.

It was actually during the period of A.D. 60 to 100 that the New Testament churches began to experience cohesiveness. Commenting on this development, Merrill Tenney says:

> The survey of the literature will show that in the last third of the first century the church was rapidly consolidating into a recognized institution. From being a scattered collection of isolated bands of believers, each with its own problems and with its own standards, it was beginning to acquire social and doctrinal solidarity and to be regarded as a potent factor in society.[4]

Obviously, the task of edifying the church during the first thirty to fifty years of its existence carried with it some unusual problems. Humanly speaking, without a body of literature there could be no systematic theology, but God had a plan—a unique plan—whereby the church was to be equipped and stabilized.

THE GREATER GIFTS

A significant passage of Scripture that seemingly has just been "discovered" in recent years is Ephesians 4:4-16. It has become the basis for many discussions, lectures, sermons, articles, and even books—particularly as it relates to church leadership.

In the Ephesian passage we read that God gave certain gifts to *some* not all, to equip *all* members of the body for service and ministry. A corollary passage is found in 1 Corinthians 12:28-31. Notice these two passages as they are compared by means of a mechanical layout.

EPHESIANS	1 CORINTHIANS
4:11 And He gave	12:28 And God has appointed in
some *as* apostles,	the church,
and some *as* prophets,	first apostles,
and some *as* evangelists,	second prophets,
and some *as* pastors	third teachers,
and teachers	then miracles,
4:12 for the equipping of the	then gifts of healing,
saints	helps,

---

4. Merrill C. Tenney, *New Testament Survey* p. 319.

for the work of service,　　administrations,
to the building up of the　　various kinds of
body of Christ;　　tongues.

12:29　All are not (apostles,) are
they?
All are not (prophets,) are
they?
All are not (teachers,) are
they?
All are not workers of
miracles, are they?

13:30　All do not have gifts of
healings, do they?
All do not speak with
tongues, do they?
All do not interpret, do
they?

12:31　But earnestly desire the
greater gifts.
And I show you a still
more excellent way.

When you compare these two passages several things become very clear:

1. Paul in the Corinthian passage classifies apostles, prophets, and teachers as the "greater gifts" and instructs the church—as a group—to desire for the local body the greater gifts (1 Co 12:31).[5]

2. The Ephesian passage lists only the greater gifts, whereas the Corinthian passage lists the lesser gifts as well.

3. There is a similarity but yet a lack of conformity in the listing of the greater gifts in the two passages. The sequence is basically the same, but *evangelists* are added in the Ephesian passage and the pastor gift is combined with the teaching gift.

---

5. The conclusion that Paul is classifying *apostles, prophets,* and *teachers* as the "greater gifts" is based on several observations. 1) Paul gives a definite order of importance where he says "first apostles, second prophets, third teachers." (2) He further places these three gifts in a distinct category when he follows this sequential listing by saying *"then* miracles, *then* gifts of healings, helps, administrations, various kinds of tongues (italics added). (3) As will be shown later, a careful comparison of this Corinthian passage with the Ephesians 4 passage helps to confirm these conclusions.

4. There is something that is even more important for the body of Christ to desire than the greater gifts, and that is a "more excellent way"—the way of love, first of all; and then the development of a strong faith and a dynamic hope (1 Co 12:13).

Why are the greater gifts listed in the Ephesian passage and the lesser gifts omitted?

First of all, consider the background of the Ephesian Christians.

If the Corinthian church represents the carnal and immature church in the New Testament, the church at Ephesus (and probably the churches in the surrounding area) represents the church that had reached a high level of spiritual maturity. This is reflected in the Ephesian correspondence, as well as in Paul's words to the Ephesian elders in Acts 20.

The Ephesian Epistle can be classified as normative in setting forth biblical truth. It was not directed to "babes in Christ" (like the Corinthians), but rather to those who were quite mature in the faith. Paul fed these Ephesians *meat*—not milk.

Of this letter, Merrill Tenney says:

> If Romans is a sample of the kind of teaching that Paul would give to churches upon his first visit to them, Ephesians is a specimen of his 'Bible conference' technique. Much of its material can be duplicated in his other epistles, and there is little theology or ethics in Ephesians which cannot be found in essence elsewhere.[6]

The "in-depthness" reflected in Paul's letter is also apparent in his personal relationship with these people. In his final meeting with the Ephesian elders at Miletus, he said:

> You yourselves know, from the first day that I set foot in Asia, how I was with you the whole time, serving the Lord with all humility and with tears and with trials which came upon me through the plots of the Jews; how I did not shrink from declaring to you anything that was profitable, and teaching you publicly and from house to house, solemnly testifying to both Jews and Greeks of repentance toward God and faith in our Lord Jesus Christ. . . . And now, behold, I know that you all, among whom I went about preaching the kingdom, will see my face no more. Therefore I testify to you this day, that I am innocent of the blood of all men. For I did not shrink from declaring to you the whole purpose of God. Be on guard for yourselves and for

6. Tenney, p. 319.

all the flock, among which the Holy Spirit has made you overseers, to shepherd the church of God which He purchased with His own blood. . . . Therefore be on the alert, remembering that night and day for a period of three years I did not cease to admonish each one with tears (Ac 20:18-21, 25-28, 31).

Verse 31 gives us a basic reason why this church was mature. Paul had spent a total of three years ministering to these people. During two of these years Paul lectured daily in the school of Tyrannus. Then, too, they had the benefit of having Timothy serve for a time as their pastor-teacher.

Here was a New Testament church that had every opportunity for spiritual growth and development. They were already on their way to discovering the "more excellent way." This is obvious from Paul's words in Ephesians 1:15-17, "For this reason I too, having heard of the faith in the Lord Jesus which exists among you, and your love for all the saints, do not cease giving thanks for you, while making mention of you in my prayers."

But Paul was not satisfied with their progress, as he never was even with his own life (Phil 3:12-14). He prayed that they might go on even further, and having been "rooted and grounded in love" might be able "to comprehend with all the saints what is the breadth and length and height and depth, and to know the love of Christ which surpasses knowledge" that they might be "filled up to all the fulness of God" (Eph 3:17-19).

It seems therefore, that the lesser gifts may not be mentioned in the Ephesian passage because these believers were beyond the infant stage that Paul describes in 1 Corinthians 13:11. They no longer spoke like children, thought like children, and reasoned like children. They were entering manhood and were doing away with childish things. The "perfect" (or maturity) was in the process of coming and the partial was passing away. The image of Christ in the mirror was coming into clear focus. They were becoming more and more conformed to His image. (See 1 Co 13:10-13.)[7]

---

7. It is important to realize that a mature church can in a relatively short period of time become immature and weak. No doubt this happened to the Ephesians. The apostle John makes it clear that they had left their "first love" (Rev 2:4). This introduces another important New Testament principle of edification; that is, that a church must never take its maturity level for granted. The local body must be constantly concerned that it is in a continuous process of becoming more and more like Jesus Christ.

This was Paul's great concern in Ephesians 4:13-16. Why were the greater gifts given to some? Why apostles, prophets, evangelists, pastors and teachers?

Greater gifts were given in order to assist the body of Christ to become full grown and mature—to attain "to the measure of the stature which belongs to the fulness of Christ"; "to grow up in all aspects into Him."

But note further the relationship between the words and ideas used in 1 Corinthians 13:10-13 and Ephesians 4:13-16.

1 CORINTHIANS 13:10-13

But when the (perfect) comes, the partial will be done away.

When I was a (child,) I used to speak as a child, think as a child, reason as a child; when I became a (man) I did away with childish things.

For now we see in a mirror dimly, but then face to face; now I know in part, but then I shall know fully just as I also have been fully known.

But now abide faith, hope, love, these three; but the greatest of these is love.

EPHESIANS 4:13-16

Until we all attain to the unity of the faith, and of the knowledge of the Son of God, to a (mature) (man,) to the measure of the stature which belongs to the fulness of Christ.

As a result, we are no longer to be (children,) tossed here and there by waves, and carried about by every wind of doctrine, by the trickery of men, by craftiness in deceitful scheming;

but speaking the truth in love, we are to grow up in all aspects into Him, who is the head, even Christ,

from whom the whole body, being fitted and held together by that which every joint supplies, according to the proper working of each individual part, causes the growth of the body for the building up of itself in love.

Note particularly the following relationships between these passages:

1. The word "perfect" or "mature" (Greek, *telios*) is used in both passages.

2. In both cases this word is describing "completeness" or "maturity" which is something that comes as a result of a process. NOTE: "But when the perfect comes, the partial will be done away" (1 Co 13:10). "Until we all attain to the unity of the faith, and of the knowledge of the Son of God, to a mature man" (Eph 4:13).

3. Both passages speak of being children or being childish as contrasted with becoming a full grown man. NOTE: The word for children or child in both of these passages comes from the same Greek word *nepios,* which means infant.

4. Also the Corinthian passage refers to the mirror (1 Co 13:12), which Paul alludes to in his 2 Corinthians letter to describe spiritual status: "But we all, with unveiled face beholding as in a mirror the glory of the Lord, are being transformed into the same image from glory to glory, just as from the Lord, the Spirit" (2 Co 3:18).[8]

This, of course, is precisely what Paul is describing in Ephesians 4:13 when he says the greater gifts are given, "until we all attain . . . to the measure of the stature which belongs to the fulness of Christ." Also, in Ephesians 4:15 he says, "We are to grow up in all aspects into Him, who is the head, even Christ." In other words, Christlikeness reflects maturity. And as the New Testament churches matured, developed, and progressed from a state of infancy to manhood, the lesser gifts seemed to no longer be manifested in their midst.[9]

There is also another interesting correlation between the Corinthian and Ephesian passages to be noted here. Paul told the Corin-

---

8. The Greek words translated mirror in these two Corinthian passages are different. In 1 Corinthians 13:12, the word is *esoptron,* which literally means a looking glass or mirror. In 2 Corinthians 3:18, the word *katoptrizo* means to reflect or to mirror an image. Paul's idea or concept in both verses, however, is essentially the same.

9. The eschatological implications in 1 Corinthians 13:12 are easily understood when it is realized that Paul's view of the second coming of Christ was "First Century." From his vantage point, he anticipated the Lord's return within his lifetime. He lived in anticipation of the fact that the body of Christ would grow toward maturity, becoming more and more like Christ, and then be translated into the presence of Christ and he would see Him "face to face." Note Paul's expression of this hope in 1 Corinthians 15:51-52. "We," he says, "shall not all sleep, be we shall all be changed, in a moment, in the twinkling of an eye, at the last trumpet; for the trumpet will sound, and the dead will be raised imperishable, and we shall be changed." Paul also uses the same plural pronoun in 1 Thessalonians 4:15. He included himself when he said, "For this we say to you by the word of the Lord, that we who are alive, and remain until the coming of the Lord, shall not precede those who have fallen asleep." It seems clear that Paul hoped that he might be among those who were yet alive when Christ returned.

thians that as a body of believers matured, three characteristics would become obvious: faith, hope, and love. These he classified as the *abiding* virtues (1 Co 13:13). The apostle confirms this in his letters to the Thessalonians, the Colossians and the Ephesians when he thanks God for the evidence of these virtues in their midst.[10]

But notice that Paul also describes these virtues in the Ephesian passage in his discussion of the process of spiritual maturation in the body of Christ. In the Corinthian letter, he simply lists them, "But now abide faith, hope, and love." As illustrated in the following table, Paul in the Ephesian letter describes the process in which these characteristics became obvious.[11]

EPHESIANS 4:13-16		1 CORINTHIANS 13:13
Until we all attain to the <u>unity of the faith</u>, and of the <u>knowledge of the Son of God</u>, to a <u>mature man</u>, to the measure of the stature which belongs to the fulness of Christ.	D O C T R I N A L	But now abide FAITH,
As a result, we are <u>no longer</u> to be children, <u>tossed here and there</u> by waves, and <u>carried about by every wind of doctrine</u>, by the trickery of men, by craftiness in deceitful scheming;		HOPE,
but speaking the truth in <u>love</u>, we are to grow up in all aspects into Him, <u>who is the head, even Christ</u>, from whom the <u>whole body</u>, being <u>fitted and held together</u> by that which <u>every joint supplies</u>, according to the proper working of each individual part, causes the growth of the body for <u>the building up of itself in love.</u>	R E L A T I O N A L	LOVE, these three; but the greatest of these is LOVE.

10. See pp. 53-54 for a discussion of these virtues (faith, hope, and love) as they were manifested in various New Testament churches.
11. See pp. 55-59 for biblical definitions of *faith, hope,* and *love.* It will then become clear how Ephesians 4:13-16 actually describes these characteristics. "Faith" and "hope" are basically *doctrinal* and "love" is primarily *relational.*

In conclusion then, it seems logical to infer that Paul omits the lesser gifts in the Ephesian letter, because he is writing to believers who had progressed beyond the infant stage that characterized the Corinthians. They no longer spoke, thought and reasoned like children (1 Co 13:11). They were already manifesting to a great degree the abiding virtues of *faith, hope,* and *love* (Eph 1:15-18). The edifying work of those possessing the greater gifts was clearly evident.

But this leads us to another interesting question:

Why is there a lack of conformity in the two lists of "greater gifts"?

Remember that Paul in Corinthians lists apostles, prophets, and teachers as the greater gifts. In Ephesians he lists apostles, prophets, evangelists, and pastors and teachers, evidently linking "pastors" and "teachers" together as a combination gift given to one person.

To discover why there is a similarity, but a lack of conformity, in the two lists of greater gifts, let's look first at the individuals who had these greater gifts in the New Testament. Who were these people and how were these gifts manifested?

APOSTLES

The term apostle almost without exception is used in the New Testament in a very distinct sense. The word refers primarily to the twelve men Jesus Christ selected out of the larger group of disciples and "named as apostles" (Lk 6:13; see also Mt 10:1-4). The Greek word *apostolos* means literally a delegate, a messenger or one sent forth with orders. When Judas turned his back upon the Lord and later took his own life, he was replaced by Matthias, who was "numbered with the eleven apostles" (Ac 1:26). Paul also classifies himself as an apostle who was "untimely born." He describes himself as one who was called to be an apostle, but who was "not fit to be called an apostle" because he "persecuted the church of God" (1 Co 15:8-9).[12] Luke's record in the book of Acts verifies Paul's claim and testimony without question. He is presented as the great apostle to the Gentiles, who in a special way left the ranks of Judaism and penetrated the pagan world with the gospel of Jesus Christ.

There is a secondary sense, however, in which the word apostle is used in the New Testament. Luke calls Barnabas an apostle when re-

---

12. See also Gal 1:1, 11-12; 2:8; 1 Co 9:1-2; 2 Co 12:11-12; 1 Ti 2:7; 2 Ti 1:11.

ferring to his "ministry" with Paul (Ac 14:4-14).[13] Also Paul seemingly classified Silas and Timothy as fellow apostles (1 Th 2:6-7), and it is also possible that he may be using the same description of Andronicus and Junias, who he says were "outstanding among the apostles" (Ro 16:7). But it is quite clear from the Scriptures that these descriptions are indeed used in a secondary sense. On the one hand they were messengers and delegates sent forth by Jesus Christ as any missionary or Christian leader involved in proclaiming the gospel of Christ. But in a primary sense, apostles were those men who were eyewitnesses of Jesus Christ, and who were taught by Him personally and particularly selected for an initial ministry in bringing into being the body of Christ—His church. Luke verifies this particular apostolic role in the book of Acts when he records their work. The apostles "solemnly testified" and "exhorted" (2:40), they taught (2:42), worked signs and miracles (2:43; 5:12), and gave witness to the resurrection of Jesus Christ (4:33).

The apostles also helped organize the rapidly developing church in Jerusalem, but did not allow themselves to get bogged down with administrative detail. Rather, they devoted themselves to prayer and the ministry of the Word (Ac 6:1-7). Interestingly, a majority of the apostles spent most of their time in Jerusalem in the early days of the church. Even when persecution drove many disciples out of Jerusalem, the apostles stayed (8:1), perhaps because they felt it was their duty. F. F. Bruce speculates also that the persecution at that time, may not have been so much directed at them, but at the Hellenists in the church.[14]

An exception to their staying on location in Jerusalem is noted by Luke, when Peter and John left Jerusalem to go to Samaria to help establish the new believers there, and to use their apostolic authority and power to lay hands on these new believers so that they might receive the Holy Spirit (Ac 8:14-17).

It is clear, however, that God had a divine purpose in planning that the apostles stay in Jerusalem. It was here that they, with the elders, hammered out the theological and practical problems of the new and growing church. Luke devotes a lengthy section to his narrative to

---

13. Though Barnabas is described as an apostle (that is, as one who is engaged in an apostolic work), he seemingly recognized that there was a special group of men who were designated as apostles of which he was not a part (Ac 9:27).
14. F. F. Bruce, *The Book of Acts* (Grand Rapids: Eerdmans, 1954), p. 175.

describe the leadership of the apostles and elders in resolving the Jewish-Gentile problems, particularly as they related to the teachings of law and grace. After much debate and discussion (15:7), the apostles and elders composed and sent a letter to the church in Antioch, clarifying some of these issues (Ac 15:22-29). Significantly, after Acts 15 the apostles are mentioned only once, and in this instance Luke records the ministry of Paul and Timothy as they traveled from city to city "delivering the decrees, which had been decided upon by the apostles and elders who were in Jerusalem" (Ac 16:4).

Hereafter the ministry of the apostle Paul receives primary attention in the Lukean account. Clearly Paul had a unique apostolic ministry compared with the other apostles who remained in Jerusalem. He was called in a special way to be a church planter. He was a multi-gifted man. He "was appointed a preacher and an apostle and a teacher" (2 Ti 1:11; see also 1 Ti 2:7). To him, above all the apostles, was revealed in a most detailed manner the mystery of the church (Eph 3:1-12; Col 1:24-28).

The apostles' work then was foundational, as described by Paul:

> So then you are no longer strangers and aliens, but you are fellow-citizens with the saints, and are of God's household, having been built upon the foundation of the apostles and prophets, Christ Jesus Himself being the cornerstone; in whom the whole building, being fitted together is growing into a holy temple in the Lord; in whom you also are being built together into a dwelling of God in the Spirit (Eph 2:19-22).

Therefore when Paul places apostles at the top of the list in both 1 Corinthians 12:28 and Ephesians 4:11, he is no doubt using the word "apostles" in a primary sense. He is not just describing an "apostolic ministry or work," but he is talking about a specific calling and appointment made by God to specific men who were to have a unique ministry of evangelism and edification in the early days of the church.

PROPHETS

The second of the "greater gifts" listed in Ephesians 4 and 1 Corinthians 12 is prophecy. To prophesy literally means "to speak forth," or "to speak out"; hence a prophet was a person who "spoke forth."

As used in both the Old and New Testaments, a "prophet" had a distinct function. This person was not just an ordinary preacher or teacher. Rather he had access to information by means of a supernatural gift from God. By means of divine inspiration he was able to communicate God's truth, particularly as it related to future events. This is abundantly illustrated in the New Testament.

Obviously the apostles were also prophets. They not only demonstrated this in their apostolic ministry as recorded in the book of Acts, but Peter, James, John, Matthew and Paul all left us with a sizable portion of the New Testament—information that was communicated by means of the prophetic gift.

But there were also individuals in New Testament days who were not apostles in the primary sense, but who were given the gift of prophecy. The first reference to a New Testament prophet other than the apostles appears in Acts 11. Several came to Antioch from Jerusalem. Luke identifies one of them as Agabus, who "stood up and began to indicate by the Spirit that there would certainly be a great famine all over the world" (11:28). As a result of this declaration, the church prepared for this future event, and believers were actually able to help Christians in other parts of the country who were in need (11:29-30).

Agabus appears later in the book of Acts and once more demonstrates his gift of prophecy when he warns Paul regarding the problems and persecution the apostle would encounter in Jerusalem (Ac 21:10-14).

There are other individuals identified by name in the book of Acts who had this same divine ability as Agabus. In the church at Antioch were Barnabas, Simeon, Lucius, and Manaen (Ac 13:1). Saul (before he was called Paul) is also classified at this time as a prophet.

Judas and Silas, who were "leading men among the brethren" in the Jerusalem church (15:22), are also classified as having this prophetic gift. Upon coming to Antioch to assist in delivering the Jerusalem letter, they "also being prophets themselves, encouraged and strengthened the brethren with a lengthy message" (15:32).

Interestingly, this special prophetic gift was not limited to men. Philip, one of the seven men appointed in Acts 6 to care for the distribution of food, had four daughters, all of whom were "prophetesses" (Ac 21:9). Thus women too were recipients of these divine abilities. This also was no doubt true in the church at Corinth, although Paul exhorts that they were not to use this gift in the church meetings (1 Co 14:27-35), but rather to allow the men to exercise their gift.

Certainly Luke and Mark and Jude also had the gift of prophecy, though it is not specifically mentioned. Rather they demonstrated this gift in the revelations embodied in their New Testament writings.

Once again then on the basis of biblical evidence, we are forced to conclude that the gift of prophecy referred to in 1 Corinthians 12 and Ephesians 4 refers to a special group of individuals in New Testament days who were given special revelations from God, in order to help the new and infant church grow and develop into a mature organism. As with the gift of apostleship, it was also a "foundational" gift. You have been "built upon the foundation of the apostles and prophets," wrote Paul to the Ephesians.

EVANGELISTS

As already noted, the gift of evangelism is mentioned in the Ephesian passage, but not in the Corinthian passage. It was no doubt also classified as a "greater gift" because of its inclusion in the Ephesian list. The word evangelist literally means a "bringer of good tidings." In the New Testament, these individuals brought the good tidings of the gospel—the good news of Jesus Christ's coming, death, and resurrection. Yet, of all the gifts listed as the "greater gifts," evangelism is the most difficult to associate with individuals in the New Testament. There is only one clear-cut reference to an "evangelist" per se, and that is Philip, one of the seven and father of the four prophetesses (Ac 21:9). His gift is abundantly demonstrated, however, in his ministry in Samaria (Ac 8:5-13) and particularly in his encounter with the Ethiopian eunuch (Ac 8:26-30).

Philip was no ordinary man in the body of Christ. His gift of evangelism set him apart. He, like the apostles and prophets, was especially gifted with unusual and supernatural abilities. He cast out unclean spirits and healed the lame and paralyzed (Ac 8:7). He received a direct revelation from the Lord regarding the Ethiopian (Ac 8:29) and after leading the eunuch to Christ, "the Spirit of the Lord snatched Philip away" (8:39). The word "snatched" is a strong word, meaning to be caught up or seized. Evidently the Lord removed Philip bodily from this place and, miraculously, Philip found himself in a different location and continued with his evangelistic work—that of "preaching the gospel" (8:40).

Though there are few references to "evangelists" per se in the New Testament, there are other ways to recognize those with this gift. For example there were the "men of Cyprus and Cyrene, who came to Antioch and began speaking to the Greeks also, preaching the Lord Jesus (11:20). The phrase "preaching the Lord Jesus" actually identifies their evangelistic ministry, for the phrase actually meant "to evangelize." We see the results of their evangelistic work for "a large number . . . turned to the Lord" (11:21).

The apostles, and particularly Paul, also demonstrated the gift of evangelism. And at this point it is important to note that all of these New Testament pioneers were frequently multi-gifted men. This gives us a significant clue as to why the list of "greater gifts" is not exactly parallel as listed in the Corinthian-Ephesian passages. This will become more obvious when we look at the gift of teaching which is mentioned next in the list.

TEACHERS and PASTOR-TEACHERS

The *didaskalos,* or teacher, is used in the New Testament to describe a person who taught concerning the things of God. The term pastor (*poimen*) means shepherd, and a pastor-teacher obviously had a dual role—that of shepherding *and* teaching the flock of God. Certainly the apostles also had the gift of teaching (Ac 4:2; 5:21, 25, 28). Of their ministry in those early days in Jerusalem we read, "And every day, in the temple and from house to house, they [the apostles] kept right on teaching and preaching Jesus as the Christ" (5:42). At least some of the New Testament prophets also had the gift of teaching. Barnabas, Simeon, Lucius and Manaen are called prophets *and* teachers (Ac 13:1). Saul (or later Paul) is also included in this list; no doubt, before his apostolic calling was made clear to him. We see Barnabas and Saul using their teaching gifts in Antioch. Luke tells us "that for an entire year they met with the church, and taught considerable numbers" (Ac 11:26).

This leads us to observe more carefully why Paul, in categorizing the "greater gifts," specifies only "teachers" in the Corinthian passage and lists "pastors and teachers" together in the Ephesian list. In reali-

ty he is doing the same thing as Luke in Acts 13:1, when he identifies these four men as prophets *and* teachers. In other words this is
why we see similarity but also variance in the two lists. As we have
already demonstrated, some men during the initial days of the church
were apostles-prophets-evangelists-pastors-teachers. Paul, it appears
had all five gifts. Others, however, were prophets-teachers. And
again some were only classified as prophets. Still others seemed to
have been evangelists-teachers. Apollos seems to be in this category.
He was an "eloquent man" and "mighty in the Scriptures" (Ac
18:24). While in Achaia, "he helped greatly those who had believed
through grace; for he powerfully refuted the Jews in public, demonstrating by the Scriptures that Jesus was the Christ" (Ac 18:27-28).

Here we seem to see a combination ministry of evangelism and
teaching. Paul also makes reference to this combination ministry in
Corinth when he asks the questions: "What then is Apollos? And
what is Paul?" He then answers these questions in this manner:
"Servants through whom you believed. . . . I planted, Apollos watered,
but God was causing the growth" (1 Co 3:5-6). Notice that evidently
the Corinthians had come to know Jesus Christ both through the
evangelistic ministry of Apollos *and* Paul, for they came to "believe"
through the ministry of these men. But note, also, that both of these
men had an edification ministry among these people in that Paul
evidently planted the seed and Apollos followed Paul's ministry by
watering the seed.

Timothy, of course, is the outstanding New Testament example of
a pastor-teacher. Paul frequently used him in this capacity, leaving
him to help a new and struggling church to get on its feet spiritually.
He sent him back to Thessalonica "to strengthen and encourage you
as to your faith" (1 Th 3:2). Likewise he asked him to go to Corinth
to teach them the doctrines that he himself was teaching "everywhere
in every church" (1 Co 4:17). He asked him to "remain on at Ephesus" so that he might "instruct certain men not to teach strange doctrines" (1 Ti 1:3).

Later Paul wrote to Timothy, "And the things which you have
heard from me in the presence of many witnesses, these entrust to
faithful men, who will be able to teach others also" (2 Ti 2:2). Perhaps this is the combination gift that Paul referred to in his two letters to this young man. There seems to be some evidence for this

conclusion. Notice the context in which Paul makes reference to Timothy's gift.

> Prescribe and teach these things. Let no one look down on your youthfulness, but rather in speech, conduct, love, faith, and purity, show yourself an example of those who believe. Until I come, give attention to the public reading of Scripture, to exhortation and teaching. Do not neglect the spiritual gift within you, which was bestowed upon you through prophetic utterance with the laying on of hands by the presbytery. Take pains with these things; be absorbed in them, so that your progress may be evident to all. Pay close attention to yourself and to your teaching; persevere in these things; for as you do this you will insure salvation both for yourself and for those who hear you (1 Ti 4: 11-16).

Note, too, that Paul in his second letter warns Timothy not to be timid, but "to kindle afresh the gift of God" (2 Ti 1:6). Undoubtedly, he had been criticized for his youthfulness (1 Ti 4:12); and his sensitive pastoral heart may have caused him to withdraw and to neglect his responsibilities. Paul encourages him not to withdraw but to continue his pastoral-teaching ministry.

Titus, too, was probably a New Testament pastor-teacher. He, like Timothy, was closely associated with Paul in his missionary travels (2 Co 2:13; 7:6-7, 13-14). Paul identifies him as his "true child in a common faith" (Titus 1:4) and as his "partner and fellow-worker" (2 Co 8:23). Paul left Titus in Crete to carry out a pastoral-teaching ministry; that is to set things in order and to "appoint elders in every city" (Titus 1:5). While there he was to "speak the things which are fitting for sound doctrine" (Titus 2:1), and to "exhort and reprove with all authority" (Titus 2:15).

There may have been other men who were closely associated with Paul who were pastor-teachers like Timothy and Titus—men such as Gaius and Aristarchus and Erastus. Luke, of course, was left behind to help establish the new church in Philippi, and, in addition to being a prophet, he may have also been a pastor-teacher.

In conclusion, therefore, we see a number of different gift combinations functioning in the book of Acts. This is why Paul is not concerned about complete uniformity, even in listing the greater gifts. There is a natural sequence, however, which is obvious in both passages, going from the foundational gifts to those that were used more

specifically in founding and establishing churches. In view of all of
the combinations it would have been awkward to attempt to come up
with a uniform list. This is seemingly why Paul spoke of "pastors and
teachers." Not all had this combination of gifts. While Apollos had
the gift of teaching, he seemingly did not have the gift of pastor or
shepherd. Interestingly, Silas may have been a prophet *and* pastor
and teacher. He is definitely identified as a prophet (Ac 15:32), and
he certainly engaged in a teaching ministry in his travels with Paul
(Ac 15:40-41). And furthermore he obviously engaged in a shepherding ministry while in Thessalonica (1 Th 1:1; 2 Th 1:1).

It is important to note once again that Paul exhorted the Corinthian
church to seek the "greater gifts." That is, as a body, they were to desire the assistance of those individuals with these gifts. In order to be
edified and to grow up and mature, they were to encourage those
who were apostles, prophets and teachers to have a ministry among
them.[15]

SUMMING UP

A study of the book of Acts, particularly, leaves little doubt as to
what is meant by those who had the greater gifts. In the most part
they were gifted men who were used of God to found and establish
the church. The *apostles* were those who were especially called, appointed and trained by Christ to form a small nucleus that would
bring the church into being.

Prophets, also classified as having a foundational ministry, were
given access to information from God by direct revelation, and were
able to predict future events in order to assist the body of Christ in
its growth and development.

Evangelists were given special abilities in preaching the gospel.
Teachers were those who could lead people into a greater understanding of God's truth. The gift was used both in evangelism and edification.

In the early days of the church, before the completion of the canon, those with the gift of teaching probably had access to doctrinal
truth by direct revelation from God. The apostles particularly were

---

15. Some of the Corinthians were rejecting the apostle Paul's ministry in favor
of others who were exercising the lesser gifts.

able to recall by means of the Holy Spirit what they had learned from Jesus Christ. While with them, He said: "These things I have spoken to you, while abiding with you. But the Helper, the Holy Spirit, whom the Father will send in My name, He will teach you all things, and bring to your remembrance all that I said to you" (Jn 14:25-26).

Pastors or shepherds were those who gave special help to new churches. They were also *teachers* that helped both in the organization of the church as well as in its growth through the process of instruction. In the first century church they seemingly had a foundational ministry, along with the others who had the greater gifts. They went from church to church assisting in the appointment of local leadership, and making sure the church learned the basic doctrines of Christianity.

It seems, therefore, that these greater gifts mentioned in 1 Corinthians 12 and Ephesians 4 were, in a *primary sense,* limited to "a church planting" ministry in the early days of Christianity, and were directly related to the universal church. These were special gifts given prior to the writing of the New Testament. These early Christian leaders were given supernatural capacities and abilities, including both knowledge and skill, in order to "equip the saints for the work of the ministry."

But, as people came to Christ and formed groups of believers in specific geographical locations, God instituted His second phase or plan for church leadership—a plan that clearly relates to the *local church.* As will be shown, this new concept called for church leaders who, though they are not classified as individuals possessing the greater gifts, were in a *secondary sense* to have a ministry that included a similar function as those who actually possessed these greater gifts.

9

LEADERSHIP IN THE NEW TESTAMENT CHURCH—PHASE 2

As pointed out in the previous chapter, New Testament church leaders faced some unusual problems during the early years of the church's existence. They had no body of inspired literature from which to teach doctrine which was distinctly New Testament. It is conceivable that some Christians even at the end of the first century had not yet been exposed to all of the gospels, Paul's letters and the other epistles.[1]

God had a plan, however, which enabled the apostles, prophets, evangelists, pastors and teachers to "equip the saints for the work of service"—even apart from having the New Testament literature. He bestowed upon these individuals supernatural capacities and abilities—involving both knowledge and skill—to enable them to edify the church.

But as churches were founded and established in the faith, it is clear from the historical record that a new plan for church leadership was instituted—one which, for practical reasons, is designated as phase two.

LOCAL CHURCH LEADERSHIP

The book of Acts as well as some material in the epistles clearly shows that, in the most part, those individuals who possess the "greater gifts"—that of apostle, prophet, evangelist, pastor and teacher—had a ministry at large. They "made disciples," founded churches, and moved from one group of believers to another, helping them to become established in the faith.

---

1. Regarding the canon of the New Testament, Tenney notes: ". . . it is evident that not all of the present books of the New Testament were known or accepted by all the churches in the east and in the west during the first four centuries of the Christian era." (Merrill C. Tenney, *New Testament Survey*, p. 411.)

The primary responsibility of the first century pastor-teacher was to help the new and struggling church to get organized and to grow spiritually. As mentioned previously, Timothy was one of the most prominent pastor-teachers in the New Testament. When the church at Corinth was struggling in its carnality and immaturity, Paul sent Timothy to teach them (1 Co 4:17). Paul also indicated his plans to send him to Philippi to have a ministry among the Christians there (Phil 2:19-20). He left him in Ephesus to instruct and guide the believers (1 Ti 1:3). On his second missionary journey, he left Timothy in Berea along with Silas (Ac 17:14), apparently to help establish the church. On the same journey, after starting the church in Thessalonica, Paul sent Timothy back to this church "to strengthen and encourage" them (1 Ti 3:1-2).

Timothy, and other men like him, such as Titus, served especially the New Testament church as God's plan for church leadership moved from phase one to phase two. The second phase was instituted as soon as there were believers in the local congregation who were mature enough to be appointed as elders. This was demonstrated by Paul and Barnabas as they retraced their steps and went back to the cities in which they had previously "made many disciples" and then "appointed elders . . . in every church" (Ac 14:21-23).

ELDERS OR BISHOPS?

The New Testament writers used two words to describe the spiritual leaders in the local churches—*bishop* (*episkopos*) and *elder* (*presbuteros*). The words are used interchangeably by several New Testament writers.[2]

The word *bishop* actually means "an overseer." This word was used as an official title among the Greeks, and Lightfoot reminds us that, "in Athenian language it was used especially to designate commissioners appointed to regulate a new colony or acquisition. . . ."[3] Synonyms for the word *bishop* might be curator, guardian or superintendent.

The word *elder,* though found in the literature of many nations, is found most frequently in the literature describing the activities of

---

2. Compare Ac 20:17 and 28; Titus 1:5 and 7; 1 Ti 3:1-2 and 1 Ti 5:17, 19.
3. J. P. Lightfoot, *Saint Paul: The Epistle to the Philippians* (London: McMillan, 1881), p. 95.

God's chosen people. Again Lightfoot has made some significant observations:

> In the lifetime of the law giver, in the days of the judges, throughout the monarchy, during the captivity, after the return, and under Roman domination, the "elders" appear as an integral part of the governing body of the country . . . Over every Jewish synagogue . . . a council of "elders" presided. It was not unnatural, therefore when the Christian synagogue took its place by the side of the Jewish, a similar organization should be adopted with such modifications as circumstances required; and thus the name familiar under the old dispensation was retained under the new.[4]

Moreover, the word *elder* appears in the New Testament more frequently than the word *bishop,* and especially in the book of Acts. Luke uses the word to refer to the "elders of Israel,"[5] and after the church was established in Jerusalem and in other parts of the world, it was used to refer to the "elders of the church."[6] Reference to being a bishop appears only once in Acts, and that is where Paul is addressing the Ephesian elders (Ac 20:28). The rest of the time it appears primarily in the Pauline epistles, and as just mentioned, is used interchangeably with the word *elder.*

Many have suggested that the term *bishop* is used to refer to the office and the word *elder* has to do with the man or person. This may be true, but it seems there is also a more significant explanation. Could it be that Paul—since he used the word *bishop* more frequently than other New Testament writers—did so to communicate more effectively to the mixture of converted Jews and Gentiles in the New Testament church? Note that the word is used in writing to the Philippians (Phil 1:1), to Timothy who was stationed at Ephesus (1 Ti 3:1-2), and to Titus who was in Crete (Titus 1:7). All of these churches were founded in a pagan world and were composed of both Jew and Gentile converts. If this be true, it means Paul was again mindful of how important it is to communicate in the language of the people. He wanted to bring both groups together in oneness, to show them there was no barrier or "dividing wall," but rather "one new

---

4. Ibid., p. 96.
5. See Ac 4:5, 8, 23; 6:12; 23:14; 24:1; 25:15.
6. Note that when used to refer to the "elders of the church" it is used to refer most frequently to elders in the church at Jerusalem, which was made up primarily of Jewish Christians. (See Ac 11:30; 14:23; 15:2, 4, 6, 22-23; 16:4; 20:17; 21:18.) There are also numerous references to "elders" in Revelation.

man." Christ has reconciled "them both in one body to God" (Eph 2:14-16. They were no longer Jews and Greeks, but the "church of God" (1 Co 10:32).

So whether we call them elders (a term well-known to Jews) or bishops (a term well-known to Greeks), it matters not, implies Paul. The important issue is what these men were like, what characterized their lives. The title was secondary, their qualifications and functions were primary.

ELDERS or BISHOPS—THEIR QUALIFICATIONS and FUNCTIONS

As you study the passages in the New Testament which refer to elders or bishops, it becomes clear that both *qualifications* and *functions* are described.[7] Significantly far more is said about qualifications than functions.

THEIR QUALIFICATIONS

1. He must be *above reproach* (1 Ti 3:2; Titus 2:7); that is, blameless or of good report. There was to be no grounds for accusing this man of improper Christian behavior.
2. He must be the *husband of one wife* (1 Ti 3:2; Titus 1:6); that is, not a bigamist. In a culture where men frequently cohabited with more than one woman, Paul needed to make it very clear that an elder in the church was to be a "one-wife man"—loyal to her and to her alone.
3. He must be *temperate* (1 Ti 3:2; Titus 1:8); that is, self-controlled. He must not be a man who is in bondage to himself and to the desires of the flesh.
4. He must be *prudent* (1 Ti 3:2; Titus 1:8); that is, sensible, wise, and balanced in judgment. He must not be given to quick and superficial decisions based on immature thinking.
5. He must be *respectable* (1 Ti 3:2); that is, he must have an orderly life. He must demonstrate good behavior.
6. He must be *hospitable* (1 Ti 3:2; Titus 1:8); that is, he must be unselfish and willing to share his blessings with others. His home life and personal life must be characterized by "hospitality."

---

7. There are three basic passages which make reference to elders and bishops: 1 Ti 3:1-7; Titus 1:5-10; 1 Pe 5:1-5. James 5:14 also makes reference to the function of elders.

7. He must be *able to teach* (1 Ti 3:2; Titus 1:9); that is, to communicate the truth of God to others and "to exhort in sound doctrine" in a nonargumentive way (2 Ti 2:24-26).
8. He must not be *given to wine* (1 Ti 3:3; Titus 1:7); that is, he must not be "addicted" to wine.
9. He must not be *pugnacious,* but gentle (1 Ti 3:3; Titus 1:7); that is, he must not be a "striker" or a person given to physical violence, but one who is characterized by forebearance and tenderness.
10. He must be *uncontentious* (1 Ti 3:3); that is, not given to quarreling and selfish argumentation.
11. He must be *free from the love of money* (1 Ti 3:3; Titus 1:7; 1 Pe 5:2); that is, not "greedy of filthy lucre," or "fond of sordid gain," or stingy with his material blessings.
12. He must be *one who manages his own household well, keeping his children under control with all dignity* (1 Ti 3:4; Titus 1:6); that is, he must have the respect of his family and be recognized as the leader of the household. Paul adds, "But if a man does not know how to manage his own household, how will he take care of the church of God?" (1 Ti 3:5).
13. He must *not be a new convert* (1 Ti 3:6); that is, one who is a new Christian and a babe in Christ. He must be a mature believer and obviously one who has been a Christian for a period of time—at least long enough to demonstrate the reality of his conversion and the depth of his spirituality.
14. He must have *a good reputation with those outside the church* (1 Ti 3:7); that is, unbelievers must also respect his character and integrity.
15. He must not be *self-willed* (Titus 1:7); that is, stubborn and one who tries to have his own way. He must not be an insensitive person, forcing his own ideas and opinions on other people.
16. He must not be *quick-tempered* (Titus 1:7); that is, one who gets angry quickly and "flies off the handle." He must be in control of his own spirit.
17. He must *love what is good* (Titus 1:8); that is, he must not follow after and desire those things which are evil and sinful. He must be the kind of person who desires to do the will of God in everything (1 Pe 5:2).

18. He must *be just* (Titus 1:8); that is, he must be fair and impartial. He must be one who can make objective judgments based upon principle.
19. He must be *devout* (Titus 1:8); that is, holy and separated from sin.
20. He must *hold fast the faithful word* (Titus 1:9); that is, he must be stable in his faith and obey the Word of God in all respects. He must not be hypocritical, teaching one thing and living another.

THEIR FUNCTION

1. He must help *shepherd the flock of God* (1 Pe 5:2, Ac 20:28; 1 Ti 3:5); that is, he must care for the church. Like a shepherd who oversees a flock of sheep, he is to guard the people of God against false teachers (Acts 20:28-30). He is to meet their needs and assist them in whatever way he can.
2. He is not to *lord it over those allotted to his charge, but he is to be an example to the flock* (1 Pe 5:3); that is, he is not to use his position for selfish gain or to demonstrate dictatorial attitudes. Rather he is to lead by example—obviously a Christlike example, as demonstrated in the qualifications just listed.
3. He is to *teach* and to *exhort* (1 Ti 3:2; Titus 1:9); that is, to instruct and warn Christians. Part of the "shepherding" responsibility is to *feed* the flock of God.
4. He is to *refute those who contradict the truth* (Titus 1:9); that is to stand up to those who teach false doctrines. They are to expose those who are "teaching things they should not teach" (Titus 1:11).
5. He is to *manage the church of God* (1 Ti 3:5); that is, to oversee the church and administer the affairs of the church. They are to be men who can "rule well" (1 Ti 5:17).
6. He is to *pray for the sick* (Ja 5:14-15); that is, along with the other elders of the church he is to go where the sick are, and pray for their spiritual and physical well being.

DEACONS

A second leader that is mentioned in the New Testament in relationship to the local church is a "deacon." The word *diakonos* means "servant," and it is from the meaning of this word that we must determine the *function* of those who have this New Testament leadership position. "Deacons" are referred to only in Paul's letter to the Philippians (1:1) and in his first letter to Timothy; and here only qualifications are listed—not function. The closest we can come to a specific reference describing the function of a deacon is in Acts 6 where seven men were appointed to *serve* tables.[8] This passage, of course, illustrates a temporary task. When the church was eventually scattered, so were the seven. The communal system was no longer continued and consequently there was no need to continue this specific leadership position assigned to these men.

Note the qualifications for a deacon as spelled out by Paul to Timothy (1 Ti 3:8-12):

1. "Men of dignity" (v. 8)
2. "Not double-tongued" (v. 8)
3. "Not . . . addicted to much wine" (v. 8)
4. "Not . . . fond of sordid gain" (v. 8)
5. "Holding to the mystery of the faith with a clear conscience" (v. 9)
6. "Beyond reproach" (v. 10)
7. "Men . . . [whose wives are] dignified, not malicious gossips, but temperate, faithful in all things' " (v. 11)
8. "Husbands of only one wife" (v. 12)
9. "Good managers of their children and their own household" (v. 12)

IMPORTANT OBSERVATIONS

Now that we have looked at local church leadership in the New Testament, note several significant things.

First *a strong emphasis is placed upon qualifications*. This is not only true in the passages just cited, but also in other instances where spiritual leadership was to be selected. The men chosen to serve tables in Jerusalem were to be men "of good reputation, full of the Spirit and of wisdom" (Ac 6:3). When Paul selected a traveling companion, he selected a man who "was well spoken of by the brethren who were in Lystra and Iconium" (Ac 16:2). And as demonstrated

---

8. The word *deacon* is not used in Acts 6, but the word "to serve" actually comes from the same root word as the word translated "deacon."

when he wrote to Timothy and Titus and instructed them regarding certain leaders in the local church, he first and foremost spelled out *qualifications*—not tasks.

Why? First, Paul knew that men who measured up to certain standards would be able to effectively organize and administer the affairs of the church. Of special significance is the special qualification regarding being able to manage his own household well (1 Ti 3:4). A man who had a well-managed family, a wife and children who respected his leadership abilities, and children who had been nurtured in the things of God, would also be a man who would be able to manage a church, gain respect from other members of the body of Christ and be able to feed the flock of God. In other words, Paul knew that a man who could function well at the family level could also function well at the church level.

Second, Paul knew that tasks change, particularly in the area of *serving,* as demonstrated so forcefully in Acts 6. This was probably *why* he gives only qualifications for deacons—not tasks. On the other hand, the function of the elders is more stabilized, for spiritual needs are relatively constant. Consequently, there is more information given in the New Testament regarding the responsibilities of these men. People will always be in need of being *encouraged, taught, exhorted, managed,* and *prayed for.* But here again, this *general* job description for elders leaves a vast amount of room for creative ministry under the leadership of the Holy Spirit. No *specific* list of spiritual tasks would be constantly relevant to *every* culture at any given moment in history.

A second observation regarding local church leadership in the New Testament is closely related to what has just been stated; that is, *Paul was not consistent in the instructions he gave regarding the appointment of elders and deacons.* Obviously in Ephesus they had both, as well as in Philippi. But in his instructions to Titus, he instructed him to appoint elders, but he says nothing about deacons (Titus 1:5).

Again, we must ask *why?* The answer seems obvious when you understand Paul's total philosophy of the ministry. He was "a free man"—not locked into patterns and structures, either in communication or in organization and administration. There is no doubt that he believed that every church needed qualified spiritual leaders who could shepherd the flock. Call them bishops, if you wish, or elders.

He was not concerned about their titles. But when it came to deacons, he obviously felt there was a need for this office in some churches, but not in others. Or perhaps, there was a "leadership shortage" in Crete, and all available men were appointed as elders. Deacons would have to wait!

It is impossible, of course, to arrive at conclusive reasons as to why there is a disparity in Paul's approach to church leadership from church to church. But, is this not part of the genius of the New Testament? Once again we see freedom in form and structure, means and methods, and patterns and programs. These are but means to achieve divine ends.

A third observation regarding local church leadership in the New Testament relates to function. Although elders are never classified as men having the "greater gifts" in the primary sense, they were, in many respects, *to do the same type of work as an apostle, a prophet, an evangelist, and a pastor-teacher.* They were not apostles, but they were to perform an apostolic ministry in the sense of being "delegates," "messengers," to the local church. Like apostles they were to exhort and defend the faith. They were not necessarily prophets in the primary sense, though they were to perform a prophetic ministry, "speaking forth" the Word of God. And primarily "forth-tellers" rather than "foretellers," they were, as the prophets of old, to "strengthen and encourage" the church (Ac 15:32). They were not "evangelists" in the primary sense, though they were to join all members of the local body, proclaiming Jesus Christ to the unsaved world —both by life and verbal witness. They were not pastor-teachers like Timothy and Titus, but were to *teach* the Word of God and to *shepherd* the flock. They were to perform the ministry of a pastor-teacher in each local congregation.

A final observation regarding leadership in the New Testament church is that *we always see a plurality of leadership.* There is no reference to the appointment of "one" elder or "one" deacon for any given church. Obviously, no one individual was ever asked to serve alone.

It is implied, however, that some would give more time to spiritual leadership than others, and some would be called upon to fill more demanding responsibilities. These men, said Paul, should be given "double honor" and be financially remunerated for their efforts. This is especially true, he said, of those "who work hard at preaching and teaching" (1 Ti 5:17-18). Plurality of leadership implies that a local church is not ready for phase two in God's plan for church leadership until more than one person is qualified to lead. But, it also reflects another very important idea regarding the New Testament church! It is a unique organism—an organism that was not designed by God to function with a pyramidal-type organizational structure. It was to be a body, as "every joint supplies, according to the proper working of each individual part. . ." (Eph 4:16). The local group needed leadership, yes, but it was to be a multiple leadership—not one individual who served as authoritative voice.

SUMMING UP

God's plan for church leadership is quite clear in the Scripture. He launched the church by giving certain men the greater gifts—men who under the direction of the Holy Spirit initiated the Christian movement and who brought local churches into existence through their preaching and teaching. As these churches were established in the faith, and when more than one man became qualified, they were appointed as elders or bishops to do a pastoral-teaching ministry in each local church. When necessary, deacons were also appointed to serve the church—particularly in meeting its more material needs. These leaders, along with all members of each local group, were a unique organism—a localized, functioning body of Christ—a microcosm and visible expression of the universal church.

But, this leads us to another important topic when discussing leadership in the local church—the functioning body of Christ. What is God's plan for "body life"?

10

THE FUNCTIONING BODY

The church is pictured in the New Testament as a unique organism. Even in its local expression it is more than an organization. Every localized group of believers is composed of individual members, who are to function and be a part of the whole.

BODY LIFE

The term "body" appears approximately forty times, directly or indirectly to describe the functioning body of Christ. The New Testament church was described as being "many members" yet "one body" and "all the members" did not "have the same function" (Ro 12:4). All had gifts that differed "according to the grace given" (Ro 12:6). One member of the body could not say to the other, "I have no need of you" (1 Co 12:21). They were "many members, but one body" (1 Co 12:20), and all members were to contribute to the growth of the body. Anything that interfered with the "functioning body" interfered with the process of edification.

This means that every member of the body of Christ is important! In a sense, every member is a leader, called of God to help other members of the body to grow and mature. Every "joint" must function and every "individual part" is to make its contribution to the life of the church (Eph 4:16).

SPIRITUAL GIFTS

In studying the concept of the "functioning body" in the New Testament, you cannot bypass reference to "spiritual gifts." It also goes without saying that there is a renewed interest on this subject in the twentieth century church, and this is understandable, for the evangelical church in general has for many years neglected the importance of relational Christianity. We have come to rely upon the "preacher" and the "pastor" to do "the work of the ministry." And on the other hand, many Christian leaders have been content to "preach and teach" and allow the members of their congregation to sit and listen.

What does the Bible actually teach about spiritual gifts? This is a difficult question to answer, which is obvious from the greatly varied opinions about this significant subject. I would like to approach this, however, by making some significant observations which grow out of our study of New Testament leadership.

First, the New Testament church which had the most spiritual gifts being manifested in its midst was also the most immature and carnal church. To the Corinthians, Paul wrote, they were "not lacking in any gift" (1 Co 1:7), but yet they were "babes in Christ." They acted like "men of flesh" (1 Co 3:1).

Second, Paul classified certain gifts as being the "greater gifts." Not all spiritual gifts listed were as important as others. The "greater gifts" were apostles, prophets, and teachers (1 Co 12:28-31), which probably also included evangelists and pastors (Eph 4:11).

Third, Paul instructed the Corinthians to seek the "greater gifts" for the body (1 Co 12:31), but nowhere are individual Christians instructed to seek spiritual gifts personally.

Fourth, Paul attributed the manifestation of certain gifts to childish and immature Christian behavior. In fact, the more mature a New Testament church became, the fewer references there seems to be to specific spiritual gifts (1 Co 13:8-11).

Fifth, Paul showed the Corinthians an even more "excellent way" than the use of spiritual gifts—the way of love (1 Co 13:13). He also showed that all of these gifts can be present, and love can be lacking; and consequently spiritual gifts can be as "nothing" (1 Co 13:1-3).

Sixth, there was no consistency in the manifestation of spiritual gifts from church to church, and . . .

Seventh, the Bible does not set forth a uniform pattern of spiritual gifts. This is obvious from the following lists:

1 CORINTHIANS 12:8-10	1 CORINTHIANS 12:28	ROMANS 12:6-8
Word of wisdom	Apostles	Prophecy
Word of knowledge	Prophets	Serving
Faith	Teachers	Teaching
Healing	Miracles	Exhortation
Miracles	Healings	Giving
Prophecy	Helps	Leading
Distinguishing of spirits	Administrations	Mercy
Tongues	Tongues	
Interpretation of tongues		

EPHESIANS 4:11	1 PETER 4:11
Apostles	Speaking
Prophets	Serving
Evangelists	
Pastors-teachers	

Eighth, when local church leaders were to be appointed, Paul did not instruct Timothy and Titus to "look for spiritual gifts"; rather to look for "spiritual qualifications."[1]

It is interesting to note that in all of the qualifications listed for elders, the closest reference to a gift is when Paul states that these men are to be "able to teach." Even here, however, it does not say he must have the "gift of teaching," but rather he must be able to communicate the Word of God effectively (compare Titus 1:9).

If having *obvious* spiritual gifts is a prerequisite for serving in the church—as some people say it is—it is very interesting that Paul himself did *not* make this stipulation for New Testament church leadership.

Ninth, "body function" is not dependent upon the list of "spiritual gifts," in the New Testament, but rather a love and concern for "one another."

This concept appears over fifty times in the Epistles alone, and it is used frequently in relationship to body function. Consider the following selected list:

---

1. It is interesting that Paul makes no reference to "elders" in Corinth. Is it possible there was no one qualified in this "gifted" but immature church to serve in this leadership position? 1 Corinthians 3:1-3 seems to imply this possibility, with the overall content of the letter supporting this hypothesis.

REFERENCE	STATEMENT
Romans	
12:10	Be devoted to one another.
	Give preference to one another.
12:16	Be of the same mind toward one another.
13:8	Love one another.
14:13	Let us not judge one another.
14:19	Pursue the things which make for peace for the building up of one another.
15:5	Be of the same mind with one another.
15:7	Accept one another.
15:14	Admonish one another.
1 Corinthians	
12:25	Care for one another.
Galatians	
5:13	Serve one another.
6:2	Bear one another's burdens.
Ephesians	
4:1-2	Show forebearance to one another.
4:32	Be kind to one another.
5:18-21	Speak to one another in psalms and hymns and spiritual songs.
	Be subject to one another.
Colossians	
3:9	Do not lie to one another.
3:12-13	Bear with one another.
	Forgive each other.
3:16	Teach and admonish one another.
1 Thessalonians	
3:12	Increase and abound in love for one another.
4:18	Comfort one another.
Hebrews	
3:13	Encourage one another.
10:23-25	Stimulate one another to love and good deeds.
James	
4:11	Do not speak against one another.
5:9	Do not complain . . . against one another.
5:16	Confess your sins to one another.
	Pray for one another.
1 Peter	
1:22	Love one another.
4:9	Be hospitable to one another.

5:5	Clothe yourselves with humility toward one another.
1 John	
3:11	Love one another.
3:23	Love one another.
4:7	Love one another.
4:11	Love one another.
4:12	Love one another.
2 John 5	Love one another.

SOME CONCLUSIONS

As we look at the New Testament in relationship to body function, and also as we consider the subject of spiritual gifts, certain conclusions become rather obvious.

First, it is very clear that spiritual maturity and the possession and manifestation of spiritual gifts are not synonymous; nor does individual maturity depend upon the presence of spiritual gifts. Paul evaluated maturity in the body by the degree of love, faith, and hope that was being manifested (1 Co 13:13).

Second, since there is no uniform list of spiritual gifts given in the New Testament, obviously the writers of the New Testament were not concerned about absolute consistency in describing spiritual gifts. Furthermore, the sum total of gifts listed in the New Testament was not manifested in every church.

Third, God obviously did not want to lock us into a "list of gifts." He has not established absolute patterns in this area—which is clear from the variation that was present—even in the New Testament churches. He perhaps has left the "gift list" open ended because He desires to manifest certain gifts at various times and at various places.

SUMMING UP

A functioning body, or "body life," as some have designated it, is absolutely essential for growth and maturity to take place in the church. The very nature of the body of Christ makes it important for every member to function and contribute to the process of edification.

It is no doubt true that every believer in the New Testament church was gifted by God in a special way to function in the body, but it was not always possible nor necessary to identify that gift by name or to be able to "pigeonhole" it by placing it in a "gift list."

It is also true that though specific spiritual gifts are mentioned on several occasions in the New Testament, the use of all of them was not essential for "body function," or for maturity to take place in the body. In fact, some of the gifts actually got in the way of unity and spiritual growth and development. This is abundantly clear as you study the church at Corinth.

The important issue, however, is quite clear as you study body function. Christians cannot grow effectively in isolation! They need to experience each other. In fact, the words "to edify," "edifying," or "edification" are used most frequently in the context of the functioning body.

Furthermore, New Testament Christians were not given the choice as to whether or not they wanted to function, they were *told* to help "one another" in many ways. Obviously "grace" is given to help each believer to function (Eph 4:7), but to do so is not dependent upon being able to classify one's "spiritual gifts," and to call them by name, before being able to participate in body life. In fact, as a Christian ministers to other members in the body, if he has a "special" gift which is recognizable, it will become increasingly clear to himself as well as to other Christians. But if it does not become recognizable, Christians shouldn't be concerned, but continue to help "one another" in the many ways specified in the New Testament.

Furthermore, if a person desires to be a spiritual leader in the church—which, says Paul, "is a fine work"—he should be primarily concerned about living up to the qualifications specified in the New Testament, not identifying his spiritual gifts.

11

PRINCIPLES OF NEW TESTAMENT LEADERSHIP

A study of leadership in the New Testament yields some very clear-cut principles for the twentieth century church. These principles can serve as guidelines and objectives for starting new churches in our contemporary culture—wherever that might be—and can also provide established churches with a criteria for evaluating their own philosophy of church leadership.

First, the most important criterion for selecting local church leadership is spiritual qualifications. In the New Testament it was not primarily abilities, talents, or even spiritual gifts.

Out of twenty specific qualifications listed by Paul in 1 Timothy 3 and Titus 1, eighteen have to do with a man's reputation, ethics, morality, temperament, habits, and spiritual and psychological maturity.

It is important to emphasize at this point, that a number of believers are confused today because of the renewed emphasis on "spiritual gifts." Though this is a good emphasis in many ways, there are some distinct problems that have grown out of a violation of the New Testament principle just stated.

When Paul gave instructions to Timothy regarding how to handle the men who wanted a leadership position in the church, he commented as follows: "If any man aspires to the office of overseer, it is a fine work he desires to do." He then listed the qualifications that each man must demonstrate to be appointed to this position. NOTE: he *did not say* he must have the gift of evangelist, the gift of pastor-teacher, and the gift of administration. Furthermore he *did not say* these men *must know* what their gifts are—a phrase that is being used frequently today, particularly in Christian colleges and seminaries.

118

We need to refocus our thinking in this area. People become qualified for a local church ministry by measuring up to the criteria set forth in the New Testament. Unfortunately we frequently look at the obvious *abilities,* and not at the more basic and fundamental *qualities.*

The qualifications for eldership listed by Paul are clearly discernible in a person who has them. But it must be noted that you cannot make accurate judgments in these cases without some careful and long-range evaluation by those who have lived in close proximity to these people. This is why a church who calls a "pastor" on the basis of hearing "him preach" may make some serious errors in judgment. The man may be able to sway the people with his oratory and yet be woefully lacking in qualifications spelled out so clearly in the New Testament.

But this introduces us to another significant New Testament principle for selecting church leadership.

Second, the true test of a man's qualifications for church leadership must be based on "quality"—not "quantity."

There is a tendency today to judge a person's qualifications for leadership on the basis of *numbers*—"how many people follow this man"; and on the basis of *loyalty*—"how many people are true to this man."

This is not to negate numbers nor loyalty as a means of evaluation, for the New Testament presents both as significant results. At least seven times in the book of Acts, reference is made to numerical increase and many New Testament believers were loyal to Paul as well as to other spiritual leaders.

But it must be remembered that any dynamic leader can develop a large organization. People are essentially followers. Many are often swayed by oratory, dogmatism, authoritarianism, and especially if it is couched in the aura of biblical terminology. Even many false leaders have built great followings, including some of the most diabolical anti-Christian cults. Unfortunately, it is also possible for a well-meaning evangelical Christian leader to build a great following; but, alas, the work is built on a weak foundation, especially if it is built around himself and his unique abilities. It may be destined to crumble and disintegrate apart from his own distinctive and dynamic leadership traits.

The apostle Paul's objective in his evangelistic missionary tours was to plant churches that were not built on a human personality but rather upon Christ Himself. He was desperately disappointed in the Corinthian Christians who were "Paulites" or "Apollosites" or "Cephasites" (1 Co 1:11-12). He wished to leave churches that would become self-contained and dependent upon the various members of the body and constantly drawing its power and dynamic from Christ, the Head.

Herein lies a delicate balance! It must be noted from the Corinthian correspondence, that even Paul himself did not always achieve this objective. People tend to extol human leaders, to put them on a pedestal, and—to make this item very personal and relevant—in a sense to become "pastor-worshipers." Most Christians would be horrified at this accusation. But, unfortunately, it cannot be denied. Loyalties can be so fixed upon a dynamic pastor that any "satisfactory" replacement is nigh to impossible. Psychologically, the people have a very difficult time shifting their loyalties to another leader.

We would do well to study carefully the life of Christ and *how* He developed such strong loyalties to Himself, and yet developed independent personalities who could function without His human presence. And further, a study of the book of Acts very interestingly reveals a strong emphasis on "leadership in the church," but also upon the "function of each member of the body." There is a balance here, an intricate balance.

Every Christian leader must constantly strive to keep his people from becoming overly dependent upon him. He must strive to "equip the saints" to minister to each other and to keep their primary loyalty centered on Christ. Unfortunately Christian leaders are human beings. To be honored and respected—both biblical injunctions—is highly satisfying psychologically. Ego-building is a pleasant experience. And it is tragic when spiritual and emotional immaturity causes a man to build a work around himself and not around the body of Christ, and particularly its Head—Jesus Christ. The work is destined for trouble, no matter how large it grows. Growth in size must be commensurate with growth in spiritual maturity. Results must be both "qualitative" as well as "quantitative."

All Christian leaders must remind themselves that we are but "human means" to achieve "divine ends." The true test of our success lies not in numbers, activities, or loyalties. We are successful *only* as we are used of God "to equip the saints" to function in the body; we are successful only when the body grows and develops and ultimately manifests the "more excellent way"—the way of love and unity—followed by a strong *faith* and a steadfast *hope*.

Third, multiple leadership in the church is a New Testament principle. The "one man" ministry is a violation of this important guideline. The Scriptures frequently stress the "mutuality of the ministry." No local church in the New Testament was ruled and managed by one person. Plurality of elders appears as the norm.

This also means that the minister or pastor as we conceive of him in many churches today is not "the head of the church" or the "president of the corporation." Unfortunately some ministers—particularly of large churches, run them like a business operation. As presidents they hire and fire, tell their elders and deacons (who function as vice-presidents) what to do, and in some instances mount the pulpit like a "benevolent dictator'—or not so "benevolent." Their flock, conditioned to such an approach, either dutifully attend each service and activity of the church and say "amen!" or they react against such un-biblical approaches and leave the church to find a more pleasant pasture in which to graze.

Naturally there will be some functional problems when more than one man is classified as the spiritual leader in the church. But this need not be, when a man who serves as a full-time pastor-teacher recognizes his position as an elder "worthy of double honor." He is only one among several qualified men designated as spiritual leaders in the church. The time he spends, or his academic training, or his remuneration does not automatically entitle him to more power. In fact, the more training he has and the more remuneration he receives, the more responsible he is to serve. Though "greatest" in one sense, in another he is to be "servant of all."

Every church leader then should take his responsibility seriously, to consult and work with other men who are as spiritually qualified as he. He must also attempt to equip every saint to do the work of the ministry; to help each member to function and to help create a warm, accepting atmosphere where each member can contribute to the other members of the body.

Practically, this means he must break the "pulpit habit"—that is, the tendency to mount the sacred platform and expostulate three or four times a week without giving his people opportunity to share their own life and ministry with other members in the body.

Please do not misinterpret. I am not advocating that we cease "to preach the Word" as Timothy was admonished by Paul (2 Ti 4:2). Nothing is more basic than teaching the truth of Scripture. This is crucial in equipping the saints to do the work of the ministry. However I *am* suggesting that a regular routine involving our present approach to the ministry, within our present church structure, is not conducive to "body function." The body *must* have an opportunity to build itself up, and this process is absolutely essential for spiritual growth to take place both at the individual and the corporate level.

This does not mean that those in positions of leadership should not be recognized as having authority. In the New Testament, elders were to be respected and obeyed. Paul in writing to the Thessalonians said, "But we request of you, brethren, that you appreciate those who diligently labor among you, and have charge over you in the Lord and give you instruction, and that you esteem them very highly in love because of their work" (1 Th 5:12-13). Again in Hebrews we read, "Obey your leaders, and submit to them; for they keep watch over your souls, as those who will give an account" (Heb 13:17). And, says Paul, those who rule well were to "be considered worthy of double honor, especially those who work hard at preaching and teaching" (1 Ti 5:17).

But the concept of authority is carefully balanced in the New Testament, which differentiates authority per se from an "authoritarian" approach. The apostle Peter, exhorting elders in various churches, said, "Shepherd the flock of God among you . . . nor yet as lording it over those allotted to your charge, but proving to be examples to the flock" (1 Pe 5:2-3). Jesus Christ set the supreme example regarding leadership when He washed His disciples' feet. He demonstrated, with this act of humility, that while He was "Lord and teacher," He was still a servant of all (Jn 13:1-16).

Fourth, local church leaders are to truly fulfill a pastoral and teaching role—particularly those who are the spiritual leaders of the church. Both functions are clearly delineated in the New Testament (Ac 20:28; 1 Pe 5:2; 1 Ti 3:2; Titus 1:9).

The greatest example of a shepherd is the Lord Jesus Christ Himself. On one occasion He said,

> I am the good shepherd; the good shepherd lays down His life for the sheep. He who is a hireling and not a shepherd, who is not the owner of the sheep, beholds the wolf coming, and leaves the sheep, and flees, and the wolf snatches them, and scatters them. He flees because he is a hireling, and is not concerned about the sheep. I am the good shepherd; and I know My own, and My own know Me, even as the Father knows Me and I know the Father; and I lay down My life for the sheep (Jn 10:11-14).

How illustrative of a man with a true pastoral or shepherd heart! He is willing to give himself to the members of the body of Christ that inhabit his fold. He stands by them no matter what the cost. He *knows* his sheep. He calls them by name! And the sheep know him; they know his voice.

There is no way to escape the implication of what it means to be a true elder. He must be *with* his people—not separate from them. He must know them personally—their needs, their concerns, their problems! He must be willing to leave the ninety and nine in the fold, and go out into the darkness of the night to find the straying lamb that has wandered away from the safety of the flock, and who has been caught up in the thicket of disillusionment and sin (Mt 18:12-13).

His door must be open to the flock. No good shepherd excludes a single sheep from the fold. He must be available—not in word only but truly available! His personality must say in no uncertain way, "I love you, I care about you, I am here beside you, you can talk to me *anytime, anywhere* and *about anything* you wish. I won't condemn you! I won't hurt you! I will help you become the person you really want to become—a mature member of the body of Christ."

Thus there is no way to circumvent people and be a good pastor. The sacred desk *must* not become a barrier between shepherd and flock. It must *never* become a place to hide, a place to defend personal weakness, a vantage point from which to unload a barrage of biblical ammunition, and then a trench in which to drop out of sight so that there is no danger of getting hit by return fire.

Yes, the elder is a shepherd, who meets the needs of his people. They shall not want. He causes them to lie down in green pastures, and he leads them beside the still waters. He restores their souls and leads them in paths of righteousness. And even if they walk through the valley of the shadow of death, he is with them and comforts them (Ps 23:1-4, paraphrase).

But a spiritual leader in the church is to be more than a shepherd. He is also to be a *teacher* (1 Ti 3:2; Titus 1:9). Here we see the public ministry of the spiritual leader. The shepherd, though working with a group, pays particular attention to each individual sheep. As a teacher he feeds his flock.

From Titus 1:9 it is clear that this man must *know* the Word of God and be loyal to it. He must be able to share its dynamic truth with the body of Christ. But here again, he is not told *how* to teach, but that he is *to* teach, and we must look elsewhere in Scripture for the "how." But we look in vain if we look for a pedagogical treatise, for what we discover is what we found out about the shepherding process—that is, we see examples, particularly of how our Lord Jesus Christ taught.

As we travel through the gospels, following this Man of Galilee, we see a Teacher reflecting many and varied characteristics. He taught individuals, small groups, large groups—and even several different groups at the same time (Lk 15:1—17:11). He was not limited to a classroom, but rather taught anywhere He saw people in need—on a hillside, in an upper room, in the synagogue, by a well, on a roof-top, in a boat in the middle of a lake, on a mountain top, and even as He hung between two thieves on the cross. Sometimes they came to Him; other times He went to them. At times He delivered a discourse and at other times He asked questions. Sometimes He told stories. Frequently He visualized His words by referring to the fowls in the air, the water in the well, the sower on the hillside, or even to people themselves. He was never stereotyped; never rigid; never without the right words. He was always meeting their needs, getting them intellectually and emotionally involved, and always penetrating to the deepest recesses of their personality. He was indeed the *master Teacher!*

How different from our stereotyped approach in the ministry today. We often mount our platforms, deliver our packages which we hope are homiletically perfect. We seldom go to the people, they come to us, and to the *usual place,* where they settle into their comfortable pews and wait to be stimulated—or put to sleep. There is seldom opportunity for questions, very little variation in the process, and visualization is classified by some as a waste of time.

And yet we are to shepherd and to teach! Don't misunderstand. I am not suggesting we cannot be effective unless we go back to the exact patterns of Jesus' example of teaching. We are living in a different culture, a different world. But may I suggest that in many instances we are not even coming close to applying New Testament principles. We assume our present forms and structures are adequate to create a dynamic learning experience. We almost worship at the shrine of a transmissive approach to communication—"preaching" particularly.[1] We glorify the scholar who knows the content of the Bible, while we ignore the body of Christ and its many members who also have something to contribute to the ministry and the building of the body.

Do we want a dynamic church? A dynamic ministry? Then I suggest that we must develop a philosophy of leadership that grows out of the Scriptures, not out of the interpretation of what others say it is or out of partial interpretation. We need church leaders who are *both* shepherds *and* teachers, and who are able to function in a structure that permits them to be and do what God intended them to be and do.

Fifth, a spiritual leader in the church must learn to establish priorities in the ministry. The apostles of old, when confronted with the problems in Jerusalem, said to the people, "It is not desirable for us to neglect the word of God in order to serve tables." They solved the problem by establishing priorities, by having seven men appointed to handle this matter, and they continued to "devote ourselves to prayer, and to the ministry of the word" (Ac 6:2, 4). Not that these matters were unimportant, nor were they matters that did not call for leaders with spiritual qualifications (Ac 6:5), but they were matters that could have taken the apostles away from their primary work.

Local church elders, too, were given priorities. They were to shepherd and teach and pray for the sick. Their primary responsibilities lay in meeting the spiritual needs of the people.

---

1. Unfortunately we have even superimposed stereotypes upon this biblical word. New Testament preaching was never only a transmissive approach. Peter's sermons in the book of Acts demonstrate dramatically the presence of group dynamics, interaction and response.

Within many of our present church structures, particularly in large churches, the pastor may find all of his time being used up in attending board and committee meetings, and making administrative decisions, conducting staff conferences, handling correspondence, and carrying out public relations responsibilities. What time is left, which may be little, is spent in serving the people as shepherd and teacher. His personal contacts with the members of the body of Christ are limited to the large group meeting, where, separated from his people by a pulpit, he expounds the Word. True, he may greet them at the door as they leave, hopefully able to call the majority by name, but woefully unaware of *who they really are*. Rather than being the true shepherd of the sheep, he is almost like the "hireling," who as Jesus said, "is not the owner of the sheep." He is carrying out a job—like a professional—who is more concerned with the smooth running organization than about the body of people who make up the church.

This, of course, in many instances, is an overstatement and an unfair evaluation. For it is true, I believe, that most evangelical ministers—men who love the Bible and the Christ it presents—desire to be true pastor-teachers. But the very structures in which they find themselves almost militate against this function. They are forced into an administrative role that is foreign to the concept of the New Testament.

It is rather interesting, too, to note those men around the country who are serving large and dynamic churches. It has already been pointed out, of course, that numbers is not *necessarily* a sign of "success," but neither is it a sign of "lack of success." Among those who are truly successful and achieve many valid biblical results, are men who are multi-gifted—they can prepare and preach three outstanding sermons a week, teach a number of classes, counsel, manage, organize, and somehow with all of this still relate to people in depth. They are characterized by an unusual charisma, and even though they stand behind the lectern or pulpit much of the time, they manage to communicate warmth and concern. Some of these men would have no trouble running General Motors, or even running a close second to the President of the United States.

As I read the New Testament, however, I am forced to ask if this is what God intended a man to have and to be in order to be the leader of a church. The qualifications given to Timothy and Titus force me to answer in the negative.

Furthermore, these multi-gifted men are few and far between, and the need for spiritual leaders in the church is far beyond the supply. Consequently, it is obvious that this is not what God intended. Rather than a multi-gifted man, God's plan is a multi-gifted body, a body made up of people who could all contribute in a special way to the building up of the church.

But what about the multigifted man? How could he better use his abilities and gifts? Rather than building a large church, he could, like Paul or Timothy, be using his gifts to build many churches, to multiply his efforts, to help equip others to serve many local groups. Whatever the solution, one thing is sure. He is violating a principle of Scripture, when he allows his own personality and abilities to inhibit other members of the body of Christ from functioning.

Perhaps the most tragic thing that can happen is when highly gifted men attempt to train ordinary men to be like themselves. Unfortunately these ordinary men (which makes up the majority of us) have neither the capacity nor the natural ability to become this kind of leader. The result is often frustration, or even more tragic, these men attempt to imitate the life of a multi-gifted man and end up a total failure—often splitting the church, hurting the body of Christ, and eventually bombing out of the ministry.

Sixth, the specific functions spelled out for New Testament leaders leave much room for creative thinking and performance on the part of twentieth century church leaders.

Interestingly, only six broad areas are spelled out for the spiritual leaders of local churches. And even more significantly, nowhere are functions specified for deacons, those who obviously are to serve the church in the more material areas. For those who were appointed as spiritual leaders, they were to shepherd the flock, be an example, manage the church, teach the Word of God, refute false teachers, and to pray for the sick. But even here, no specifics are given as to *how* this was to be done.

This, again, points to the uniqueness of the New Testament literature. Here are absolutes for the twentieth century spiritual leader; here are guidelines that are relevant until Christ comes again.

But here also are broad directives that allow for a great amount of freedom under the creative leadership of the Holy Spirit. Whatever the culture, whatever the time in history, the Christian leader who understands New Testament leadership principles will have his feet firmly planted upon the absolutes of Scripture, but at the same time he will not be locked into functional patterns and forms that are neither contemporary nor effective in doing the work of the ministry.

It must be stated, however, that creativity in church leadership must be guided by the other significant leadership principles in the New Testament. To have God's fullest blessing come on our work, we must not get locked into secondary issues. Rather we must put our primary emphasis on biblical qualifications and the function of church leaders. And where qualifications are given, but no functions (as with deacons), we must recognize the freedom that the Holy Spirit is allowing. We must evaluate success by means of quality— not quantity. We must emphasize the mutuality of the ministry and body function. And as Christian leaders, we must establish biblical priorities, so that we are not sidetracked into areas of responsibility that can be officiated by other qualified men.

Seventh, Christians need not be "locked in" to certain titles and names to describe church leaders.

Paul demonstrated this principle clearly. He did not hesitate to use more than one title in order to communicate the meaning or idea behind a leadership position in the church. To the Christians converted out of the Greek culture, the term "bishop" had significant meaning when talking about church leadership. To the Jewish Christians, the term "elder" was obvious and clear. But both were "good" words to describe those men who were to lead the local churches in the New Testament.

It is also obvious that the Holy Spirit allowed Paul to borrow words from both the religious and secular culture that surrounded these people. It was not necessary to come up with a word that was uniquely "Christian." Though an "elder" in Israel performed a leadership function within Judaism, and a "bishop" served in the secular community as an overseer of certain colonies, both words could be used to adequately describe the "overseer" of a local church. The important point, of course, is that this man needed to be *uniquely* qualified to oversee this *new* and *distinctive* group of people.

Today the twentieth century church does not need to get "locked in" to titles and "terminology." We should be free to select and choose titles that will clearly describe New Testament function in the twentieth century.

On the other hand, we should not hasten to change. Instead, the criterion for change is when certain terms become a hindrance, rather than a help to the function of a church. This was Paul's criterion. He felt free to "become all things to all men. . . . for the sake of the gospel" (1 Co 9:22-23). The "end" is the most important issue. Any means —providing it does not violate other Christian doctrines and principles—may be used to achieve New Testament objectives.[2] Note, however, that because Paul was flexible in terminology when describing leaders in the church, it does not mean that he was indefinite in other areas. When it came to leadership qualifications and functions, he was definite, precise, and consistent. This helps us to differentiate absolutes from nonabsolutes in the area of leadership.

Summing Up

1. The most important criterion for selecting local church leadership is spiritual qualifications.
2. The true test of a man's qualifications for church leadership must be based on quality—not quantity.
3. Multiple leadership in the church is a New Testament principle.
4. Local church leaders are to truly fulfill a pastoral and teaching role.
5. A spiritual leader in the church must learn to establish priorities.
6. The specific functions spelled out for New Testament leaders leave much room for creative thinking and performance on the part of twentieth century church leaders.
7. Christians need not get "locked in" to certain titles and names to describe church leaders.

---

2. I am by no means advocating that the "end" justifies the "means." This is heresy from Satan himself. Rather the Scriptures teach that any *legitimate* means may be used to achieve New Testament objectives. Legitimacy must be determined on the basis of the total teachings of the New Testament. And in relationship to terminology, one thing is clear: because a word or term or title was used in the non-Christian community, it was not automatically disqualified from being used in the Christian community.

12

BIBLICAL EXAMPLES OF ADMINISTRATION AND ORGANIZATION

The Bible is relatively silent regarding organizational and administrative patterns. But this is not without design, for nothing becomes obsolete so quickly as structural forms. They are but a means to divine ends. Furthermore, life is made up of so many variables and unpredictable events that creativity in this area must be constant.

But the Bible *does* speak in this area, and when it does, its examples yield some dynamic and powerful principles.

Both Old Testament and New Testament illustrations of organization and administration surface the same basic principles. This again helps to show that the patterns are not absolute, but the principles are.

The purpose of this chapter is to present four structural examples—two from the Old Testament and two from the New Testament. First we'll look at an Old Testament example and a New Testament example in close alignment, to show how clearly they compare in the nature of the problems, the solutions, and the results. The second two examples are uniquely different but again demonstrate similar principles.

A Comparative Study

Two of the most obvious problems calling for organization and administration are found in Exodus 18 and Acts 6. The former involved a mass of people, no doubt two million plus, camped in the wilderness. The latter involved a rapidly multiplying group of Christians in Jerusalem, by then numbering in the thousands.[1]

---

1. It is interesting to note the references to numbers in the first part of the book of Acts. The church was launched with approximately one hundred and twenty (Ac 1:15); in 2:41 about three thousand were added to the original one hundred

The following chart will help to isolate the *problems,* the *solutions,* and *results* recorded in these passages.

MOSES IN THE WILDERNESS (Ex 18:13-27; Deu 1:9-18)	THE NEGLECTED WIDOWS (Ac 6:1-7)
PROBLEM	PROBLEM
Exodus 18 v. 13—The people stood about Moses from morning until the evening. v. 14—Moses sat alone trying to do the job all by himself. vv. 15,16—Moses was attempting to resolve the problem of the people; he served as the judge in matters of interpersonal relationships and taught the people the laws of God. v. 18—T h i s laborious process caused undue stress for Moses and for the people as well.	Acts 6 v. 1—The disciples were increasing rapidly. W i t h s u c h growth: —the communal system was put under stress. —certain individuals among the Hellenistic Jews were being overlooked in the daily serving of food. —consequently, the Hellenists began to complain. v. 2—The Twelve apostles got involved in the details of this discussion and the results of this discontentment caused them to begin to neglect their primary responsibility . . . to teach the Word of God.
SOLUTION	SOLUTION
Exodus 18 v. 19—Moses' father-in-law, Jethro, served as his consultant. Jethro advised Moses to establish priorities —to serve as a mediator between the people and God —to teach them as a group	Acts 6 v. 2—The Twelve called a meeting of the disciples. vv. 3,4—In this meeting they informed the people regarding their major task as the twelve apostles — prayer and the ministry of the Word.

and twenty; in 4:4 we are told that "the number of the men came to be about five thousand." Some believe that the mention of "men" refers to five thousand households. If so, the number of disciples would have been four or five times this number, or maybe more, at the time the events in Acts 6 took place.

the statutes and laws of God.

vv. 20,21—To delegate the responsibility for handling the interpersonal problems of everyday life to a select group of qualified men — "able men, who fear God, men of truth, who hate unjust gain."

v. 22—These men were to handle the minor matters, and only the major problems would be filtered through to Moses.

Deuteronomy 1

vv. 9-12 — Moses communicated his problem to the people.

v. 13—Moses instructed each tribe to "choose wise and discerning and experienced men"; Moses in turn appointed them as heads.

vv. 16-18—Moses carefully instructed the leaders in everything they were to do.

v. 3—They instructed the Christians to select seven qualified men to care for the need that existed . . . "men of good reputation, full of the Spirit and of wisdom."

v. 5 — The congregation chose seven men—obviously Hellenists.

v. 6—The apostles confirmed the choice of the people through prayer and the laying on of hands.

RESULTS	RESULTS

Exodus 18

v. 22—Moses was assisted in his responsibilities.

v. 23—Moses was able to endure the demands of his leadership role.

  —The people's needs were met and they were satisfied.

Acts 6

v. 7—Evidently the needs of the people were met; unity was restored; the apostles were able to fulfill their primary work

  —the Word of God kept on spreading

  —the number of believers kept on increasing greatly.

Though these two events took place at different times, in different settings, and under a different set of circumstances, and though there were many other differences surrounding the details of these two situations, the nature of the problems, the way in which the problems were solved, and the results are strikingly similar.

THE NATURE OF THE PROBLEM

Problem-wise, both Moses and the apostles had more than they could do personally, and both were becoming involved in details that kept them from fulfilling their primary responsibilities. Moses particularly was unable to endure the physical and psychological stress.

Furthermore, in both situations the people themselves were under stress and became discontented because their personal needs were being neglected. The children of Israel came to Moses to be instructed, to have him work out problems among them, to state their grievances, and to make their petitions. Evidently, some people stood in line all day long and perhaps even then did not get a chance to have a hearing with their leader (Ex 18:13).

In view of the previous problems Moses had with these people— their desire to return to Egypt, their complaints against him for getting them into this wilderness experience, their carnality and sin—it does not take too much imagination to reconstruct the tense mood and emotional outbursts that must have taken place among these people.

The disciples in Jerusalem must have faced similar problems. Though hopefully more "spiritually mature" than their forefathers, these new Christians also became very unhappy when their physical needs were not met. Furthermore, it may be that we see, in Acts 6, favoritism being shown toward a certain class or group.

It was the Hellenistic Jews against the Hebrews. The Hebrews were Palestinian Jews, whereas the Hellenists were residents of other countries, such as Syria, Egypt, and Asia Minor. The Palestinian Jews spoke their own language, whereas the Hellenists spoke Greek. Furthermore, the Hebrews probably composed the majority of Christians, and the Grecians were in the minority. Added to this, the Palestinian Jews no doubt reflected the more rigorous aspects of pure Judaism, whereas the Hellenists reflected the influence of Greek customs.

Consequently, we have a combination of factors that may be strongly parallel to some of the problems of prejudice that exist in the church in the twentieth century. But perhaps of more importance was the fact that the growth of the church was so rapid that the natural tendency to neglect certain people may have become the primary factor in causing this problem.

THE WAY THE PROBLEM WAS SOLVED

Though the specific steps taken to solve the problems that existed differed in certain particulars, there were four important similarities. First, both Moses and the apostles *established priorities.* In Moses' case it was his father-in-law, Jethro, who helped him to see and analyze the problems. He advised Moses to give primary attention to serving as a mediator between the people and God (Ex 18:19), and to be the one who taught the people the Word of God (Ex 18:20).

When the apostles became aware of the problems in Jerusalem, they immediately communicated to the multitude of Christians that they could not be burdened with the details of waiting on tables, but must continue to give primary attention to teaching the Word of God and to prayer (Ac 6:2-4). They were not negating the importance of these details, but knew they would be unable to carry out their primary objectives and be personally involved in meeting the physical needs of the people as well.

The second similarity in these two sets of circumstances is the *delegation of responsibility to qualified men.* Moses chose able men— men who were *God-fearing, honest,* and also men who *hated unjust gain* (Ex 18:21).[2] The apostles instructed the people to select seven men who had a *good reputation,* who were *filled with the Holy Spirit,* and who were *wise* (Ac 6:3). Here it is important to note the high spiritual standards set for selecting men to fulfill the responsibility of meeting the physical needs of people.

Actually, these high standards in both situations were a secret to the effectiveness of the step in solving the problem. Moses and the apostles needed men they could trust. Men who were dishonest, unspiritual, selfish, and tactless would have only accentuated the problem. Qualified men, on the other hand, would resolve the problems.

The third similarity is that they *organized to meet the need that existed at that moment and in those peculiar circumstances.* In the Old Testament situation, "Moses chose able men out of all Israel, and made them heads over the people, leaders of thousands, of hundreds,

---

2. In Deu 1:13, these men are described as "wise and discerning and experienced men."

of fifties and of tens" (Ex 18:25). This was obviously the best strategy for the occasion. This organizational plan was a fitting structure for a nation on the move, and no doubt "this arrangement was linked on to the natural division of the people and the tribes and families, etc."[3]

Jamieson comments:

> The arrangement was an admirable one, and it was founded upon a division of the people which was adopted not only in civil but in military affairs; so that the same persons who were officers in war were magistrates in peace (see Num. 31:14). . . . Care was thus taken by the minute subdivision to which the judicial system was carried, that, in suits and proceedings at law, every man should have what was just and equal, without going far to seek it, without waiting long to obtain it, and without paying an exhorbitant price for it.[4]

The apostles, on the other hand, had the people (no doubt the Hellenistic Christians only) select from among themselves seven men. This was a wise move, for the people themselves knew those who would meet the qualifications that the apostles had prescribed. Moreover, if the people selected these men, there would be no accusation of a prejudicial choice on the part of the twelve (note that all seven men chosen had Greek names).

Again the structure set up on this occasion was appropriate to the situation. No doubt the number seven was recommended because the apostles estimated that this was the number it would take to do the job.

A fourth similarity is that in both of these circumstances, the *structure set up was temporary.* When the children of Israel settled in the land, the organizational plans changed. Also in a relatively short period of time, persecution drove the Christians out of Jerusalem, and some of the men who were serving tables became evangelists (Ac 7-8). The whole situation changed, creating new needs, and called for new forms and structures, particularly as permanently located churches were established in various communities.

---

3. C. F. Keil and F. Delitzsch, *The Penteteuch* (Grand Rapids: Eerdmans, 1949), 2:87.
4. Robert Jamieson, *Genesis-Deuteronomy* (Grand Rapids: Eerdmans, 1948), pp. 348-49.

THE SIGNIFICANCE OF THE RESULTS

The results of the organizational steps taken to resolve the problems in Exodus 18 and Acts 6 are clearly delineated in the Word of God. Simply stated, the problems were resolved—at least for the time being (organizational problems are never permanently solved). Moses and the apostles were able to carry out their primary tasks. The people's needs were met and they were satisfied. Moses' physical and psychological needs were also met, and as a result of the appointment of the seven men in Acts, the "word of God kept on spreading; and the number of the disciples continued to increase greatly in Jerusalem, and a great many of the priests were becoming obedient to the faith" (Ac 6:7).

REBUILDING THE WALLS
The Book of Nehemiah

The Problem	
1:2-3	Nehemiah, cupbearer to the king of Persia, received a report that the remnant in Judah who had returned were in great distress and reproached because the walls of Jerusalem were broken down and burned with fire.
1:4	Nehemiah's response was one of depression and sadness.

The Solution	
1:4-11	Nehemiah fasted and prayed.
2:1-2	He did not hesitate to reveal his sadness to the king.
2:3	He told the king why he was depressed.
2:4	The king asked Nehemiah: "What would you request?"
2:4	Nehemiah asked God for guidance in responding to this question.
2:5	He asked the king to send him to Judah to rebuild the walls.

2:6	The king responded positively.
2:7-8	Nehemiah asked the king for official letters so he could travel freely and also obtain timber from the king's forest.
2:12-16	When Nehemiah arrived he spent three nights secretly surveying the situation. At this time he no doubt developed a strategy for rebuilding the walls.
2:17-20 3:1-32	Nehemiah then revealed his plan and asked the people to help him rebuild the walls.
4:1-13	When the enemies of Israel tried to stop their work the people did two things: they prayed and set up a guard day and night.
4:14	When the people grew fearful, Nehemiah told them (1) not to be afraid, (2) to remember the greatness of God, and (3) to fight for the sake of their families.
4:15	As soon as the word got out to their enemies that they were ready to defend themselves, they returned to the wall to continue building.
4:16-23	Nehemiah devised a new plan for working and guarding so that they could continue building, but also be ready for war.
6:15	They completed the walls in fifty-two days.

The Immediate Results

12:27-29, 31-42	The people sang and praised God.
12:30	The people purified themselves and the city.
12:43	They offered sacrifices to God.
6:16	When the enemies of Israel witnessed this impossible feat and heard the rejoicing of Israel, "they lost their confidence." They recognized that this could have been achieved only "with the help of God."

THE NATURE OF THE PROBLEM

The problems in Jerusalem focused on the broken walls. This condition resulted in ridicule, reproach, and humiliation for the people of Judah. They were mistreated and abused. Many of the Jews were afraid to even live within the city. They remained a scattered, fearful people, even though they were living in the land of Judah. They had little security from their enemies round about, and lived in constant fear and anxiety.

Consequently many were living out of fellowship with God. They did not worship God nor were they being exposed to the laws of God. Some of the Jews were even taking advantage of their own people (Nehemiah 5). Neither did they pay tithes, nor did they keep themselves pure and separated from the paganism and idolatry that surrounded them.

THE WAY THE PROBLEM WAS SOLVED

Nehemiah's approach to solving this problem was a tremendous example of organizational and administrative skill that included both the human and divine dimensions. They are so carefully blended throughout the narrative that it is difficult to separate the two, but they are both there.

First, Nehemiah sought wisdom and help from God (1:4-11).

Struck with the terrible plight of his people, Nehemiah's initial step was to pray and fast. He acknowledged God's greatness, confessed their sins (including his own), reminded God of His promises to regather the children of Israel if they repented, and then asked the Lord to grant him mercy before the king whom he served.

Second, Nehemiah built bridges to the king (2:1-10).

No doubt he had already laid the groundwork for this bridge. He had been a good servant. His sadness was very obvious to the king against a backdrop of his constantly happy countenance. And furthermore, Nehemiah was not afraid to reveal his true feelings to the king, evidence of a certain degree of rapport—and faith.

Nehemiah's prayer was answered. The king asked why he was so downcast.

But even at this moment Nehemiah relied upon God. Moving from a purely human factor (revealing his sadness), he breathed a prayer to God for wisdom to answer the king's question. Here was the opportunity he had been hoping for. His response and the *way* he answered and *what* he said were critical!

God answered Nehemiah's prayer as quickly as he had prayed. Nehemiah's answer was clear-cut but tactful. He asked that the *king* might send him to rebuild the walls.

When given a favorable reply, Nehemiah took another step—a bold one! He asked for official letters from the king to be able to pass through various countries unhindered. He even went so far as to ask for the privilege of cutting down trees from the king's forest.

Request granted! And with these credentials Nehemiah had not only built bridges to the king, but he had built bridges all the way to Jerusalem and to his own people. To the surprise of the enemies of Judah, he even arrived with army officers and horsemen assigned to him by the king.

Third, Nehemiah secretly surveyed the situation in Jerusalem and developed his strategy (2:11-16; 3:1-32).

On three successive nights he quietly but carefully inspected and evaluated the damage to the walls. Here, read between the lines, is administrative wisdom personified. Nehemiah knew that he needed to have his facts in hand before he challenged the people to rebuild the wall. Furthermore, to even let them know the purpose of his coming before developing his strategy would be lethal. Humanly speaking, he might have lost the people before he even got the plan off the ground. And furthermore, to release the information early would have unveiled the plan to the enemies of Israel, who would have scoffed even more.

The people, of course, didn't need any more demoralization. They were already at a low ebb. Nehemiah's great challenge was to build their morale and convince them the job could be done. So he proceeded to develop a strategy that was unique. The priests were to work on the Sheep Gate, inferring that this was an assignment that appealed to them personally. Some scholars feel that this gate was near the temple and it would be through this gate that they would bring small cattle for sacrifice. The men of Jericho were assigned to work on the part of the wall that was nearest to their city. In like manner, if archaeological speculation is correct, the goldsmiths and perfumers were assigned a section of the wall nearest their shops.

Whatever the specifics, it is clear that Nehemiah had mapped out his plan carefully and with wisdom. Over twenty-five times the phrase "next to him" (or "them") or "after him" (or "them") is used to designate the organizational structure. Every person or group who could work, including some women, was assigned to a task.

Fourth, Nehemiah revealed the plan to the people, motivating them with both human and divine factors (2:17-20).

He appealed first to their wretched condition—the *reproach* they were bearing because of the broken walls, and the *desolate condition* of Jerusalem. Next, he told them how *God* had helped him to win the favor of the king and his support in this venture.

The results were positive. "Let us arise and build!" was the response; and so they did. When the enemies heard about it and saw the people taking their places around the wall, they responded with mockery and hatred! But the people were prepared, so their goals were set—their strategy outlined! They did not submit to their enemies' demoralizing attacks.

Note how Nehemiah said "we" will arise and build (2:20). He *was* their leader, but he was also "one" with them. He was a part of the team, and he too was on the front line engaging in the same difficult work (5:16). This is dynamic leadership. This is a basic reason why these people saw this project through to completion against almost impossible odds. Nehemiah's example went far beyond what is ordinarily expected. His life was such a contrast to those of "the officials" and "leaders" around him that he generated unusual loyalty and motivation.

Fifth, Nehemiah supervised the work closely, facing and solving unforeseen problems as they arose during the process (4:1-12; 6:15).

Laying the groundwork for any venture is only part of the organizational-administrative picture. Even though the people "had a mind to work," they were to face consistent ridicule and hostility. The work went on; and when it became obvious the enemies were planning to attack in order to stop the work, Nehemiah prepared for the battle by placing people all around the wall. Significantly he stationed them by families (4:13). This was shrewd—but necessary. It guaranteed performance if attacked. For, if their families had been in another place in the city or outside the walls, the temptation would be to run to them. Now they would have to fight to protect them—on location!

This is exactly what Nehemiah knew would arouse and appeal to them. So when he saw their fear, he gave them three charges: (1) "Do not be afraid of them"; (2) "Remember the Lord who is great and awesome"; and (3) "Fight for your brothers, your sons, your daughters, your wives, and your houses" (4:14).

Fortunately the battle never materialized. The enemy, evidently overawed by this determination and the bold stand of the Jews, backed away from their threat (4:15). And everyone once again took up his task at the wall.

Nehemiah devised a new strategy. From then on some worked and some guarded; some worked with one hand and carried their weapon in the other; those who had to work with both hands kept their swords at their sides. And a trumpet would be used to gather the people together quickly in case of attack. No one was to go out of Jerusalem at night; rather they were to stand guard. And in the final days of building, Nehemiah and many of his workers and guards never removed their clothes nor laid down their weapons, even when they stopped for a drink of water (4:23). Against almost impossible odds, *they completed the wall in fifty-two days!*

THE SIGNIFICANCE OF THE RESULTS

The results of Nehemiah's organizational and administrative skill are obvious all the way through the building program. This was a long-range project, and at every step along the way he achieved certain siginificant goals. He won the favor of the king, motivated the people to begin the work, kept the people at the task in spite of threats from their enemies, and finally they rebuilt the wall. Here it must be noted that, while doing all this, he helped straighten out social and financial problems (5:1-19), and warded off a subtle attack on his own life by Sanballat and Gesham (6:1-14).

But the final results of this project were far more rewarding. Nehemiah must have been overwhelmed with thanksgiving and praise to God; for, all the way through this intense experience, he praised the God of heaven for every accomplishment.

Imagine the thrill when he heard the people singing and praising God at the dedication of the wall (12:27-29; 31-42). The two great choirs on top of the walls must have been an unbelievable sight to the enemies of Judah. The sounds of their voices and rejoicing were so loud that they could be "heard from afar" (12:43), and their enemies were so overwhelmed with this fantastic accomplishment that "they lost their confidence" (6:16). In the words of Nehemiah himself, "They recognized this work had been accomplished with the help of our God."

Other results followed. The people were able to develop a system of defense which provided security against their enemy (4:17). There were more social reforms, as they were able to reorganize and develop order in the community (11:1, 12). And most important of all, there were religious reforms. The people were once again able to come together to hear the law of God (8:1-18). No doubt the most rewarding result of all for Nehemiah was to see the people— as a reunited people—confessing their sins, worshiping the God of heaven, and making a covenant with Him.

THE JERUSALEM COUNCIL

Acts 15:1-35

Problem

15:1	Certain men were teaching false doctrines in Antioch —"you must be circumcised to be saved."
15:2	Paul and Barnabas debated the issue publicly but could not solve the problem.

Solution

15:2-3	The church at Antioch decided to seek guidance from the apostles and elders at Jerusalem.
15:4	The Antioch delegation reported how Gentiles were being converted through faith alone.
15:6	The apostles and elders met in a closed session to discuss the matter.
15:7-11	Peter reminded the people of what God did for Cornelius and his household.
15:12	Paul and Barnabas gave specific testimony regarding the "signs and wonders God had done through them among the Gentiles."

15:13-18	James made reference to the work of the Old Testament prophets and how they had predicted Gentile conversion.
15:19-21	James proposed a solution to the problem.
15:22	The apostles, elders, and the whole church agreed to this proposal.
15:22-30	A letter was written spelling out the solution.
15:22	Judas and Silas were chosen by the church to deliver the letter.
15:30, 32	Judas and Silas delivered the letter and also a "lengthy message."

Results

15:31	The congregation rejoiced when they heard the contents of the letter.
15:33	Judas and Silas were sent back to Jerusalem in peace.
15:35	The work of God continued unhindered.
16:4-5	The instructions in the letter were delivered by Paul, Silas, and Timothy to many of the new churches.

THE NATURE OF THE PROBLEM

Here was a problem that was destined to affect all of the newly formed churches. Antioch was a prominent center of Christian activity, and it would not be long until the news of the disagreement and debate would spread to the new believers scattered throughout the New Testament world. The result would be confusion, disillusionment, and disunity.

This was no minor eruption! Here were Paul and Barnabas in open debate against men from Jerusalem, the birthplace of the whole Christian movement. The issue was just as crucial—either man was "saved by grace through faith," or it also involved works. It could not be both. The results of this controversy would either unite the churches or split them.

THE WAY THE PROBLEM WAS SOLVED

It did not take long for the leaders in the Antiochian church to recognize the explosive nature of this problem. They *acted quickly* and *with wisdom*. They faced the problem *head on*. They met together and decided this problem was beyond their ability to handle. They needed assistance. Acting with perception, they decided to take the problem back to its original source. They chose a delegation—to accompany Paul and Barnabas—and set off for Jerusalem.

Note their approach when they arrived. *No attack on personalities!* No accusation against the Jerusalem church! They simply reported what God was doing in the Gentile world. And it was this noncritical and objective tactic that set the tone for this whole conference.

The immediate result was disagreement from certain people—whom Luke identifies as coming from the "sect of the Pharisees" (15:5). But rather than allowing the issue to become a matter for public debate which would have quickly degenerated into emotional name calling, the apostles and elders went *into a closed session* to discuss the matter.

Exact sequences and what was involved are somewhat unclear in the biblical account. But there is sufficient information to draw some accurate conclusions. There was more discussion and debate, probably within the smaller group (15:6-7).

Eventually, Peter stood up publicly before the whole congregation (15:7-12), and substantiated the initial report by reminding the people of something they already knew (15:7): his own personal experience with Cornelius. God had saved him and his household "by faith" and gave them the Holy Spirit, just as He had done at Pentecost (15:9). There were the same "signs" as at the beginning (Ac 10:44-46).

At this juncture Paul and Barnabas added more support to the case by building on Peter's testimony. While the multitude listened in silence, they, too, related what signs and wonders God had done through them among the Gentiles (15:12).

The next move was crucial! James (undoubtedly the brother of Christ, and obviously the most respected leader in the church in Jerusalem) spoke on the issue. He began by adding support to Peter's testimony, and then in a marvelous demonstration of wisdom and insight, summarized the teachings of several Old Testament prophets that related directly to the problem. He then made a proposal—in actuality suggesting a compromise—one that would not violate "justification by faith," but one that would also pacify the Jewish Christians who still found it difficult to understand "freedom from the law" (15:19-21).

No doubt there was consensus. Whether the proposal was first made to the apostles and the elders or to the whole church is not clear. Obviously the letter had to be composed by a select group. The scriptural record *does* make it clear that the "whole church" felt good about the decision and was involved in the selection of Judas and Silas to deliver the letter.

So step by step under the leadership of men who were seeking God's will, the immediate problem was solved. No one could really predict what was going to happen in the actual process. An objective approach to the problem, being willing to face the issue squarely and openly, and using much wisdom and administrative skill, the meeting in Jerusalem was successful. They accomplished there what they were unable to accomplish in Antioch—achieving results that were more far reaching and significant than had they merely stilled the local storm.

The Significance of the Results

The usual results of a problem well solved are immediately obvious. People were happy and content. There was peace among the brethren, and the work of God continued without interruption and without being sidetracked onto peripheral issues. It is perhaps most significant that the apostle Paul was happy with the decision. He, personally, with his missionary team, delivered the letter from Jerusalem to all the churches which he had established. Previous encounters with Paul had evidently convinced Peter and James that he would tolerate no inconsistency in crucial theological matters. Legitimate compromise was one thing, but to vacillate and be inconsistent was another (Gal 2:1-21).[5]

---

5. Some believe the account given by Paul in Galatians 2 is also a description of the Jerusalem meeting recorded in Acts 15. Because of certain "seeming" discrepancies in this account as compared with Luke's account, there are some serious problems with this view. Consequently, some believe the Galatian account took place earlier, when Paul and Barnabas delivered the contribution to the Jerusalem brethren (Ac 11:27-30). Still others believe it took place after the event in Acts 15.

Summing Up

Here, then, are four biblical examples of organizational and administrative structure and skill. Though all vary, they all have several things in common: a problem arose, a solution was sought, and results were achieved. More than that, each problem was attacked with a variety of approaches which yielded basic principles. And it is to these principles we turn in the chapter to follow.

13

PRINCIPLES OF BIBLICAL ADMINISTRATION AND ORGANIZATION

As Christian leaders functioning in the twentieth century, we face a multitude of problems. The rapidly changing world has not helped to reduce the number of problems nor their complexity. But God's people have always faced problems, and in many instances those that face us today are—in their roots—the same old problems. But all problems—old or new—call for certain administrative actions and organizational structures to solve them. This was true among the people of God, both in the Old and New Testaments.

There are relatively few examples of administrative action and organizational structure in the Bible; and those that do appear vary greatly. Obviously, because of the lack of conformity, these patterns and structures cannot be classified as normative. But what do appear, however, are several well-selected examples which provide us with profound and normative principles of organization and administration. It is these biblical principles which can provide us with guidelines in developing patterns and structures, and in turn can help us carry out biblical directives and reach New Testament objectives in the twentieth century.

Principles of Administration

First, face the reality of problems. Do not ignore them. If we do, they will not go away! They get worse! We may "sweep them under the rug," but eventually they reappear—in double measure. We can "hide our heads in the sand," but when we develop enough courage to "look up" they will be bigger and more foreboding than ever. And

147

if we manage to "imagine they are not there," eventually the people to whom we minister will painfully remind us that reality exists.

It does not take much creative imagination to project what could have happened in Israel if Moses had ignored Jethro's advice, or if the apostles had closed their eyes to the murmuring of the Hellenists. What if the Antiochian Christians had "looked the other way" and not faced the heresy that was being taught by the Judaizers? It could have had negative repercussions all over the New Testament world.

Nehemiah's problems were different! He could have conveniently ignored the plight of his people. No one (except his Father in heaven) would have known or even cared. But he could never have gotten away from his conscience and the pain he felt in his heart. Though the task was tough and filled with unpredictable events—some that even threatened his very life—he fulfilled the will of God. And the people benefited from his selfless efforts.

There are occasions—but very few—when we, as Christian leaders, can ignore problems in the church—sometimes without too many outward repercussions. But, in our hearts we must live with the decision to withdraw from desperate situations in order to have an easier path to walk. When people's needs go unmet because of our selfishness and our unwillingness to face problems, we must live with our decisions. And as often happens, God bypasses us to achieve His purposes through another vessel, who is far more sensitive to human needs as well as to His Spirit.

Today, as in the New Testament, churches are facing problems. Some are purely organizational; some are theological; some are cultural. Many, of course, involve all three. Though some of these problems are as old as man himself, and though some are new and contemporary, they *are* problems and they must be solved for God's richest blessing to rest on the local church.

Never ignore problems. For if you do they may overwhelm you, defeat you and cause you to leave the work of God, feeling hostile and bitter or depressed and discouraged. And worst of all, you may rationalize your failure, putting the blame on others for your own unwillingness to face problems head on.

Second, develop a proper perspective on the problem before seeking concrete solutions. Sometimes this can be done quickly, and at other times it takes a period of careful evaluation.

In Acts 6 it did not take the apostles long to pinpoint the nature of the problem and to arrive at a solution. The cause was obvious, as well as "what was" and "what was not" the best approach to solving it. It did not take a long period of prayer, evaluation, and seeking God's will to arrive at a solution.

For Nehemiah it was a different story. He was far removed from the actual environment in which the problem existed. His only source of information was an oral report (Neh 1:1-2), and what he actually learned from this report was very limited (1:3). Consequently, he spent a lengthy period of time seeking God's guidance, and his first step when arriving in Jerusalem was to spend three nights carefully inspecting and evaluating the walls of Jerusalem. Because of the complexity of the problem and the explosive nature of the situaiton, he in wisdom decided to get "personal perspective" before publicly announcing his strategy.

For the leaders in the Antiochian and Jerusalem church, the problem in Acts 15 was yet different. It was a theological problem—one that had grown out of Judaism and the law of Moses. It emerged in the transition from the old dispensation to the new, as the apostles themselves attempted to clarify even in their own minds "how a man is saved." God's choosing these men to "be with Jesus," and "to launch the church," and "to speak the truth of God," did not automatically guarantee them "complete perspective" on the whole redemptive plan. We often fail to realize this factor, which is so obvious in the unfolding of biblical revelation.

In Jerusalem it took time to solve the problems of Judaism versus Christianity. It involved a process of reports, debate, and discussion, both in private and in public. It involved historical and biblical research as well as an analysis of what God was doing on the contemporary scene. And it was the result of this process that led to perspective and an "organizational and administrative" answer—a letter and its deliverance to the churches.

Moses, as he led the people through the wilderness, appears to have been totally unaware that he even had a problem, or that it could be solved with a good organizational and administrative plan. It took his father-in-law Jethro to reveal the problem as well as the solution.

One of the problems of being a leader is that sometimes we get so close to a situation that "we can't see the forest for the trees." This was Moses' difficulty. He knew he had a lot of work to do and that he was working with a group of "unspiritual" and "unpredictable" people, but he did not have the "big picture" that would have helped him facilitate his responsibilities. Here is where others can help us solve a problem. It took a "Jethro" to help Moses to even *see* his problem. It took the Jerusalem church to help the Antiochian church solve the problem they were *already* aware of. Pinpointing it more specifically, it took the assistance of Peter and James to help Paul and Barnabas to bring the problem of law and grace into clear focus.

A great danger that faces every Christian leader is to become threatened by advice. Somehow we feel it is a reflection on our competency, and so we proceed to try to solve the problem alone. Unfortunately, if the problem is beyond us, we will probably end up a failure, far more humiliated than if admitting we needed help. Actually to seek advice is a sign of strength and not weakness. This does not mean that we execute every bit of advice we get from others. Rather it means listening, sorting ideas carefully, and selecting a course of action in dependence upon the Spirit of God.

Third, establish priorities. This may actually be one of the main reasons we cannot solve our organizational and administrative problems. We do not run away from problems; rather we try to solve them all by ourselves.

This was Moses' problem until he took his father-in-law's advice. He was in the process of physical and psychological deterioration caused by undue stress. He could not do everything; fortunately he recognized this fact and did something about it.

The apostles, too, in Acts 6, were aware of this principle. They quickly established their priorities and made them known to the people. This did not mean that "serving tables" was unimportant—far from it—but it did mean that they had certain spiritual responsibilities that they had to fulfill. They could not do both.

Today pastors and other spiritual leaders are bombarded with many demands on their time. Contemporary culture and its pressures have complicated the lives of people, creating greater needs. A "big society" and "big business" have created a "big mentality." We automatically demand more of our leaders and ourselves. Therefore, it is absolutely essential, especially for spiritual leaders in the church, to establish priorities. If we don't, we will neglect our primary calling to "shepherd" and to "teach" the flock of God.

Fourth, delegate responsibility to qualified people. This principle follows naturally the "establishment of priorities." We have seen it demonstrated remarkably by Moses, by the apostles, and by Nehemiah.

This principle, we can conclude, has been the secret to *every* leader's success. Peter Drucker, who has made a careful study of executives, concludes that a significant mark of every successful leader—whether he be the President of the United States or the president of General Motors—is that he knows how to "use all the available strengths—the strength of associates, the strength of supervisors, and one's own strength."[1]

But notice that the Bible clearly emphasizes that delegation of responsibility must be to *spiritually qualified* people. This is what Moses and the apostles did in Exodus 18 and Acts 6. They looked for men who were honest and full of faith, men who were wise and discerning and experienced. They knew that to appoint men of weakness rather than men of strength would be devastating to the whole operation. They also knew that men of quality could handle organizational problems.

Nehemiah, of course, had a similar problem. However, he needed every available person to rebuild the walls, and he used them. But significantly, when it came to administering the affairs of Jerusalem after the walls were rebuilt, he appointed Hananiah, who had been commander of the forces, to be "in charge of Jerusalem." Nehemiah chose this man because "he was a faithful man and feared God more than many" (Neh 7:2). He had already proved himself as a qualified leader.

The selection of spiritually and psychologically qualified people for leadership positions in the church is one of the most obvious administrative principles in the New Testament. This is why most all of the qualifications of elders and deacons in 1 Timothy 3 and Titus 1 relate to the man's reputation, ethics, morality, temperament, habits, and spiritual and psychological maturity.

---

1. Peter F. Drucker, *The Effective Executive* (New York: Harper & Row, 1966), p. 71.

Many churches today are guilty of filling positions with *people*—but not *qualified* people. We often make judgments based on "skills" (sometimes falsely classified as spiritual gifts), but if these skills are practiced in a context of carnality it can be devastating. Unfortunately, "ability" and "carnality" mix well, for ignoble ends. Far better to have a person who has undeveloped skill and who is strong in spiritual and psychological qualities. If he is strong in the latter, he will *become* strong in the former. And if he has special gifts of the Spirit, they will soon become obvious.

Fifth, maintain a proper balance between divine and human factors.

The temptation for all leaders is to go to extremes. On the one hand, we may rationalize indecision and inaction on the basis of God's sovereign will and grace. This can easily become a "cop out" for irresponsibility and—God forbid—even laziness. On the other hand, we may take matters into our own hands and ignore the will of God, His power, wisdom, and guidance.

Both extremes of course are wrong. Nehemiah, of all the biblical examples, demonstrates most forcefully the balance. He prayed and then "acted." And sometimes he "acted" and then "prayed." And at times he prayed *while* he acted. As he consistently sought guidance from God, he at the same time proceeded to use the mind and energy that God had given him to do what he *knew* needed to be done.

Perhaps the clearest example of this principle in the life of Nehemiah was when he arrived in Jerusalem. He "arose in the night" and went out and surveyed the walls. But, said Nehemiah, "I did not tell any one what my God was putting in my mind to do for Jerusalem" (Neh 2:12). Here it is clear that he was formulating his plans as he inspected the walls, but he was also fully convinced that God was guiding his thoughts.

Christian leaders functioning in the twentieth century church must maintain the same balance. How easy it is to go to extremes, to attempt to solve problems in our own strengths and with our own abilities; and to neglect prayer, God's help, and direction and blessing. On the other hand, how easy it is to withdraw, spend time in prayer or in Bible reading; and to neglect human responsibility. And God help us to put a proper emphasis on both the divine and human—and in that order.

Sixth, take an approach to problem solving and decision making that takes into consideration the attitudes and feelings of everyone who is involved.

Basic to effectively applying this principle is *communication.* Before taking specific steps to solve his problem, Moses *explained* to the people he was not able to bear up alone under the heavy responsibility (Deu 1:9). At the appropriate time, Nehemiah called the people together and *explained* his strategy to rebuild the walls (Neh 2:17). The apostles in Jerusalem "summoned the congregation" and *explained* the situation (Ac 6:2), and in Acts 15 the whole church was involved in solving the problem of "law and grace." Organizational and administrative problems cannot be satisfactorily solved without proper communication. Obviously circumstances vary (as they did in the scriptural examples), affecting what is said, how much, when, and with whom. But there was always communication with as many people as possible.

Another factor which appears in all four biblical case studies is group involvement in the decision-making process. Again we see variance in the particulars, but there was always group participation and consensus. Moses instructed each tribe to select leaders to represent and rule them (Deu 1:13). The apostles charged the "congregation" to choose seven men to serve tables (Ac 6:1-3). And though the apostles and elders evidently met in closed session to hammer out some of the aspects of the problem of law and grace that obviously could not be handled in a large group, the whole church *was* involved in making the final decision (Ac 15:22).

Nehemiah's problem was a different one indeed. The primary responsibility of rebuilding the walls lay on his shoulders. He was *the* leader. It was *his* idea and strategy. But Nehemiah knew he could *never* achieve his goal without the consensus of the people. Consequently, he carefully communicated his ideas to the people and then issued a call to "come" and as a team to rebuild the walls of Jerusalem. The results of his success as a leader are reflected in their response when they said, "Let us arise and build" (Neh 2:18).

Many problems are created in the twentieth century church by ignoring this important biblical principle. We are only asking for trouble if we attempt to railroad things through and operate as a dictator. Even the apostles—direct representatives of the Lord Jesus

Christ—did not use their apostolic authority to bypass this principle. Naturally there are many problems which need not be brought to the whole congregation for debate and discussion, but again our biblical examples give us significant guidelines in applying the principle of "congregational involvement."

In Exodus 18 and Acts 6 minor details were solved by *people selected by the group.* This was the crucial point at which there was group involvement. Note, however, that in Acts 6 it is conceivable that *only* the Grecian Christians were involved in solving the problem. There was no need to call the *whole* Jerusalem church together to solve a problem that affected only a certain segment of the church.[2] In Acts 15 the whole church seemed to be involved in being made *aware* of the problem, but the basic proposal was formulated as a result of debate and discussion by the apostles and elders. But it was the *whole* church that approved the proposal and was involved in the selection of men to implement the plan.

Here in Scripture we see four significant guidelines in determining when the whole group should be involved:

1. Involve the people that are directly related to and affected by the problem.
2. Communicate the nature of the problem to this group.
3. Involve the group in selecting qualified men to represent them in helping to solve the problem.
4. Secure the group's approval of the final solution to the problem.

Seventh, solve every problem creatively under the leadership of the Holy Spirit. Never allow yourself to get locked in to administrative routines that may have worked before.

We must remember that in the Bible there was no one way of either attacking or solving a problem. Every situation was different. Circumstances varied, the nature of the problem varied, and solutions varied.

Christian leaders today frequently allow themselves to get locked in to administrative patterns. They attempt to "borrow" patterns and approaches from other churches, or they continue to use patterns that have worked before. When we do, we are closing our minds and hearts

---

2. The argument for this is based on the fact that only men who had Greek names were selected. It is further supported by the fact that it was the Grecian Jews who were being neglected. It seems the apostles called *these* people together and helped them solve their particular problem.

to God, who has always used means creatively throughout history to administer His work. In order to find the will of God in every matter, we must be guided by biblical principles, current circumstances, and the Holy Spirit.

One thing is clear from a study of administration in the Word of God—*principles are normative! Patterns are not!*

PRINCIPLES OF ORGANIZATION

First, organize to apply New Testament principles and to reach New Testament purposes.

Throughout these chapters principles are stated which are believed to be biblical principles. If the principles are applied, they will give the twentieth century church New Testament guidelines.

Put another way, principles that are normative also become purposes or objectives. They are not only principles to be applied, but they become ends to be attained.

Organizational structures in the Bible are always presented as a means to an end. They were never ends in themselves. Therefore, the first and most important biblical principle of organization is always to develop structures for the church which will help us to reach New Testament objectives.

This, in fact, becomes one of the criteria whereby we are able to evaluate our organizational structures. Are we truly functioning according to New Testament principles? Are we reaching New Testament purposes? If not, perhaps we do not have adequate forms to do the job.

Second, organize to meet needs. This was a distinctive mark of the New Testament church. The church did not just organize to organize. Rather it organized when the need arose, whether it was to "feed people in need" or to "solve a theological problem."

The first and most all-inclusive and continuous need faced by the New Testament church was to carry out the Great Commission. They were under obligation to "make disciples" and to "teach those disciples." Obviously, they organized to do so. But as pointed out already, very few illustrations are given as to "how" this was done. Unfortunately some today interpret the lack of organizational detail in the New Testament as an indication that the church is to function without structure. This is, of course, an impossibility. To quote Dr.

George Peters, Professor of Missions at Dallas Theological Seminary, "Wherever there are people, there is function; and wherever there is function, there is form." This is a reality.

True there *is* limited reference to organizational structure in the Scriptures, but again this is not without design. There *are* sufficient illustrations to show it *is* necessary and there is sufficient *variance* to show that particular structures *are not absolute*. And the illustrations we *do* have yield dynamic principles that are applicable to any culture, and at any time in history. All of this, of course, points to freedom to design and create organizational structures that will be the most effective to reach New Testament objectives in today's world.

Donald Guthrie has spoken to this issue in his commentary on the Pastoral epistles:

> There is, therefore, considerable evidence to show that Paul was not unmindful of church organization. The absence of uniformity of government in Pauline churches is capable of other explanations than that Paul was completely disinterested. He appears to have been sufficiently flexible in his approach to allow any system which suited local conditions and was dictated by the Holy Spirit.[3]

It has already been demonstrated that Paul was more concerned about qualified men than specific patterns of organization. He *was* interested in organization for he charged the Corinthians to "let all things be done properly and in an orderly manner" (1 Co 14:40). He also instructed Titus to remain in Crete so he could "set in order what remains" (Titus 1:5).

But he also knew that every culture (even the various subcultures in the New Testament world) called for different approaches to specific organizational problems. He therefore bore down on the absolutes—qualifications for leadership positions—knowing that men of God who are wise and prudent could develop the structures necessary to meet the specialized demands of any culture at any time in history. As Dr. Francis Schaeffer has said, "Any thing the New Testament does not command, and regard as church forms, is a freedom to be exercised under the leadership of the Holy Spirit for that particular time and place."[4]

---

3. Donald Guthrie, *The Pastoral Epistles* (Grand Rapids: Eerdmans, 1957), p. 28.
4. Francis Schaeffer, *The Church at the End of the Twentieth Century,* p. 67.

Third, keep organization simple. This principle is closely aligned with the former; that is, organizing to meet needs. If organization is to be functional, it must be as simple as possible. Complicated organizational patterns frequently become "ends" in themselves.

This does not mean that organizational patterns are never complex. For example, the pattern in Exodus 18 was very intricate, but it was also designed for over two million people who were traveling through the wilderness. But it *was* functional, though complex, and carefully designed to meet the needs of the children of God at that particular time in their lives.

A good test of whether or not simplicity is being lost, even in a complex pattern, is whether or not the structure is serving biblical objectives. If it is not, it needs to be carefully evaluated in the light of scriptural criteria.

It is important for every Christian leader to realize that a "smooth running church" does not mean it is successful as measured by the Word of God. The world, and many Christian groups as well as pseudo-Christian groups, have produced dynamic organizational structures. Some because of their efficiency are reaching more people and raising more money than evangelicals.

Reaching objectives? Yes, but the wrong ones! You see, good organization can be used to reach any purpose or end—noble or ignoble, biblical or non-biblical. And unfortunately, some non-Christians use biblical principles to reach non-biblical objectives.

Fourth, keep organization flexible. The structures set up in the wilderness for a people "on the move," were changed when they "settled in the land." When the walls were complete, a new approach was devised to govern Jerusalem. When persecution hit Jerusalem, the structure of Acts 6 was terminated, and when the specific "law and grace" problems recorded in Acts 15 were solved, they went on to *new* ways of solving *new* problems. Biblical leaders were never locked in to organizational structures.

Organizational patterns that develop rigidity and "hardening of the categories" are in danger of being treated as authoritative, and absolute. This is wrong. We are not free to make unchangeable what God intended to be changeable. "In a rapidly changing age like ours," says Dr. Schaeffer, "an age of total upheaval like ours, to make non-absolutes absolute guarantees both isolation and the death of the institutional, organized church."[5]

There are many areas today where the evangelical church needs to rethink its organizational structures—areas that we have allowed to become absolute and nonflexible. The following questions are designed to probe our thinking and to "break us loose" from rigidity and inflexibility.

HOW MANY MEETINGS AND WHEN?

Who is to say *how many* meetings should be conducted in a given week in the church? The Bible certainly does not dictate any patterns in this area.

Furthermore, who is to say *when* these meetings are to be held? Other than a few references to meetings on the "first day of the week" (Ac 20:7; 1 Co 16:2), there is little said in Scripture about when the New Testament church met. Some would even question that meeting on Sunday is an absolute guideline for the church, but rather an example of when the church met.

The Corinthians, no doubt, met on Sunday evening to partake of the Lord's Supper and to exercise their spiritual gifts (1 Co 11), but is this an absolute pattern? I think not! If so, the majority of churches have been out of step with Scripture for many years. But even in view of this scriptural evidence (or lack of it) regarding *when* believers are to meet, there are many Christians who feel you are tampering with scriptural authority if it is suggested, for example, that the Sunday night service be cancelled in favor of a more qualitative meeting at some other time.

Midweek prayer meeting has probably become the most rigid pattern of all, for to suggest a change (in the minds of some) is synonymous with "being opposed to prayer." The fact is, there is no biblical injunction for the church to "meet for a midweek prayer meeting." It may be an excellent idea, but there is nothing sacred about a "midweek prayer meeting" per se. What makes it sacred is what happens there, for there is no question but that believers are to *pray*. But *when* they meet to pray is but a means to an end.

It is interesting, too, that many Christian leaders evaluate the spiritual climate of the church by how many attend midweek prayer

---

5. Ibid.

meeting. There may be some truth to this, but a more basic question is whether or not the body of believers represent a praying church. *When* they meet or *how many* meet at one time is not nearly so significant. A quantitative answer to "how many attend midweek prayer meeting" may be an indicator of spiritual maturity—or the lack of it. But it may also be true that a midweek prayer meeting, as it has come to be traditionally practiced, may no longer be the best means or pattern for the twentieth century church. Because of work schedules, school activities, and other cultural changes, perhaps the hour and evening chosen in a previous era is no longer the best time. Perhaps this is a major reason why believers are not actively attending this service as they once did.

WHAT KINDS OF MEETINGS?

In recent years the various *kinds* of meetings conducted by the church have multiplied. The twentieth century church has meetings for children, meetings for youth and meetings for adults. We have Bible classes, fellowship meetings, training sessions, worship periods, preaching services and prayer meetings. We have Sunday school sessions, vacation Bible schools, training hour, children's church, youth church, adult church, women's missionary meetings, home Bible studies, child evangelism classes and youth rallies. We have board meetings, committee meetings, teachers' meetings and choir practice. Other types of meetings, of course, could be added to this list depending on the church and situation.

Actually it is difficult to find any pattern in the New Testament that illustrates the present approach to meetings and agencies in our average church today. We know the first century Christians had meetings, but what kind and what the specific characteristics of these meetings were is very difficult to determine.

This, of course, does not mean it is wrong to have the different kinds of meetings and agencies we have today. The very freedom allowed in the New Testament is the basic reason there *is* so much variety. The important New Testament principle, of course, is *why* these meetings are held; in other words, do they exist to achieve New Testament objectives?

But the point I am making here, is that the very freedom that has allowed us to develop the forms and structures we have today has been stifled by allowing what we are doing at the present time to become *the way.* For example, is the typical Sunday school the best form of Christian education in our contemporary society? Is the usual training hour on Sunday evening the best way to equip various members of the body of Christ for Christian service? Is our morning church service the best kind of meeting to help believers learn the Scriptures and worship God?

It is time for the church to evaluate the kinds of meetings it has, and to justify their existence on the basis of New Testament principles and purposes.

WHAT ABOUT THE PATTERNS AND FORMAT WHICH
CHARACTERIZE MEETINGS?

In some churches if you dare change the order of the morning worship service, you get the distinct feeling you are tampering with the Scriptures themselves. Who is to say how a service is to be ordered? There is very little in Scripture to suggest specific answers to this question.

We *do* have mention of what *experiences* Christians should have when the body of Christ meets, but *how* all of this is put together is not illustrated in detail. We do have some reference to what the Corinthians did in their Sunday evening meetings, but the specific format is difficult to reconstruct.

It is my opinion that what we see in Corinthians is illustrative of the way *they* met and, with the exception of certain aspects of *what* they did, provides no absolute guidelines for the church. This is logical when we realize that the whole tone of Scripture emphasizes freedom in "organizational structure." And this point becomes even more forceful when we realize that the Corinthians, who were using this freedom, were doing so as a very carnal group of believers. All the more reason not to get locked into *their* patterns.

The body of Christ, therefore, needs to determine its meeting patterns and format, first of all, by setting forth clear-cut biblical objectives for these meetings. The patterns which are chosen should then be the best possible means to achieve these biblical ends within the context of the contemporary culture, taking into consideration the many variables which affect a group of people who live in a particular time in history, and in a particular part of the world, and in particular communities. This is also true, of course, in determining the number of meetings, when the meetings are held, and the various kinds of meetings. To allow our present patterns to lock us in to a particular approach is to make non-absolutes absolute, and this is a definite step in the direction of institutionalism.

WHAT ABOUT THE PLACE FOR MEETINGS?

An interesting trend in churches today is to conduct meetings off the church property. But more interesting than this phenomenon is the attitude of certain Christians toward this trend. Some people are highly threatened, for they feel the church hierarchy may lose control of what is happening. To some, anything that decentralizes the body of Christ rather than centralizing it (that is, bringing everyone together in one place) is a danger signal.

It is also interesting to get the feedback from some Christians that the "church building" is *the* scriptural place to meet. This is of special interest since the New Testament Christians had no church buildings to meet in. At first they met in the temple in Jerusalem and in homes. When the Jewish leaders eventually rejected Christianity, some had to meet in their homes exclusively. This is one reason why we have many references to "house churches" in the New Testament.

Does this mean that "house churches" is the New Testament way— an absolute pattern which we must go back to if God's richest blessing is to rest upon the church? Again, I think not! However, I would add that there is something unique about the "house church" that assists in creating a "family atmosphere" for the body of Christ. It is unfortunate that the strong emphasis on church buildings has led us away from the concept of a home as a meeting place for believers to experience New Testament Christianity.

But there are many problems created by our culture in exclusively holding a regular church meeting in a "house church." Extensive traveling for business purposes by the head of the home, vacation periods, trends in weekend living habits, the various needs of all age levels, a limited time for families to even get together as a single family in their homes—all of these factors make a "house church" difficult to maintain in many communities.

But to say that the "church building" is *the* biblical place to meet is to be totally unscriptural. To say that *any* particular place is *the* biblical place is to make a non-absolute an absolute. Because of the various cultural changes and the needs of people today, the body of Christ needs to be flexible as to where it meets. A Sunday school class for college youth that meets on the university campus may be far more effective than meeting in the church. Using a number of homes for midweek Bible study and prayer sessions, led by a number of mature lay Christians, may be far more significant than trying to get everyone to meet at the church under the leadership of the pastor.

Then, too, renting facilities other than church buildings may be a greater use of the Lord's money than building a huge church plant. Some churches use YMCA buildings, public schools, college campuses, and other available buildings. On the other hand, in some locations it is difficult to function this way. In other parts of the country it works out well, depending on a variety of factors.

But the important point is that the body of Christ be *flexible* in determining *where* its meetings are to take place. There are no biblical absolutes dictating the answers to these questions.

SUMMING UP

What forms and patterns are developed to carry out these administrative and organizational principles is a matter of creative leadership under the direction of the Holy Spirit. It is impossible to derive specific patterns and structures from the New Testament (which is also abundantly demonstrated by the many different types of church government in existence today among evangelical believers).

It seems, however, that the Holy Spirit definitely planned this "ambiguity." Because of the variety of environments, cultures, and mentalities in the world today, God knew that to issue absolutes in the area of structure and form in organization and administration would be to provide specific guidelines that would be difficult to implement in various areas of the world. The principles He has given us, however, are supracultural and can and should be applied to the twentieth century church, wherever it may be.

These principles are:

ADMINISTRATION

1. Face the reality of problems.
2. Develop a proper perspective on the problems before seeking concrete solutions.

3. Establish priorities.
4. Delegate responsibility to qualified people.
5. Maintain a proper balance between divine and human factors.
6. Take an approach to problem solving and decision making that takes into consideration the attitudes and feelings of everyone involved.
7. Solve every problem creatively under the leadership of the Holy Spirit.

ORGANIZATION

1. Organize to apply New Testament principles and to reach New Testament purposes.
2. Organize to meet needs.
3. Keep organization simple.
4. Keep organization flexible.

14

COMMUNICATION IN THE NEW TESTAMENT

The *way* in which New Testament Christians communicated is another broad and significant area for study. Actually, many facets of communication have already appeared in our investigation of first century believers, and the way in which they proceeded to carry out the Great Commission.

Among the unsaved they taught, declared, spoke, proclaimed, preached, testified, witnessed, exhorted, praised, reasoned, refuted, explained, demonstrated, persuaded, and gave evidence for what they believed.

As a church "gathered" for edification they taught and exhorted one another. They engaged in fellowship, broke bread, prayed, and praised God. They encouraged and strengthened one another, and reported and described God's work and blessings in other parts of the world. And when they had theological and ethical difficulties, they debated, wrote, implored, and admonished one another.

All of these words are used in the New Testament to describe the process of communication, both as the believers evangelized (made disciples) and as they gathered to be built up and edified. A careful study of these words in context makes it very clear that they are used to describe a process that was characterized by much variety and many different approaches. Whether it involved Peter's sermons recorded by Luke, or Paul's communication with various individuals and groups, there is obviously no consistent pattern in the *way* their content was presented. And of course, the New Testament letters *all* reveal a variety in literary style and form. Even among and within the Pauline epistles, there is no consistent approach in form and structure.

All of this points to "freedom" in communication. But the many examples in the New Testament, like so many other areas of first century church life, yield some profound principles which can assist the twentieth century church to be a "communicating" church—as a church "in the world" and as a "gathered community."

Because Paul said, "Be imitators of me, just as I also am of Christ" (1 Co 11:1), two basic communication models follow. The first presents Jesus Christ Himself, the supreme model! The second presents the ministry of Paul, as well as two of his co-workers. Both models, however, yield New Testament principles of communication.

A COMMUNICATION MODEL FROM JESUS CHRIST

The communication methods of Christ have been studied and researched for many years, and the process has yielded some outstanding observations and principles. But there is an "overall" perspective that has not, to my knowledge, been explored, or at least presented in written form.

A careful listing of the specific communication situations, beginning with Christ's public ministry and up to the time He was taken into custody, yields approximately 184 examples. Assuming that all such cases recorded in the gospels are generally representative of Christ's three-and-one-half-year ministry on earth, some very interesting observations can be made from the chart "Communication Situations in Christ's Ministry."[1]

These communication situations can be broken down into the various cases listed in table 1. When these cases are divided into two categories by identifying those who were either neutral or negative and those who were definitely positive, we have the statistics given in table 2. If these cases are divided into those involving individuals and those involving groups, table 3 is the result. By dividing the "Group"

---

1. A. T. Robertson's *A Harmony of the Gospels* (New York: Harper, 1922) was used for this study. The specific analysis began with "Christ's public ministry," Part VI, page 19, and was terminated at Part XIII, page 205, entitled, "The Arrest, Trial, Crucifixion, and Burial of Jesus." Before His public ministry there are no references to specific communication situations, and following His arrest the references are quite limited.

Obviously certain judgments were made as to what was a "specific" communication situation. Furthermore, general references were excluded from this list; such as, "And Jesus was going about all the cities and the villages, teaching in their synagogues, and proclaiming the gospel of the kingdom, and healing every kind of disease and every kind of sickness" (Mt 9:35; see also Mk 16:20).

situations into those who were positive toward Christ and those who were either neutral or negative toward Him, thè comparison in table 4 is made.

COMMUNICATION SITUATIONS IN CHRIST'S MINISTRY

TABLE 1

A Distribution of the Percentage of Times Christ Spent Ministering to Various Individuals and Groups

COMMUNICATION SITUATION	NUMBER	PERCENTAGE
The disciples (larger group of followers)	29	15.8
The scribes and Pharisees (as a group)	28	15.5
Two or more apostles	24	13.0
Sick people (includes only individual healings)	22	11.9
A general group (other than disciples)*	20	10.8
Individuals generally**	19	10.3
Individual apostles (the 12)	19	10.3
The multitudes	18	9.7
Sick people (involving group healings)	5	2.7
Totals	184	100

TABLE 2

The Percentage of Times Christ Spent Ministering to Various Individuals and Groups Positive Toward Him Compared with the Percentage of Times Spent with Those Negative

DEFINITELY POSITIVE		EITHER NEUTRAL OR NEGATIVE	
Disciples	15.8%	Scribes and Pharisees	15.5%
Sick people (individual		General group	10.8%
and group)	14.6%	Individuals generally	10.3%
Two or more apostles	13.0%	Multitudes	9.7%
Individual apostles	10.3%		
Total	53.7%	Total	46.3%

*Indicates such groups as the "Jews," the "servants," etc.
**Such as Nicodemus, the woman at the well, a scribe, etc. This does not include individuals who are definitely classified as disciples. They are included under the first item in the table. Out of 29 references to the disciples, only 8 are "individual" disciples.

TABLE 3

The Percentage of Times Christ Spent with Individuals Compared
with the Percentage of Times He Spent with Groups

INDIVIDUALS		GROUPS	
Sick individuals	11.9%	Disciples	15.8%
Individuals generally	10.3%	Scribes and Pharisees	15.5%
Individual apostles	10.3%	Two or more apostles	13.0%
		General group	10.8%
		Multitudes	9.7%
		Sick people (a group)	2.7%
Total	32.5%	Total	67.5%

TABLE 4

The Number of Times Christ Spent Ministering to Groups Positive
Toward Him Compared to Those with Groups Negative or Neutral

GROUPS POSITIVE		GROUPS NEGATIVE OR NEUTRAL	
Disciples	29	Scribes and Pharisees	28
Two or more apostles	24	General group	20
Sick people	5	Multitude	18
Total	58 (46.8%)	Total	66 (53.2%)

From these categorizations, note the following specific observations:

1. Christ *balanced* His ministry by communicating with many different kinds of people. Taking into account all of the sub-groups and individuals He ministered to, the percentage of times He spent with each of these various groups ranges from approximately 10 percent to 15 percent (table 1). He neglected no one.

2. He spent approximately *half* of His times communicating to those who were *positive* toward His ministry and the other *half* communicating to those who were either neutral or negative (table 2).

3. He spent about *one third* of the times with individuals, and about *two thirds* of the times with groups (table 3).

4. Of the two-thirds of the times He spent communicating with groups, He spent about half of them with groups who were positive toward His ministry and the other half communicating with those who were either neutral or negative (table 4).

5. Of the 32.5 percent of the times that He spent with individuals, He spent about one-third communicating with individual sick people, one-third communicating with individuals generally, and about one-third communicating with individual apostles. Interestingly, all three categories involving individuals approximate 10 percent (see table 3).

All of these observations indicate that Jesus Christ neglected no one. He had His priorities, but He was as interested in those who were positive toward Him as those who were negative or neutral. He also divided His time between groups and individuals. And even among the kinds of individuals He ministered to, He evenly distributed His efforts.

There is no more outstanding communication model! But more than the overall picture, the way He trained the twelve is even more magnificent. They were His special group. Even though it appears that He spent as many times communicating with individuals generally as He did with individual apostles, in reality He spent nearly 100 percent of His time with the twelve.

How could this be? Note His general approach to training these select men. First, after calling them to follow Him, along with the general group of disciples, He then called them to be with Him in a special way: to watch, to observe, to listen as He preached to the multitudes, as He debated with the scribes and Pharisees, taught the larger group of disciples, and ministered to individuals. Then He sent them out to do what He had been doing. Finally, He began a special concentrated ministry with them, preparing them for His death, His resurrection, and the Great Commission.

As Christ carried out His general ministry communicating with all classes of people, He, in a special way, spent His total time training these twelve men. No doubt every time He spoke to the multitudes, the apostles heard what He said. Every time He healed a person, they observed. Every time He dialogued and debated with the Pharisees, they looked on with amazement. In almost every instance when He talked with individuals, they also listened in—or at least got firsthand feedback (for example, as with the woman at the well).

Notice, too, the unique pattern that frequently emerged in Christ's overall ministry. At times He would be teaching the multitudes; then He would turn to the larger groups of disciples and speak to them more personally. And on occasions, He would turn to the twelve and speak even more specifically and intimately about the truth He was teaching the larger group. Going a step further, He would at times turn to one individual or perhaps two or three of the twelve, to share with them some truth even more forcefully. (See fig. 3.)

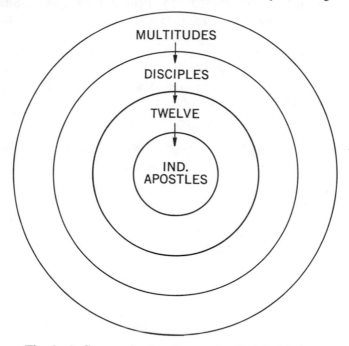

Fig. 3. A Communication Pattern in Christ's Ministry

What we see in Jesus Christ is an unequaled communication model. While He reached the multitudes, He was equipping a group of twelve men for an in-depth ministry. And while He was equipping twelve men, He was especially equipping Peter and John for a more foundational ministry that would go beyond even that of the other apostles. This is obvious from the ministry of these two men as revealed in the book of Acts, as well as by the New Testament literature they wrote. It was no secret to the twelve that Jesus Christ had a special ministry for these men, and particularly for the apostle Peter. The way He singled out Peter for special instructions and lessons verifies this point beyond doubt.

A COMMUNICATION MODEL FROM PAUL, SILAS, AND TIMOTHY

These three New Testament leaders are chosen for a reason. First, they represent three men who in a special way exemplify those who had the greater gifts (1 Co 12:31). Paul was an apostle; Silas is classified as a prophet (Ac 15:32); and Timothy was definitely a teacher.[2]

A second reason these men are chosen for this model is that they have left for us, through Paul's writings, one of the most comprehensive communication patterns found anywhere among those who founded and established churches.

THEIR MINISTRY IN THESSALONICA

Luke records the basic events leading to the founding of the church in Thessalonica (Ac 17:1-9). We note from this passage that Paul himself "reasoned" in the synagogue for three Sabbaths, probably covering a three-week period (vv. 2-3). Some Jews were converted and a large number of Greeks and leading women (v. 4). Other than these basic facts, Luke tells us very little about the actual ministry of these three men in this Macedonian city.

However, when we come to Paul's first epistle to these new Christians, a large portion of the letter is given over to describing their initial ministry with these people. These reflections by Paul give us some exciting insights into the way these men as a team communicated with these people—before and after they became Christians.

The First Thessalonian Letter	Communication Characteristics
1:1 Paul and Silvanus [Silas] and Timothy to the church of the Thessalonians in God the Father and the Lord Jesus Christ: Grace to you and peace.	Paul wrote this letter representing his two co-workers, Silas and Timothy, who served with him when the church was founded in Thessalonica.

---

2. There is biblical evidence that all of these men had multiple gifts. For example, Paul classifies himself not only as an apostle but as a preacher and a teacher. Luke also classifies Paul as a prophet. There is no doubt that he was also an evangelist. Silas was not only a prophet, but seemingly a teacher and a pastor. Timothy had both the gift of teaching and that of pastor.

1:2 We give thanks to God always for all of you, making mention of you in our prayers;

Part of their follow up with these people was *prayer*.

1:3 constantly bearing in mind your work of faith and labor of love and steadfastness of hope in our Lord Jesus Christ in the presence of our God and Father;

The criteria for evaluating the effectiveness of their ministry was the degree of *faith, hope,* and *love* manifested by these believers.

1:4 knowing, brethren beloved by God, His choice of you,

They recognized *God's sovereign work* in the lives of people.

1:5 for our gospel did not come to you in word only, but also in power and in the Holy Spirit and with full conviction; just as you know what kind of men we proved to be among you for your sake.

They did not depend upon their oratory and communication skills alone, but primarily upon the *power* of the *Holy Spirit*.

1:6 You also became imitators of us and of the Lord, having received the word in much tribulation with the joy of the Holy Spirit,

They lived in such a way as to be living *models* of the Christ-life which these people could imitate.

1:7,8 so that you became an example to all the believers in Macedonia and in Achaia. For the word of the Lord has sounded forth from you, not only in Macedonia and in Achaia, but also in every place your faith toward God has gone forth, so that we have no need to say anything.

One of their objectives was to *multiply themselves;* they also measured the effectiveness of their work by the outreach of these believers.

1:9,10 For they themselves report about us what kind of a reception we had with you, and how you turned to God from idols to serve a living and

Paul never hesitated to give *positive feedback* in order to encourage his converts to continue to live dynamic lives for Jesus Christ.

true God, and to wait for His Son from heaven, whom He raised from the dead, that is Jesus, who delivers us from the wrath to come.

2:1,2 For you yourselves know, brethren, that our coming to you was not in vain, but after we had already suffered and been mistreated in Philippi, as you know, we had the boldness in our God to speak to you the gospel of God amid much opposition.

When first communicating with the non-Christians in Thessalonica, they preached the gospel with *boldness*.

2:3 For our exhortation does not come from error or impurity or by way of deceit;

These men were *honest, open,* and *sincere*.

2:4 but just as we have been approved by God to be entrusted with the gospel, so we speak, not as pleasing men but God, who examines our hearts.

They wanted to *please God first* of all, not men.

2:5 For we never came with flattering speech, as you know, nor with a pretext for greed —God is witness—

Their motives were *pure*.

2:6 nor did we seek glory from men, either from you or from others, even though as apostles of Christ we might have asserted our authority.

They did not demand honor because they were Christ's representatives; rather they won *respect* through their behavior.

2:7 But we proved to be gentle among you, as a nursing mother tenderly cares for her own children.

They ministered to these people in a spirit of *gentleness*—like a mother nursing her child.

2:8 Having thus a fond affection for you, we were well pleased

They were *unselfish,* being willing to literally give their lives if to impart to you not only the gospel but also our own lives, because you had become very dear to us.

necessary to win these people to Christ.

2:9 For you recall, brethren, our labor and hardship, how working night and day so as not to be a burden to any of you, we proclaimed to you the gospel of God.

They worked night and day so as not to have their *motives* misinterpreted.

2:10 You are witnesses, and so is God, how devoutly and uprightly and blamelessly we behaved toward you believers;

They lived *exemplary lives* among those who came to Christ (see 1:5-6).

2:11,12 just as you know how we were exhorting and encouraging and imploring each one of you as a father would his own children, so that you may walk in a manner worthy of the God who calls you into His own kingdom and glory.

They maintained an *individualized ministry* among these new Christians; they literally taught and encouraged "each one," just like a father would work with each one of his children.

2:13 And for this reason we also constantly thank God that when you received from us the word of God's message, you accepted it not as the word of men, but for what it really is, the word of God, which also performs its work in you who believed.

They *exalted* the Word of God; not their own ideas or philosophy.

2:17-20 But we, brethren, having been bereft of you for a short while—in person, not in spirit—were all the more eager with great desire to see your face. For we wanted to come to you—I, Paul, more than

They *continued their interest* in these people after they had to leave them.

once—and yet Satan thwarted us. For who is our hope, or joy or crown of exultation? Is it not even you, in the presence of our Lord Jesus at His coming? For you are our glory and joy.

3:1,2 Therefore when we could endure it no longer, we thought it best to be left behind at Athens alone; and we sent Timothy, our brother and God's fellow-worker in the gospel of Christ, to strengthen and encourage you as to your faith;

They *followed up* their ministry by having Timothy return to Thessalonica to strengthen and encourage these believers.

3:3-5 . . . so that no man may be disturbed by these afflictions; for you yourselves know that we have been destined for this. For indeed when we were with you, we kept telling you in advance that we were going to suffer affliction; and so it came to pass, as you know. For this reason, when I could endure it no longer, I also sent to find out about your faith, for fear that the tempter might have tempted you, and our labor should be in vain.

They were *straightforward* and *honest* with these people about the realities of Satan, and the trials they would have to endure because of their decision to follow Christ.

3:6-9 But now that Timothy has come to us from you, and has brought us good news of your faith and love, and that you always think kindly of us, longing to see us just as we also long to see you, for this reason, brethren, in all our

They *did not hesitate to share their human feelings* with these people—they were desperately concerned about them, and when they received a positive report of their progress in the faith, they were encouraged in the midst of their own trials and tribulations.

distress and affliction we were comforted about you through your faith; for now we really live, if you stand firm in the Lord. For what thanks can we render to God for you in return for all the joy with which we rejoice before our God on your account,

They did not hesitate to share these inner feelings.

3:10-13 as we night and day keep praying most earnestly that we may see your face, and may complete what is lacking in your faith? Now may our God and Father Himself and Jesus our Lord direct our way to you; and may the Lord cause you to increase and abound in love for one another, and for all men, just as we also do for you; so that He may establish your hearts unblamable in holiness before our God and Father at the coming of our Lord Jesus with all His saints.

They *wanted to return as a team* and assist these believers to go even further in their Christian development.

4:1,ff. Finally then, brethren, we request and exhort you in the Lord Jesus that, as you received from us instruction as to how you ought to walk and please God (just as you actually do walk), that you may excel still more.

Paul *used this letter as an additional means of follow up.* No doubt Timothy reported certain areas where they needed additional instructions — about morality (4:2-8); about their business life (4:10-12); about the second coming of Christ (4:13-17); about their attitudes toward their spiritual leaders, those in special need, and all men (5:12-15); as well as about their church life (5:16-21).

SUMMING UP

From Christ's model, we have looked at an overall strategy in the area of communication. The Lord Jesus demonstrated in a unique way how to meet the needs of all, but at the same time to communicate in a special way with special groups for in-depth training and development.

The communication model representing Paul, Silas, and Timothy demonstrates in a more specific way how these men won people to Christ, and then how they helped them grow spiritually. In summary, their communication was marked by the following characteristics:

THE TEAM AS MEN

1. They were living examples of the Christian way of life.
2. They were sincere and honest, and kept their motives pure.
3. They were bold and unintimidated.
4. They were gentle and loving.
5. They were unselfish and sincerely interested in people.

THEIR METHODS AT THE DIVINE LEVEL

1. They included a ministry of prayer.
2. They recognized God's sovereignty.
3. They relied upon the Holy Spirit.
4. They exalted the Word of God.

THEIR METHODS AT THE HUMAN LEVEL

1. They won respect through performance.
2. They maintained an individualized ministry as well as a ministry to groups.
3. They followed up by sending back Timothy to teach them.
4. They were honest and open about their own humanness.
5. They planned to return as a team to continue the process of edification.
6. They gave positive feedback to these new believers regarding their progress in the Christian life.
7. They maintained a written ministry by sending letters to encourage and instruct them.

THEIR EFFECTIVENESS

1. They evaluated it by the degree of faith, hope, and love present and manifested in the local body of believers.
2. They evaluated it by the way these believers were multiplying themselves in their sphere of influence.

15

PRINCIPLES OF NEW TESTAMENT COMMUNICATION

A study of communication models in the New Testament, from the life of Christ and the lives of New Testament leaders, surfaces some significant principles. These principles can serve as guidelines to enable church leaders today—as well as every member of the body of Christ—to be more effective in presenting the Word of God, both to those who know Christ, as well as to those who do not.

First, Christian communication is a distinctive process including both human and divine elements. As illustrated in figure 4, it can take place, and quite effectively, at the human level. God's common grace gives men the ability to communicate with one another.

But Christian communication includes some unique elements that go far beyond the purely horizontal level. Even when communicating with non-Christians, the Word of God, the Holy Spirit, and God Himself are involved in the process. A leader who is sensitive and open to spiritual guidance will find God Himself waiting to communicate through His Word and by His Spirit. (See fig. 5.) In turn, the believer has access to God's heart and power through prayer. At the same time all of these elements are at work in the communication process, God is working in the heart of the unbeliever through His Holy Spirit (Jn 16:7-8).

But Christian communication becomes a totally unique process when all individuals involved are Christians. (See fig. 6.) Here we have the concept of the "body." Communication can now move in all directions—from God to Christian leader, to individual members of the body of Christ, and from God to each member of the body to "one another." This is why Paul told the Colossians to teach and admonish one another (Col 3:16), the Ephesians to

177

speak to one another (Eph 5:19), and the Galatians to serve one another (Gal 5:13).

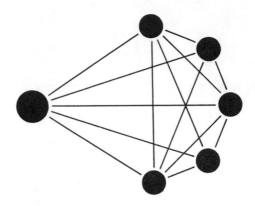

Fig. 4. Communication—Effective at the Purely Human Level

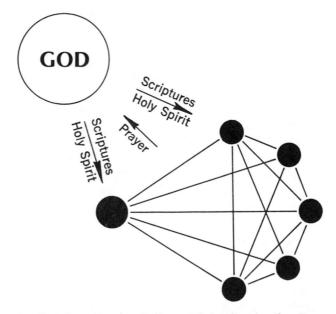

Fig. 5. Christian Communication—Distinctive in the Process of
Evangelism

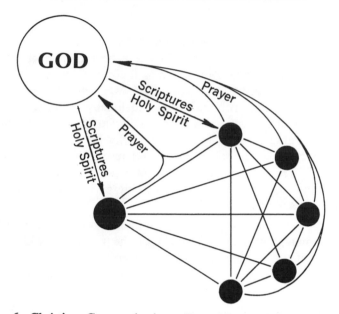

Fig. 6. Christian Communication—Even More Distinctive in the Process of Edification

God's plan definitely calls for those who are specially qualified to communicate to the church. This is very clear in the qualifications spelled out for spiritual leaders. But the Scriptures are also very clear that God's plan calls for every member of the body to communicate with one another in order to be properly edified.

But, as we consider this distinctive process including both the human and divine elements, it is obvious that some Christians tend to overemphasize, on one hand, the human elements; and on the other hand, the divine elements. New Testament leaders demonstrated beautifully the importance of both. They maintained a unique balance.

Paul, Silas, and Timothy recognized that "no one can say, 'Jesus is Lord,' except by the Holy Spirit" (1 Co 12:3). This is why, in writing to the Thessalonians, they gave testimony to the fact that the gospel did not come to these believers "in word only, but also in power and in the Holy Spirit and with full conviction" (1 Th 1:5). It was God who was at work in their hearts, causing them to respond to the Word of God (1:4). They knew the power of prayer (1:2) and the supernatural influence of the Word of God (2:13).

They were also aware of the importance of human effort. They were definitely cognizant of the fact that God has chosen to use human instrumentality to achieve His sovereign purposes. This is why they spent time with each one individually (2:11). After they had left Thessalonica, this is why they sent Timothy back to strengthen and encourage them (3:2). This is why Paul wanted the whole team to return to Thessalonica to continue a ministry among them (3:11-13). They did not hesitate to give positive feedback to these people. And they sat down and wrote letters to give them additional instructions and help.

All of these factors clearly point to human responsibility in Christian communication. In fact, most of the principles which follow grow out of the "human dimension" of communication in the New Testament setting. It is these factors which stand out on the pages of Scripture as you study the biblical examples. We cannot ignore them, but neither should we substitute them for the divine elements in the unique process of Christian communication.

Second, Christian communication should be to all kinds and classes of people.

Jesus demonstrated this principle forcefully. He went everywhere communicating with everyone! Whether Pharisee or disciple, apostle or another individual in need, He included them all. Whether to admirer or critic, He distributed His efforts in an amazing way.

Paul too said, "I am under obligation both to Greeks and to barbarians, both to the wise and to the foolish" (Ro 1:14). There were no class distinctions in this man's mind. Everyone needed the gospel. There was no one too poor or too rich, too religious or too pagan, or too near or too far, who did not come within the circle of Paul's concern.

Christians, like all human beings, can become prejudiced. It is easy to "pick and choose" those to whom we want to communicate. James blasted this kind of "personal favoritism," when he said:

> For if a man comes into your assembly with a gold ring and dressed in fine clothes, and there also comes in a poor man in dirty clothes, and you pay special attention to the one who is wearing the

fine clothes, and say, "You sit here in a good place," and you say to the poor man, "You stand over there, or sit down by my footstool"; have you not made distinctions among yourselves, and become judges with evil motives? (Ja 2:1-4).

This is wrong! These things ought not so to be, exclaimed James. "If you show partiality, you are committing sin" (2:9).

All Christians, but particularly spiritual leaders in the church, should evaluate their sphere of communication. Obviously we must establish priorities—especially as spiritual leaders. Our primary calling is to "feed the flock of God." But this in no way excuses us from a ministry to the *total* flock of God, and also to the unsaved man, wherever and whoever he may be. And as shepherd and teacher, we must communicate this concept to the whole family of God.

Third, Christian communication should be carefully balanced between a ministry to groups and a ministry to individuals. Again, Jesus Christ as well as Paul, Silas, and Timothy demonstrated this principle.

You may have wondered why these New Testament leaders frequently left a strong and thriving church. It did not just happen! If the Thessalonians are representative of their philosophy of communication, they spent a significant amount of time discipling individuals as well as speaking to groups.

The tendency today among evangelical Christians is to be satisfied to speak "to the multitudes." Pastors frequently spend most of their time behind the pulpit or in front of the group. To do so is to ignore a dynamic principle of Christian communication, demonstrated by both our Lord and the church leaders in the New Testament.

Certainly this takes time! But it is time well spent. For without this balanced approach, Christian communication becomes impersonal and wooden. It loses its dynamic and power. The individual is lost in the crowd, and we become guilty of communicating to a congregation—not individuals; to groups and not persons; to classes and not individual students.

Aren't you glad Jesus Christ died for *you*—as well as the world? Remember, in His mind you are one among many, but also the very hairs of your head are numbered!

This New Testament principle is particularly important in our present culture where technology and mass communication are in vogue. The tendency is to forget the individual.

There is no substitute for personal contact. Paul's illustration of ministering to the Thessalonians like a "mother nursing a child" and communicating with each one "as a father would [with] his own children" are powerful examples (1 Th 2:7, 11). People respond to personal attention. This is the way God made us. Therefore mass communication *must* never become a substitute for face-to-face interaction.

Interestingly, some evangelicals react against technology per se. It must be emphasized that technology in itself is not "evil." In fact, technology—if used appropriately and with wisdom—can greatly help us to put the personal touch back in communication. But, ironically, many of those Christians who react the most against technology are often the ones who violate the principle of personal contact. They do so by substituting a "pulpit only" type ministry. Their primary outreach is to groups, and their main approach is verbalization. Unfortunately they are striking out at the wrong thing. A deeper concern—and far more significant—is their violation of a biblical principle of communication so clearly demonstrated in the Word of God. We *must* carefully balance our ministry to groups, as well as to individuals.

Fourth, effective Christian communication must include an in-depth ministry to a select group as well as a ministry to the larger group of Christians.

Once again we see this principle demonstrated, both in the communication model of Christ and particularly in the ministry of Paul. While Jesus Christ was ministering to a variety of groups and individuals, He was at the same time preparing the twelve for a specialized ministry. While Paul was traveling about preaching and teaching, he was building his life into Timothy, who was his traveling companion.

The results of Paul's "discipling process" in the life of Timothy were capsuled when he wrote to this young pastor-teacher while he was stationed at Ephesus: "And the things which you have heard from me in the presence of many witnesses, these entrust to faithful men, who will be able to teach others also" (2 Ti 2:2).

In these words of Paul to Timothy we have, of course, not only a tribute to Paul's unique approach to communication, but here is also a reinforcement of the communication principle under consideration. This process was to be continued. Timothy was to select "faithful men" that he in turn could disciple. And these men were in turn to "teach others."

We cannot communicate with all people in depth. It is a human impossibility! Even Christ, our Lord, concentrated on a select few. But we can, while "equipping all saints to do the work of the ministry," equip a few chosen individuals in a specialized way. It will be these people who will in a unique way multiply our ministry.

But here again many Christians get off balance. It is either the "multitude" or the "individual." It is either the "large group" or the "small group." It is either an "in-depth ministry" or a "general exposure." The Bible, of course, teaches it must be "both-and"—not "either-or."

Fifth, for communication to be qualitative, it must get beyond the verbalization level. This is particularly true in training people in depth.

Christians often stop at the "word" level. We are so conditioned to thinking "verbally" that we feel awkward in a context that is characterized by total involvement.

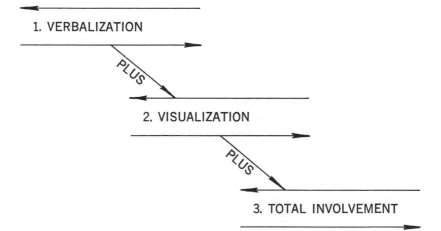

Fig. 7. Biblical Communication Levels

With Christ, it was verbalization, plus visualization, plus actual involvement. (See fig. 7). He did not stop at the first level. He verbalized, yes, but visualized wherever possible, and as He trained the twelve, He got them totally involved in the process. They learned by doing. Their failures, as well as their successes, became the backdrop against which Christ spoke the deep truths of God. And even after they had *experienced* many things, He still remarked: "I have many more things to say to you, but you cannot bear them now" (Jn 16:12). They had not yet "experienced" the separation from Him and the trauma of His arrest, crucifixion, and His resurrection. *Then* they would understand His words even more fully.

"Words," of course, are basic to communication. They are God's unique invention, and through the *written* Word of God they have become a primary means by which He has revealed His will to mankind.

But if we are to follow the example of New Testament leaders, particularly in equipping individuals for a ministry in depth, we must get beyond the verbalization level, particularly in a culture that is more and more oriented toward sensory experience. The "Sesame Street" generation is on us, and in many respects McLuhan is correct: "The medium has become the message." No amount of criticism or reaction will change this reality. It is here! Our responsibility then is to respond to this challenge with effective Christian communication.

These "new" concepts should not be new at all to Christians. God *always* intended communication to get beyond the verbalization level. It was *always* His desire for us to *experience* Christian truth, not just hear it. This is why the concept of the body of Christ is so unique. It creates a context in which we can not only experience Christ, but we can actually "experience one another." It provides opportunities for relational experiences that are two-dimensional— with God and with each other. When the body functions as God intended it to function, Christians will get beyond the verbalization level in their communication, and beyond the knowledge level in their learning of divine truth.

The body of Christ also is God's divine means for getting beyond the verbalization level in our Christian witness. It is as non-Christians *see* the body funtioning in *love* and *unity* that they become convinced of the reality of Christianity. Once again it must be emphasized that this becomes the experiential backdrop against which "words *about* Jesus Christ" take on meaning and true significance. McLuhan's phrase then, "the medium is the message," is actually a biblical concept. It is the *medium* (the body of Christ) that actually *becomes* the message to the unsaved world. And it is the "functioning body" that becomes the context in which believers can grow to maturity.

But this leads us to another significant New Testament principle of communication.

Sixth, in Christian communication, example is foundational to effective verbalization. No amount of words can overcome the power of hypocrisy. Nor will words alone do what the power of positive example can achieve.

This was the distinctive characteristic of Paul, Silas, and Timothy. This is the basic reason why these Macedonian missionaries obtained such outstanding results. "You are witnesses and so is God," they wrote, "how devoutly and uprightly and blamelessly we behaved toward you believers" (1 Th 2:10). No individual could point his finger at these Christian leaders and accuse them of inconsistent Christian living. They demonstrated with their lives what they were communicating with their lips.

This, of course, is why Paul lays such great emphasis on proper moral and ethical behavior as a criteria by which church leaders should be selected. This is why he chose Timothy; he was "well spoken of by the brethren" (Ac 16:2). This is why all of the New Testament writers emphasized the importance of "walking worthily" before each other, and particularly the unsaved world. It is as Christ becomes incarnate within the body of Christ that Christian communication develops its power, and "words" become meaningful. People may forget "what we say" but they never forget "what we are."

This leads to another important point when discussing the principle of exemplary living. Frequently the *way* something is said is far more important than *what* is said. "And the Lord's bond-servant must not be quarrelsome, but be kind to all . . . with gentleness correcting those who are in opposition" (2 Ti 2:24-25), wrote Paul to Timothy. Elders too must not be "self-willed" or "quick-tempered" (Titus 1:7). Many Christians have not even "been heard" because of a bad example or the tactless use of words. There is truth in the maxim: "the way we live speaks so loudly they cannot hear what we say."

Have you ever wondered why Paul could say some of the things he did and get away with it? After all, he "pulled no punches" when writing to the Corinthians, and he "minced no words" in his communication with the Galatians.

Actually the answer is quite simple. When people know "you love them," it is amazing what you can say and still be heard. But let them doubt your love, and concern, and sincerity, and your words will become "as a noisy gong or a clanging cymbal."

Seventh, effective Christian communication doesn't just happen— it takes self sacrifice and hard work.

There is something very demanding about getting involved in the lives of people. There is a price that must be paid. You not only exert physical energy, but there is an emotional and spiritual drain that often leaves the dedicated Christian leader exhausted.

While on earth Jesus Christ was, of course, the most selfless Person who ever lived. He gave *everything*—including His life—that men might live. But at the human level, the apostle Paul is an amazing example. While in Thessalonica, he and Timothy and Titus worked "night and day" so as not to be burdensome to these people. Paul was so intent on not communicating false motives that he at times did not take what was rightfully his (1 Co 9:1-15).

But Paul paid a price for his devotion to Christ's work. He himself testified that his greatest burden was "the daily pressure" upon him because of his "concern for all of the churches" (2 Co 11:28). He often agonized over believers who were immature and in need of spiritual growth and development (Gal 4:19-20). He, like no other servant of Jesus Christ, bore in his body the "brand-marks of Jesus" (Gal 6:17).

To be an effective communicator, we cannot resist hard work and involvement. To reach all classes of people—both groups and individuals—and to build our lives into certain people in depth, all of this calls for effort and hard work. God never called us to a life of ease and leisure. Our lives are not our own. We are bought with a price! Responsibility calls for accountability.

Here again we see the uniqueness of the body of Christ. God did not call each one of us to carry out the Great Commission alone. He did not even call each one of us to be an "apostle Paul" or even "a Timothy." But He does expect each member of the body to function and contribute to the work of Christ. With the grace that is given to each of us "according to the measure of Christ's gift" (Eph 4:7), we must participate *diligently* in God's great plan.

Eighth, Christians must never get locked in to certain patterns and forms in communication, but be free and flexible.

As evangelicals we have allowed ourselves to absolutize in the use of various communication forms. We have tended to fixate on certain approaches to communication, particularly in our preaching and teaching methodology.

Where in Scripture are we told to preach three-point sermons, or to deliver thirty-minute messages without interruption?

Where are we told to prepare and deliver lectures on various books of the Bible? Or to expand on topics which we trace through the Scriptures?

Don't misunderstand! This may be an effective way to communicate. But the problem is that there are some who seem to believe that this way is the *biblical* way.

The fact is that we are hard pressed to find illustrations of the way we preach and teach today. Most examples in Scripture are greatly varied and far more spontaneously developed and delivered than our particular approaches. And we certainly cannot find any consistent form or pattern in the way Scripture was written. We have a great variety of approaches to written communication from one Bible book to another, with a majority of New Testament books being personal letters. Most of these are not highly structured. Each one varies in form and literary style, depending on the need of the recipients.

We fail to realize, of course, that communication patterns are relative, and very much related to the culture in which we live at any given moment in history. Even in our own American culture we are seeing some tremendous changes in the way communication takes place and what people respond to. As McLuhan points out, we have moved from what he calls an emphasis on "hot" to "cool" communication. Eventually we will shift in another direction, particularly in this technological age, which is creating a number of upheavals in many areas of our lives.

It is very important to realize that many Christians have superimposed upon Scripture certain methods which they feel are biblical but which are purely cultural. For example, what do *you* think of when you hear the words of Paul to Timothy, which instructed him to "preach the word" (2 Ti 4:2)? If you are typical, you will not think of this imperative per se, but you will think of the *way* you have experienced preaching taking place in your lifetime. The tendency is to equate the *way* we preach with the biblical imperative *to preach*. Actually Paul does not tell us *how* to preach, and the word here correctly means *to proclaim*. But again he doesn't tell us *how* to proclaim the Word. He did, however, demonstrate in his own way a variety of ways to carry out this injunction.

The preaching methodology, which we have come to accept as the "biblical way," has come to us through cultural and educational developments. "One way" communication, particularly, is a product of the development of oratorical skills which have grown out of the Greek and Roman culture.

All of this is not to say that to use these methods is wrong. They have proved to be very effective in certain situations and under certain circumstances. What *is* wrong is to get locked in to a "way" of communication that is purely a means to a divine end. What makes it doubly wrong is to classify it as a biblical norm. We must be free to develop new approaches to communication and free to disband old and ineffective forms and structures. The challenge is to allow ourselves to be guided by the principles of Scripture which will keep our eyes focused on guidelines and which will help us to be contemporary, though biblical.

SUMMING UP

Communication is a current subject in our contemporary society. Whether it is described as "cool" or "hot," it is nevertheless a topic of deep concern.

Evangelical Christians, too, are challenged with a task of communicating the message of Christ and His Word to a people who are bombarded with the latest in communication technique. In a day of Telstar communication and earth-lunar dialogues, Christians need to focus clearly the New Testament principles of communication. These principles both guard us against extreme influences by science and technology, and set us free to be creative under the leadership of the Holy Spirit.

1. Christian communication is a distinctive process, including both human and divine elements.
2. Christian communication should be to all kinds and classes of people.
3. Christian communication should be carefully balanced between a ministry to groups, as well as a ministry to individuals.
4. Effective Christian communication must include an in-depth ministry to a select group, as well as a ministry to the larger group of Christians.
5. For communication to be qualitative it must get beyond the verbalization level.
6. In Christian communication, example is foundational to verbalization.
7. Effective Christian communication doesn't just happen—it takes self-sacrifice and hard work.
8. Christians must never get locked into certain patterns and forms in communication but be free and flexible.

PART II
THE LENS OF HISTORY

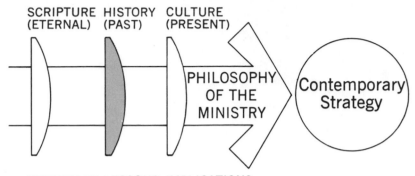

Fig. 8. The Lens of History

The second part of this study is designed to assist you in viewing the contemporary church through the lens of history. Part I, of course, treats biblical history, particularly, New Testament history.

But Part II focuses in on a particular kind of church history—the history of forms and structures. It surveys especially the reflections of institutionalism from the pages of the past. But, perhaps most important, are the lessons we can learn from the *immediate* past, those lessons that grow out of the study of the church in the twentieth century.

16

INSTITUTIONALISM IN HISTORY

One mistake that has been repeated several times by God's people on earth is to fall into the subtle trap of institutionalism. What makes this pitfall particularly dangerous is that it is not a phenomenon that is exclusively related to the church or other religious organizations. It seems to happen naturally wherever you have people who band together to achieve certain objectives. People, plus structure, plus age, seemingly, more often than not, equals institutionalism.

And all elements are necessary, for wherever you have people, you have function; and wherever you have function, you need some kind of form and structure. And *age,* of course, is inevitable, for time marches on.

But more specifically, what is "institutionalism"? Let's look at it first as a natural phenomenon.

WHAT OF THE SECULAR WORLD?

John W. Gardner, past president of the Carnegie Corporation, has said: "Like people and plants, organizations have a life cycle. They have a green and supple youth, a time of flourishing strength, and a gnarled old age."[1]

Rather than defining "institutionalism" per se, it may be easier to look at the symptoms of institutionalism—when has it happened? Or, when is it beginning to happen? Some of these symptoms are as follows:

1. The organization (the form and structure) becomes more important than the people that make up the organization.
2. Individuals begin to function in the organization more like cogs in a machine.

3. Individuality and creativity are lost in the structural mass.
4. The atmosphere in the organization becomes threatening, rather than open and free; people are often afraid to ask uncomfortable questions.
5. The structural arrangements in the organization have become rigid and inflexible.
6. People are serving the organization more than the objectives for which the organization was brought into existence. In other words, means have become ends.
7. Communication often breaks down, particularly because of a repressive atmosphere and lots of red tape.
8. People become prisoners of their procedures. The "policy manual" and the "rule book" get bigger, and fresh ideas are few and far between.
9. In order to survive in a cold structure, people develop their own special interests within the organization, creating competitive departments and divisions. The corporate objective gives way to a multitude of unrelated objectives which, inevitably, results in lack of unity in the organization as a whole.
10. Morale degenerates; people lose their initiative; they become discouraged and often critical of the organization and of others in the organization—particularly its leaders.
11. As the organization gets bigger and as time passes, the process of institutionalization often speeds up. A hierarchy of leadership develops, increasing the problems of communication from the top to the bottom and the bottom to the top. People toward the bottom, or even in the middle of the organizational structure, feel more and more as if they "really don't count" in the organization.

When you have these symptoms in an organization, institutionalism is already in its advanced stages.

But there is a note of optimism that grows out of the study of the history of organizations and institutions. Again, let me quote Gardner:

> Organizations differ from people and plants in that their cycle isn't even approximately predictable. An organization may go from youth to old age in two or three decades, or it may last for centuries.

---

1. John W. Gardner, "How to Prevent Organizational Dry Rot," *Harper,* October 1965, p. 20.

More important, it may go through a period of stagnation and then revive. In short, decline is not inevitable. Organizations need not stagnate. They often do, to be sure, but that is because the arts of organizational renewal are not yet widely understood. Organizations can renew themselves continuously.[2]

Interestingly, the principles of organizational renewal actually work. More and more, even secularists are discovering what these rules are and are beginning to apply them in the secular community.

WHAT OF THE PEOPLE OF GOD?

Church history reveals at least three major periods of institutionalism among the people of God, with many smaller segments and periods of institutionalism in between.

JUDAISM

The first main period of institutionalism involves the children of Israel after they returned from Babylonian captivity. For a while, under the leadership of Ezra and Nehemiah, new life was evident among God's chosen people. But by the time Jesus Christ arrived on the scene, the nation of Israel as a whole, and its religious system particularly, had become so encrusted with institutionalism that it was nigh unto impossible to recognize truth from tradition.

It was at this "religious system" that Jesus directed His sharpest barbs. For example, when His disciples were criticized by the Pharisees for plucking the heads of grain on the Sabbath, Jesus retorted: "The Sabbath was made for man, and not man for the Sabbath" (Mk 2:27). In other words, He was saying, "You have taken a *means* and made it an *end* in itself. You have completely lost sight of the spirit of the law. You have lost the individual in your religious system. All you have left is an empty form."

Again and again Jesus put His finger on the devastating results of institutionalism. He reminded the religious leaders that they had successfully preserved their religious system, their "orthodoxy" and their tradition, and had even led the majority of the people into an external conformity with the outward expressions of their religion. But they had lost the individual; they had no deep understanding of God's truth; their followers had no vital and real experience with the living God.

---

2. Ibid.

ROMAN CATHOLICISM

In the panorama of church history, the vibrant, pulsating New Testament church that grew out of Judaism eventually gave way to a stagnant, lifeless Roman church. As always, there were pockets of vitality and pure Christianity; but as a whole, the church was doomed to hundreds of years of institutionalized religion. When the Edict of Milan gave legal status to Christianity, many became "Christians" because it was the popular thing to do.

It was against this religious system that the Reformers rose up to defend biblical truth and personalized Christianity. Religion had become a matter of form and ceremony, not of life and experience. All kinds and varieties of tradition began to overshadow biblical truth. Abuses and pagan practices became rampant.

But notice! The Roman church was preserved—in all of its "bigness" and power—even to this day. Its authoritarian approach to education and its transmissive communication preserved the church's "orthodoxy," and until very recently, very few within the system questioned its demands and dogmas.

It is important to point out at this juncture that "bigness" is not necessarily a sign of true spiritual success. "Numbers" can be very deceiving. "Followers" are relatively easy to find, if one works hard enough and shouts loud enough to make his voice heard above the many that are crying for the attention of people today.

But what are they following? What do they believe? What of their lives? Where are we leading them?

These are the crucial questions! Let us not be deceived by numbers, for if Jesus Christ's success on earth had been measured by numbers, He must be classified as a failure. There were times, of course, when multitudes followed Him, when His disciples multiplied; but there also came a time when "many of His disciples withdrew, and were not walking with Him any more" (Jn 6:66). The price was too great for these people to follow Jesus Christ (Jn 6:60).

This is not to say that numbers are not significant. In the early days of the church, thousands were added to the company of believers (Ac 2:41), and "the number of the disciples continued to increase greatly" (Ac 6:7). But true success was measured by the results that were being achieved in the lives of people. Just so today, we must measure our success by biblical criteria—not by how many people attend on Sunday morning, or Sunday evening, or on Wednesday night, or how many we have enrolled in our Sunday school. Some even measure success by the total number of meetings that have been conducted in a given period of time. Activity per se is not a correct measuring rod. The results of these activities (biblical results) are!

REFORMATION CHURCHES

And so the reformers reacted against the institutionalism and the dead orthodoxy of the Roman church. But with what did they replace it?

For a time—life and vitality! The authority of the Bible, justification by faith, and the priesthood of every believer became cardinal doctrines once again. Conversion became a matter of personal relationship with Jesus Christ, particularly among adults who saw the light. But what of their children? What of their tolerance of others? What of their forms and structures and approaches to communication. What of their eventual outcome?

You cannot *force* Christian community. Some leaders eventually refused others the same liberty and freedom they had demanded for themselves. Education was controlled and directed by Protestant state churches, and degenerated into the same stereotyped, traditional and authoritarian system from which they came. Correct doctrine per se was not the answer!

THE FREE CHURCH MOVEMENT

Out of the institutionalized religion that soon developed in the Reformation churches came a variety of groups that wished to maintain the vitality and freshness they saw reflected in the New Testament. The discovery of America provided a natural means by which many could begin anew. But in many instances, even in these early days, the same "institutionalism" was transferred from the Continent to the New World. It was a constant struggle, as it has always been, for the true believers to keep a proper focus on biblical objectives and principles, and to keep from becoming institutionalized.

An interesting phenomenon, however, hit the shores of America in the nineteen hundreds that was destined to be a blessing in disguise for the evangelical church. The stormy winds of liberal theology threatened the very life of Bible-believing Christians. Battering away at the very foundations of historic Christianity, liberal theologians and natural scientists made Bible-believing Christians study, think and pray and act as never before.

True, the majority of seminaries went liberal and many Christian colleges followed suit, but in their place came the Bible institutes and the Bible conference movement, and eventually the evangelical seminaries. And from these training institutions, came men and women who believed the Bible as the Word of God; believed in personal conversion; and generally speaking, believed in the local church as God's primary means for the edification of believers.

In the forties and fifties liberalism began to retreat—not necessarily because of the fervor of evangelical Christians—but more because of liberal theologians themselves, who began to question the very presuppositions of their own theology. Two world wars blasted hard at the very core of their thinking—that man is basically good and that the world is destined to get better. In its place came the new theology, frequently called neo-orthodoxy, but with little in common with classic Christianity, except in its terminology. This is particularly true in America. Its proponents are trying desperately to be relevant, and contemporary, and to meet the needs of mankind in a world that appears on the brink of disaster. Racial hatred, wars, pollution, overpopulation, conflicting ideologies, and the threat of nuclear disaster are common topics for discussion among the leaders of the world in both religious and secular circles.

THE CHURCH AT LARGE

The Protestant church at large is, without doubt, institutionalized. It is criticized by young and old alike. It not only has become a victim of its form and ceremony, but it has lost its direction. It no longer has an absolute guide to determine its objectives and from which to get its principles to guide it in its function.

Many religious leaders recognize the symptoms of institutionalism in the church at large. They are trying desperately to pump new life into a dying corpse by means of "form" changes and a renewed emphasis on the individual. They really *try* to care—to interact with the issues that surround us on every hand—in many cases putting evangelical Christians to shame.

But they are no more successful than the university or the social organization in obtaining ultimate success, for even though they can meet the physical and psychological needs of man, they have no way to change his heart, his inner being. The true message of Christianity —personal conversion and a supernatural new birth through the indwelling and living Christ—has been basically eliminated from their theology and their contemporary strategy. A comfortable universalism has replaced the hard realities of eternal lostness outside of Jesus Christ. And without this message and truth, all efforts towards helping man are ultimately doomed to failure. No amount of organizational renewal can save the church at large.

THE EVANGELICAL CHURCH

What of the Bible-believing church? No doubt it has grown and become more popular than ever before and *has* penetrated society. Some of its key spokesmen are household names among the leaders of the world.

There is no doubt that evangelicalism, particularly in America, has come into its own as a movement. There are many signs of encouragement. In spite of the pressures of secularism and materialism, and the obvious moral decline in our culture as a whole, evangelical Christianity is continuing to make an impact. The advent of the drug culture, sensualism, and the mystical cults have actually created a vacuum into which Bible-believing Christians have been able to enter with the message of Jesus Christ. Youth, particularly, who have been subtly led into a way of life that has left them in a whirlpool of despair, have responded to the authority of the Bible and its redeeming message. Campus organizations, such as Campus Crusade for Christ and Inter-Varsity Fellowship, are experiencing unparalleled opportunities and success in communicating the gospel of Christ to disillusioned youth.

But what about the local church in the evangelical community? Here, too, there are some obvious encouragements. Generally there is a strong faith in the authority of Scripture and the need for personal salvation. Many Christians, though affected in their thinking by materialism and secularism, still have a deep desire to be in the will of God. There is a strong commitment on the part of many to the local church itself; even among those who head extra-church organizations. Many pastors and teachers are preaching the Word of God (with varying degrees of effectiveness), and there is a general concern for evangelism and edification. Never before have we had so many educational agencies within the church, and so many excellent materials and tools available to reach all age levels.

But somehow, with all of these strengths, the voice of the ancient apostle comes echoing across the centuries: "I know your deeds and your toil and perseverance. . . . I know your deeds, and your love and faith and service. . . . But I have this against you" (Rev 2:2, 4, 19-20). Something is wrong with the evangelical church! This, of course, is not strange language, for something is always wrong and will always be wrong with the church on earth. We can never be perfect while in bondage to mortality. But there seems to be something distinctly wrong in the local church, a lack of focus that need not be; something that can be corrected by means of making some proper adjustments.

Here we can learn a vital lesson from history. Every movement eventually faces the threat of creeping institutionalism. There is no doubt that evangelical Christianity is facing this threat today. It is in particular danger because it has moved from the crisis of fighting for its life into a period of unparalleled popularity—a trend that usually accompanies institutionalization.

At this juncture we need to remind ourselves of what happened to previous movements among the people of God. We need to look carefully at the results of institutionalized religion.

REFLECTIONS OF INSTITUTIONALISM IN JUDAISM, ROMAN CATHOLICISM AND IN THE REFORMATION CHURCHES

All of these movements preserved their religious system, but they lost sight of the individual. In fact, the system—its dogmas and traditions and its forms and structures—eventually became more important than the people themselves.

These movements also preserved their "orthodoxy," but their adherents failed to appropriate a deeper and personal comprehension of God's truth. People gave mental assent to doctrine, but there was little relationship to their daily living. Being a part of the movement was no different than belonging to a club, society, or group in the secular world. In many cases traditions overshadowed the Word of God.

These movements all gained external conformity on the part of their followers, but apart from inner experience. People religiously performed routines and rituals, but without true spiritual meaning. Their religion became a matter of form and ceremony, not life and experience. A personal relationship with God was replaced with an impersonal relationship with an organization.

All of these movements perpetuated themselves by means of an education that was authoritarian, stereotyped and transmissive. They utilized indoctrination with little room for creative thinking and freedom. The learning atmosphere became nonpermissive.

All of these movements developed a hierarchy of leaders, who in turn developed a careful and logical system of theology. It was the leaders who did the "thinking" and the "communicating," while the ordinary people became the recipients and followers of the wisdom of the sages.

As these movements grew and enlarged, structure and form became rigid and inflexible. In fact, their means and ways of doing things eventually became ends in themselves and as sacred in the minds of people as their beliefs.[3]

SUMMING UP

It is the thesis of this chapter that history can tell us something very important about many evangelical churches. Clearly we are in danger of confusing form and function, and of moving rapidly in the direction of becoming thoroughly institutionalized.

But what are some of the specific symptoms? It is to this question we turn in the chapter to follow.

---

3. For a helpful treatment of the problems of institutionalism in the church, see Findley B. Edge *A Quest for Vitality in Religion* (Nashville: Broadman, 1963).

17

REFLECTIONS OF INSTITUTIONALISM IN THE EVANGELICAL CHURCH

The phenomenon of creeping institutionalism in the evangelical church as we enter the latter part of the twentieth century is unique. In some respects it is a different kind of institutionalism than at any other time in history.

True, the institutionalism we see today has many similarities to that of the past. There are certain common elements wherever and whenever institutionalization takes place.

But there are also some unique elements, the most important being our *biblical* orthodoxy. Is it possible to believe the Bible is the Word of God, and to communicate it to others with expertise, and yet be a victim of institutionalism?

1. Our greatest strength has helped create some of our greatest problems. The strongest feature of the evangelical church has been its adherence to the Bible as its final authority in faith and practice. Though there are a variety of interpretations in some areas of theology, most evangelicals are in agreement regarding the Bible as being the inspired Word of God.

This emphasis, of course, has helped greatly to preserve historic Christianity. Wherever groups have departed from this basic starting point, there is a movement away from the clear and obvious teachings of the Scriptures regarding Jesus Christ and salvation, as well as other important fundamental doctrines.

Our fight for survival in the early nineteen hundreds against the inroads of liberalism successfully preserved the fundamentals of the faith. This was really the beginning of a strong, evangelical scholarship, which has continued to give evangelical Christianity a decided respectability and sophistication.

But something happened, particularly in our strong Bible-teaching churches. By emphasizing the Bible as the Word of God—and rightly so—as well as its doctrinal teachings, we put a strong emphasis on studying the Bible and transmitting it to others. This, in turn, became a primary objective of many evangelical churches, a worthy objective, to say the least.

Several things transpired. First, to carry out this objective, we began to train qualified people to teach the Bible. Evangelical schools—first Bible institutes and colleges and later seminaries—designed curricual to teach young men a knowledge of the content of the Scriptures, so that they might transmit it to others through a pulpit ministry.

Second, the young men trained in these schools went into churches and taught as they were taught. Many became ardent expositors (in some instances, "little professors") and the people were their "students." In Sunday morning services, on Sunday evenings, during the midweek service, and in Sunday school classes, people listened to three or four or even five expositions a week. In the twenties and thirties, when people were starved for the Word of God which had been ripped from the pulpits of the land, this was a refreshing breeze from heaven.

However, a problem arose. Many laymen became ardent "listeners." There was little opportunity for personal interaction with other members of the body of Christ, or little opportunity for expressing the Word in their own lives. The functioning body was replaced with a trained and gifted man.

Fortunately, young pastors could take what they learned in schools and transmit it to others, as they turned their churches into miniature Bible schools and seminaries. But, for the most part, those who were on the listening end in the churches absorbed the Word but had no similar outlet.

Third, church structures and patterns were designed to carry out this Bible-teaching objective. Church sanctuaries, functionally speaking, often became "lecture halls," and educational buildings became academic centers. Preaching well-organized sermons (or put another way, delivering high-powered Bible lectures) became the primary means of teaching the Word of God.

Thus our concentration on biblical authority, and the importance of learning and transmitting its message, has led some evangelicals to neglect some other *very* important emphases in the Scriptures. True, learning the Word of God is foundational to Christian growth, but what of the other experiences Christians need to have to become mature believers? What about the New Testament atmosphere that emphasizes the importance of the body of Christ functioning in all of its parts, in order to build itself up? How can all members of the body use the grace God has given them to build up the rest of the body, when they are consistently "forced" to sit and listen to one man teach or preach?

And what about the New Testament atmosphere that emphasizes *koinonia,* that unique fellowship with one another, where Christians bear one another's burdens, and "thus fulfill the law of Christ." To what extent do our church structures and patterns lend themselves to bringing about this kind of New Testament experience?

And what about that unique New Testament experience of worship and fellowship with God that grows naturally out of a heart full of gratitude to God, not only for His Word, but for fellow believers? To what extent do our typical "worship services" and "prayer meetings" result in true worship and body function? Basically, there are often preliminary activities leading up to the culminating experience—a message from the Word.

Our present patterns are in many ways inconducive to worship, for an attitude of worship grows out of a vital experience with the Word and with other believers.

Our failure to provide balanced New Testament experiences for believers has resulted in an emphasis on correct doctrine and a knowledge of the Scriptures, but has neglected other important needs that create mature Christian personalities. Consequently, we have moved toward a sterile, though biblical orthodoxy, a very dangerous move in the direction of institutionalized religion. One well-meaning layman put it well when she said, "I take notes in my Bible at every meeting of the church, and I have all of this wonderful Bible information, but something is really lacking in my life. Something is wrong in my Christian experience."

2. *Emphasizing the church as a soul-wining station has also contributed its share to the process of institutionalization.* This is really a different kind of problem than the one just described. In a sense, it is an opposite-type problem, one you don't really find in the strong

Bible-teaching church. In the "evangelistic-oriented" church we often find a decided lack in good Bible teaching. The frequent complaint is that "all the preacher ever preaches is the simple gospel message." And often he preaches these "gospel messages" to a church full of Christians. Pastors of these churches put a strong emphasis on bringing unsaved people to the church to "hear the gospel." The church becomes the center of all activity in reaching the unsaved world. Laymen are taught by word and example that their evangelistic task is to "bring them in" to hear the gospel.

Interestingly, this approach brought rather successful results in the early nineteen hundreds, primarily because many unsaved people were religiously oriented. Many had already been exposed to the fundamentals of the faith and were at one time "church people." But times have changed! Many neighbors and work associates (with the exception perhaps of those in certain segments of what remains of the "Bible belt") are pure pagans. They could care less about ever going to church—especially evangelistic meetings. And as times have changed, so have the number of non-Christians that consent to come to church. But in many churches the preacher is still preaching the gospel as if they were there. Consequently, Christians are starving for good Bible teaching.[1]

Incidentally, this is why many Christians leave these churches and seek out good Bible-teaching churches. Their initial response in their new environment is one of great satisfaction. But over a period of time they become saturated with Bible truth, and then their experience parallels that just described in the previous section.

But what about the church as an evangelistic center? First of all, let it be reemphasized strongly that one of the basic objectives of the church *is* to reach the unsaved world. But let it also be emphasized that the purpose of the "church gathered," as described in the New Testament, is not evangelism—but edification. God never intended for the pastor's primary responsibility to be that of evangelism; that is, to preach to unsaved people who are brought to church by church members.

---

1. It is recognized, of course, that there are a number of exceptions within this general situation. Soul winning was a very important objective of the New Testament church. But their basic approach was not to make the "church gathered" an evangelistic center.

Again, don't misunderstand! This does not mean that unsaved people should not be welcomed in the church or even invited. Otherwise, they may not see the body of Christ functioning in love and unity, a vital means of reaching non-Christians. However, there is not a single reference in the New Testament to structuring a church service for unsaved people. Only in 1 Corinthians do we see Paul instructing the Christians to be orderly in their service, lest some unsaved person come in and think these Christians are out of their minds (1 Co 14:23). But here again Paul is emphasizing the importance of a service properly ordered for Christians, where the Word is taught by various individuals in the church (1 Co 14:24). The non-Christian, observing the body of Christ functioning properly to build up itself, would then be in a position to become convicted by the Holy Spirit and respond to the message of the gospel (1 Co 14:24-25).

Many churches that function as evangelistic centers often have greater problems with institutionalism than the Bible-teaching churches. Without a good diet in the Word of God, activity and meetings become even more superficial and void of real spiritual meaning. Even fellowship opportunities degenerate into social contacts that are little different from social gatherings in the world. Fellowship, or *koinonia,* in the biblical sense is *more* than "coffee and doughnuts," and human beings relating to each other on the human level. Within the context of *biblical koinonia,* even partaking of food will become a more meaningful experience (Ac 2:42).

In addition to superficial experiences (a distinct reflection of religious institutionalism), many Christians in these churches have their eyes focused on the church as a meeting place. They hear and experience so frequently that the church is the place for spiritual activity that they become "building oriented."

An emphasis on the "church gathered" is commendable and biblical. But a church in the biblical sense is not a building, or an organization, or even a place of meeting—but an organism, a body of believers meeting together. And "why" Christians meet is of utmost importance! From a biblical point of view, it is *not* to listen to a pastor preach the gospel to unsaved people. Nor is it to just listen to the pastor-teacher expound the Word. Rather, it is to be a time when believers edify themselves through total body function. It *is* to be a time when the Word of God is taught. But it is also to be a time when believers are to experience true "family of God" relationships. As a result of these vital experiences, they are in turn to go out and minister to their own families, minister to other believers, and be effective witnesses for Jesus Christ in the unsaved world.

3. We are beginning to support the "institution" rather than its reason for existing. Put another way, we are more concerned *with* existence than our *cause* for existence.

This problem is reflected in the way we evaluate success. As long as we have lots of activity, lots of people coming, lots of "decisions," an enlarging income, a growing pastoral staff, and an ongoing building program—we feel comfortably successful and evangelical. "The Lord is blessing," is our repeated evaluation.

Frequently we show little concern for the content of our activities, as long as they are "going on." Whether or not "decisions" result in mature discipleship is often overlooked in the midst of everything else that is "happening."

And the people who come? Well, so long as *new* people are coming, it really doesn't matter *who* they are and *where* they come from. As long as they come, we report we are reaching people. The facts seem to be that many churches grow because Christian people are on the move—from the center of the city to the suburbs, and from city to city, and from church to church. Very few seem to be new Christians, reached for Christ by the local body of believers as they share their faith with neighbors, friends, and work associates.

Yet we feel successful because we are *growing*—and really without reaching a New Testament objective of penetrating the pagan community in which we live.

The problem of being concerned with "existence" more than our cause for existence, is also reflected in the way we evaluate "spirituality, particularly as a pastoral staff. Our people "measure up" as long as they come and listen to our sermons, bring their children to all the activities we've planned for them, support the church with their offerings, willingly serve on boards and committees, and help keep the agencies of the church functioning by filling leadership slots. In short, as long as people support the program, we evaluate them as spiritually mature.

But what about their home life? Is the father the spiritual head of the home, spending time with his children individually and collectively? What about the relationships between mother and father? What about the spiritual climate, as measured by biblical criteria?

Is each home a dynamic force in the community, reflecting Jesus Christ? How is the family relating to unsaved neighbors? Are they given to hospitality, both among non-Christians as well as Christians?

What about the father's ethics in the business world? Is he a dynamic Christian witness in the way he lives as well as in the way he talks?

What about other aspects of their church life? Are believers really ministering to other members of the body of Christ, or do they use all of their time and effort to just keep the machinery of the church running smoothly? Are they really growing and developing in their Christian lives? Or are they frantically running on a religious treadmill, getting wearier and more numb as each week passes by, and at the same time keeping their guilt level down because of their "Christian service"?

What about the overall climate in the church? Is it warm and inviting and personal, or do people come Sunday after Sunday, sit side by side in long pews, take notes in their Bibles, say "Amen," drop their money in the offering plate, and walk out without really *knowing* other members of the Christian family, and without making any contribution to other members of the body of Christ?

All of these questions can go unanswered in many evangelical churches—even be answered in the negative—and yet we can evaluate our church as very successful. The truth is, it may be existing beautifully as an organization, but woefully lacking as a functioning New Testament organism. It is not achieving certain fundamental, biblical objectives.

4. We are emphasizing correct doctrine and frequently neglecting the quality of one's life. An important criterion for evaluating spiritual maturity is often "what a man believes"—and not "the way he lives."

What a man believes, of course, is basic and fundamental, but the Bible is explicit and clear that it is "both-and," not "either-or." Paul's letter to the Romans gives the first eleven chapters over to doctrine and the last five to Christian living. Likewise, the Ephesian epistle devotes the first three chapters to doctrine, and the last three chapters to the Christian's walk. The Bible is clear that we are to be "doers of the word, and not merely hearers" (Ja 1:22).

It is possible to go into some evangelical churches and discover there is very little difference in the life style of its members and that of non-Christians. They may know the Bible, but their lives reflect little of the fruit of the Spirit. On the other hand, many evangelical churches have developed false criteria for evaluating spirituality—an unfortunate legalism that reflects the same spiritual sickness of the Pharisees. Spiritual depth is measured primarily by externalities—certain "thou shalt nots" that have become standard in some Christian circles. If Christians *don't do* certain things, they are automatically classified as spiritual. It is possible, of course, to refrain from many activities and be extremely carnal, and yet to feel "comfortably spiritual." And when it comes to basic Christian attitudes toward both fellow Christians and unsaved people, particularly an attitude of love, there is a decided lack.

This is not, of course, to advocate total freedom—a concept that is very nonbiblical. But both extremes—license or legalism—are a reflection of institutionalized Christianity. Again, we must evaluate spiritual maturity by means of proper biblical criteria. "By this all men will know that you are My disciples, if you have love for one another" (Jn 13:35).

5. *We have allowed nonabsolutes to become absolute.* This way of thinking is the most subtle of all in leading the church into institutionalism. That which is meant to be a *means* to an end, becomes an *end* in itself. We allow ourselves to get locked in to patterns and structures that are no longer relevant and adequate, to help us minister to the people who live in our contemporary culture.

It is vitally important for every believer to be able to differentiate between those areas of the Word of God that are absolute and never changing, and those areas that are relative and simply illustrative of the *way* the people of God in years past attempted to reach biblical objectives.

It is obvious from a careful study of the Scriptures that New Testament Christians considered certain doctrines absolute: that God exists; that He is a Spirit; that Jesus Christ was God in the flesh and that He came to die for the sins of the world; that man is in need of a Saviour; that salvation is by grace through faith; that there is a diabolical spiritual world which includes Satan and his evil forces; that Jesus Christ died, arose, ascended to heaven, and will come again. These and many other truths cannot be changed if a church is to be "Christian" in the biblical sense.

Another area of obvious absolutes has to do with directives and objectives. The New Testament church consistently took the Great Commission seriously, both in the task of evangelism and edification. And there were certain qualifications for Christian leaders! There was to be no "give and take" in these matters.

But there is also much scriptural evidence to show that New Testament Christians did not consider certain forms and patterns and structures to be absolute. Rather, these were but means to carry out New Testament directives and reach New Testament objectives. When patterns do appear, they vary from situation to situation in the areas of both communication and organization and administration.

But it is very important to note that these biblical examples are given for a purpose: to yield absolute principles for the church. A careful study of the *way* the first century church proceeded to carry out the Great Commission reveals certain obvious guidelines that will enable the twentieth century church to function as a New Testament church—*absolute in the essentials,* and *free and creative in devising contemporary approaches* to evangelism, edification, leadership, communication, and organization and administration. An important task facing Christian leaders of every generation is to make sure these principles and guidelines are accurately formulated and correctly focused.

Summing Up

The evangelical church in the twentieth century has a unique challenge to break the shackles of institutionalization that have already begun to bind and inhibit her from being a dynamic organism. One of the most encouraging lessons from history is that we need not be "locked in" to a continuous cycle of institutionalism. It can be broken; renewal can and must be constant. The church, as no other group of people on earth, has the resources always to be what God intended her to be. If secular organizations can apply the principles of renewal and be successful, how much more can the family of God, particularly when it has principles that emerge from the eternal Word of God.

PART III
THE LENS OF CULTURE

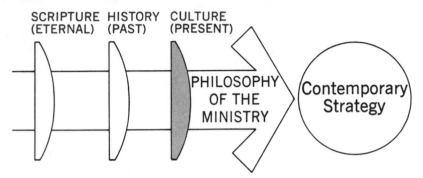

SCRIPTURE HISTORY CULTURE
(ETERNAL) (PAST) (PRESENT)

PHILOSOPHY OF THE MINISTRY

Contemporary Strategy

PRINCIPLES LESSONS IMPLICATIONS

Fig. 9. The Lens of Culture

Section III is a brief treatment of some of the most crucial problems in contemporary culture and how they affect the church. It is not designed to be exhaustive, but it is a place to begin.

This is a challenge that faces every generation of God's people. To ignore the changing world is to ignore reality and biblical responsibility.

If any lesson is clear from the New Testament, it is that the first century church did not withdraw from society. Rather, it existed, expanded, and even thrived in a pagan culture. The twentieth century church must do the same!

18

UNDERSTANDING CULTURE

"Culture is a stern reality," acknowledged Dr. George Peters, Professor of World Missions at Dallas Theological Seminary. "It is as extensive as man and as comprehensive as his ways, thoughts, sentiments, and relationships. It is the all-encompassing nonbiological atmosphere of his being as well as the institutions that make his life tolerable and mold him into the being he actually is."[1]

Cultures, of course, vary even within a particular geographical area. Within a large city, for example, there are many subcultures, each with its own beliefs, attitudes, patterns of behavior, distinctive social relationships, value systems, and thought forms.

But in spite of the variety of cultures that exist, never before has the world been "so small." We *do* live in a "global village." People everywhere are being affected by similar influences which precipitate cultural change. Environmental factors and variables are in constant motion, accelerated particularly by technology. Beliefs once held as sacred and absolute are being challenged, altered, and even abandoned. Hence a shift in attitude and behavior follows naturally.

Christians, more than any other group, should face the need to understand culture. This is an imperative. First, so that we might effectively penetrate our society with the gospel of Jesus Christ; and second, so that we may be truly Christian in the midst of a culture that is increasingly becoming antagonistic to our biblical presuppositions.

The church's cultural concern must be universal! We can do no less. The Great Commission included the world. The followers of Christ in the first century were to "make disciples" everywhere—in "all the nations."

---

1. George Peters, *Saturation Evangelism*, p. 193.

But let's begin where most of us are—at home—in America. What about our particular culture? How do we differ in our thinking, attitudes, and behavior compared with those who have gone before? What are some of the factors that have affected us all, both young and old alike, and consciously as well as unconsciously? Why is America different today?[2]

It is possible to approach these questions with an attitude of simplicity. But the very nature of the problem (America and its "bigness" and its relatively short, but intricate history) ought to tell us immediately that *what* exists today, and *why* it exists, is not the product of a simple cause-effect relationship. Rather there are many intricacies and complexities.

What follows is an attempt to unravel some of the interweaving threads that have formed the American cultural web that all of us, whether we recognize it or not, are entangled in today.

One important cause in precipitating our present American crisis is the natural process of institutionalization. America began its existence with wide-open doors for individual fulfillment. There was lots of room "to move." The pioneering spirit captivated the creative minds of our forefathers. They explored the vast areas and established new frontiers. They invented and prospered in a land of unprecedented opportunity.

This kind of free environment naturally beckoned people everywhere. America began to grow, and as she grew the inevitable happened! There was a need for organization—organization which evolved from family units to community units; from communities to colonies; and from colonies to a large federal government. And within this developing governmental structure came big business. Mergers, consolidations, mass production and corporate labor moved people away from individualism. Rural communities, small farms, individual vocational interests, and small towns began to pass off the scene. Of course, this process was advanced even more rapidly by developing technology.

Eventually the corporate state and its forms and structures became

---

2. This limitation is not as restrictive as it may seem. What has happened in America over the last several years is affecting the world. An understanding of American culture is a good beginning point to help understand the emerging "world culture."

This is not a proud statement. Unfortunately, from a Christian perspective, the American influence has probably been more negative than positive.

so big and unwieldy that what was designed to serve the people began to enslave the people. We began to function more like cogs in a machine rather than as free personalities. Individuality and creativity were lost in the structural mass. Rigidity and inflexibility set in, making significant changes in structure almost an impossibility. Freedom of the people and by the people was replaced by hierarchy in government.

President Richard Nixon spoke dramatically to the problem of institutionalization in government, in his State of the Union message delivered to a joint session of Congress on January 22, 1971. That evening, in his opening remarks, he told Congress he was going to ask them "to change the framework of government itself—to reform the entire structure of American government, so we can make it again fully responsive to the needs and the wishes of the American people."[3]

Later in his address the President hit at the issues more specifically with statements such as the following:

> Let's face it. Most Americans today are simply fed up with government at all levels. They will not—and they should not—continue to tolerate the gap between promise and performance in government. . . .
>
> The fact is that we have made the federal government so strong it grows muscle-bound, and the states and localities so weak they approach impotence. . . .
>
> As everything seems to have grown bigger and more complex in America, as the forces that shape our lives seem to have grown more distant and more impersonal, a great feeling of frustration has crept across the land.[4]

Unfortunately very little has been done about the President's proposal. This is testimony itself to the extent of institutionalization that exists in America. We have become prisoners of our procedures.

Charles Reich also speaks to the problem of institutionalization in America in his penetrating book, *The Greening of America*. He defines the American crisis as follows:

> We no longer understand the system under which we live, because the structure has become obsolete and we have become powerless; in turn, the system has been permitted to assume unchallenged power

---

3. Richard M. Nixon, "State of the Union Message," *Vital Speeches of Today* 36 (February 1971): 226.
4. Ibid.

to dominate our lives, and now rumbles along unguided and therefore indifferent to human ends.[5]

No one who understands the natural tendency for structure to get
in the way of function will deny that America is in bondage to its
bigness. This is an important cause in creating our present crisis. But
it is only *one* cause. There is another, even more significant, that is
so interwoven with the process of institutionalization that it is difficult to separate the two.

*Another cause is that America, functionally speaking, has de-
parted from its founding principles.* There are those who still believe
that as a nation we are in essence what we were in days gone by.
But this is merely a "dream," a figment of the imagination. There
may be reference to our founding principles in our laws, in our
speeches, and in our conversations. But in reality we function "as a
people" as if they do not exist.

American life was launched and built upon the principles embodied in the Protestant ethic:

> A universal belief in the sovereignty of God, the divinely revealed
> law of God, the God-given freedom of the individual, and the over-
> ruling direction of Divine Providence. Coupled with this was the
> conviction that by God's help, any worthy ambition was within the
> range of achievement.[6]

Don't misunderstand! This did not make us a "Christian nation,"
as so many people seem to believe. We were simply a nation built
upon Christian principles; and they worked! That is, they worked as
long as men did not get in each other's way. A rapidly developing
system of big business and marketing soon surfaced the fact that the
majority of American people were "Christian" in name only.

In the early days of our society, a philosophy of rugged individualism blended with the Protestant ethic. The American way of life
actually combined the principles of the Bible with a great deal of
self-centered behavior. These two concepts co-existed because man
had lots of room to move about, plus new areas to pioneer, combined with opportunities for creativity, inventiveness and self-styled
living. Each individual family was the focus of most activities, with

---

5. Charles A Reich, *The Greening of America* (New York: Random, 1970), p. 14.
6. James DeForest Murch, *Teach Or Perish* (Grand Rapids: Eerdmans, 1961),
p. 19.

very little competition in vocational areas. There were no empire builders and great tycoons. "Business mergers, consolidations, mass production, corporate labor, governmental bureaucracy, and highly developed societal organization" were still future.[7]

But as America grew big, Americans generally were unable to adjust to the problems because of their basic moral incompetence. Murch has put it well:

In the ensuing fight for survival, the ethics of the jungle were revived. Lying, double dealing, cheating, stealing, and the like were camouflaged with an uncertain respectability and condoned if they achieved success and brought material prosperity.[8]

The complexity of the American problem can now be seen more clearly. We are not only in bondage to a huge machine (institutionalism), but we have departed from our foundation. The American people have nothing to go back to, except a new ethic. Absolutes have been replaced with relativism.

Many non-Christian cultural analysts do not recognize this as a "cause" of our problems. In fact, they feel this is "good" because it is a return to "freedom" and "individualism," both having been taken away by the process of institutionalization and replaced by the corporate state. To many of these people, an environment that will allow individuals "to think" and "to be" what a man "wants to be" is the important principle that will once again set man free. What a man *thinks* and *does* is not nearly as important to them as the fact that he *has* the freedom to do so. This, they believe, is the important principle that made America great. Our country prospered "in spite of" the Protestant ethic, which they feel was a shackle on the American people that has now been thrown off.

Unfortunately this is not a correct picture. Mankind has never built a satisfactory society on "freedom" per se. It has always been "freedom within form," as Dr. Francis Schaeffer states in his analysis of the student revolution.[9] The form he is referring to are those principles which are in harmony with God Himself.[10] But the belief

---

7. Ibid., p. 21.
8. Ibid.
9. Francis Schaeffer, *The Church at the End of the Twentieth Century*, p. 25.
10. The seedbed for the American crisis was sown even before the American dream existed. For a penetrating analysis of the root factors leading to our present dilemma, particularly in our Western culture, read Dr. Francis Schaeffer, *Escape from Reason* (Downers Grove, Ill.: Inter-Varsity, 1968), *The God Who Is There* (Downers Grove, Ill.: Inter-Varsity, 1968), and chapters 1 and 2 in *The Church at the End of the Twentieth Century*.

in "freedom" per se as a means to American reform is what has led many analysts to interpret the recent uprising among our youth as a "bright spot" on the horizon. The hippie movement, reaction against the corporate state, unwillingness to be just a cog in the machine— all are interpreted as a breath of fresh air and, if properly channeled, will be the "greening of America."[11]

Many brilliant minds have analyzed our problem, unfortunately, as purely environmental and cultural. To them lawlessness and disorder have resulted because our "social order" was destroyed by the corporate state. They see the destruction of our natural environment caused by exploitation. And our democracy and liberty have been threatened by the "impersonal lordship of our economic and technological system."[12]

These men fail to recognize that at the heart of the problem they so carefully analyze is the nature of man; that he is spiritually separated from God and incapable of facing the intricate problems of culture apart from being regenerated by the Holy Spirit. Man is incapable of loving his neighbor as himself, apart from the power of God within him. He always wants more than his share, and he will eventually lie and cheat to get it—if he has to.

And so America finds itself in a desperate plight. Well-meaning individuals are striving to renew the nation. They know we are in deep trouble. But apart from an intervention by God Himself they will never turn the tide. For even if they are successful at structural reform that once again recognizes the individual and restores his freedom, they no longer have the foundations upon which to build— biblical principles that helped make America great.

A third reason the American culture is in crisis, is that we have become a pluralistic society. This fact, of course, is very closely interwoven with the two previous "causes."

Pluralism in our culture—both a blessing and a curse—has evolved for several reasons. *First,* the very nature of the American society opened the door to a variety of viewpoints. Man was free to believe what he wanted to believe, and as long as he did not force

---

11. This is Charles Reich's hope in his book *The Greening of America.* He does not condone radical means to reform America, but he believes that the recent reaction by youth against the plastic culture, which he classifies as a new consciousness, is America's hope for the future.

12. Reich, p. 35.

people against their wills, he could propagate and indoctrinate others at will. This, of course, is why classical Christianity flourished in America. It was, first of all, in basic harmony with the foundational principles upon which America was built; and second, man was free to evangelize. But this freedom—and rightfully so—allowed other religions and ideologies to also flourish in America. Religious cults and isms of all kinds and varieties were born as a result of our "freedom of religion."

But pluralism has also evolved in the American culture because man has become unhappy with the "system." When he became a cog in the machine and when he was exploited, he began to ask *why?* And the natural answer was that we had the wrong ideology. Unable to see clearly the problem in its roots, many people were open to Communism. They were, and are, open to anything that they think will set them free.

More than we like to admit, Karl Marx saw some of the problems in our system of government long before we did. His observations, of course, led him to conclude that man was not capable of being free. Rejecting the idea that God exists and that man has a soul, he made no apologies for propounding the doctrine that the state must be superior. He felt this was the only way to guarantee equality.

Seen against the backdrop of the American dilemma, it is not difficult to understand why many people are soft toward Communism. They are confused, bewildered, and unhappy. They know that something is wrong with the American system, but they do not clearly understand *why.* They are reaching out for an answer—and they are willing to listen to a philosophy that is, at least, bent on "changing" things around. They do not realize, of course, that they are exchanging one "set of problems" for another: a system that "promises" ultimate freedom, but eventually destroys what freedom they have.

Liberal theologians also have contributed their share to the American crisis. They have added another voice to those already "crying in the wilderness." It is to them we must attribute much of the *humanistic* view of man that has deceived so many, even some of our most prominent national and political leaders. Failing to recognize and admit that man is sinful by nature and morally incompetent, they go on dreaming that if man is trusted and given freedom he will inherently do what is "right" and "good." This explains why the efforts of many sincere national leaders are so pathetic. They actually believe we can revive America by setting man free from the cultural machine. With this improper view of man, their solutions cannot and never will be successful in our present culture, while the population explosion continues to complicate human relationships, and where we are constantly "thrown together" and continue to get in each other's way.

Closely aligned with and interwoven with theological liberalism is the voice of *existentialism*. It is the voice of despair. It sees no hope apart from a "leap of faith." It has departed from a rational approach to life and existence. It is this philosophy that has led many youth to "drop out" of society, and others to experiment with oriental mysticism and the occult.

In essence it is one of the most significant roots of the "student revolution." Youth particularly have become victims of existentialism. Not too many years ago they were told that "science" had the answers to the world's problems. The supernatural presuppositions they were reared on were destroyed, and in their place came the scientific method. Many bought the idea—hook, line, and sinker—that this was the way man was going to be "made good." But as the members of the younger generation looked around them and saw the selfish and materialistic lives of their parents, teachers, and their leaders, they were left in a state of total disillusionment.

But one thing came clearly into focus in their minds. Science was not the answer. Nor was the federal government solving their problems. And tragically, what they knew of the church was but a caricature of reality. None of these were bringing in the good life or the "great society." And most tragic of all, at this juncture their supernatural presuppositions were gone—ruthlessly blasted from under them and replaced with an ideology that was failing to do what it was supposed to do. So many (listening to the voice of a Timothy Leary and others like him) "turned on to drugs" and "dropped out." Seeking a deeper and more valid experience in life, they began to dabble in the occult and supernatural world of Satan.

The drug problem, of course, in itself has created a tremendous social problem in America, and will continue to plague a culture that is already overburdened with seemingly insurmountable problems.

So our pluralistic culture continues to contribute its share in helping to perpetuate the American crisis. Our "ideological confusion and futility" has placed our society in a "moral vacuum."[13]

As Dr. Robert Fitch stated in *Christianity and Crisis,* ours is

an age when ethics is becoming obsolete. It is superseded by science, deleted by psychology, dismissed as emotive by philsosophy; it is drowned in compassion, evaporates into aesthetics, and retreats before relativism . . . . The usual moral distinctions are simply drowned in a maudlin emotion in which we have more feeling for the murderer than for the murdered, for the adulterer than for the betrayed; and in which we begin to believe that the really guilty party, the one who somehow caused it all, is the victim, not the perpetrator of the crime.[14]

A fourth factor that is contributing greatly to our cultural crisis is a rapid period of change that has pervaded almost every area of American life. This is the thrust of Alvin Toffler's book, *Future Shock.* He believes that many of the problems and conflicts that exist today between parents and children, and generations, and culture can be traced to "the acceleration of change." According to Toffler, we live in an age of "transcience"—a new "temporariness" in everyday life. It can be defined as the rate at which our relationships with things, places, people, and information turn over.

We are, he says, a throw-away society. Things flow into and out of our lives at high speeds. We are as never before a mobile society; with a professional and technical population being the most mobile of all.

People, too, flow through our lives at a faster clip, allowing us to develop deep friendships with very few.

All of these rapid changes, says Toffler, including our information overload through the modern media, are producing a kind of illness. Quoting psychologist Ardie Luben to support this idea, he says:

If you overload an environment with novelty, you get the equivalent of anxiety neurotics—people who have their systems continually flooded with adrenalin, continual heart pumping, cold hands, increased muscle tone and tremors.[15]

---

13. Murch, p. 33.
14. As quoted in ibid.
15. Alvin Toffler, *Future Shock* (New York: Random House, 1970), pp. 298-99.

All of us have experienced what Toffler has discussed in his book. And when the changes he describes are combined with the other changes in our society, which are discussed in this chapter, it becomes even more obvious why America is in deep trouble.

The fifth significant factor contributing to the American crisis is the communications revolution. Radio, film, colored television, portable tape recorders, paperback books and multi-colored magazines —all are having a profound impact upon the American culture. All ages are bombarded with these media, day after day, from morning until evening. We wake up to automatic radios and go to sleep watching television.

Special programming for the younger set has produced the Sesame Street generation: a breed of youngsters who has learned more than any children of their age in previous generations. The Hollywood film and the world of print have educated youth in the ways of man as in no other time in history. Adults, too, are greatly influenced by what they read, see, and hear. None of us is unaffected.

Unfortunately media can be used for good and bad purposes. The use of these media for pornographic purposes is, of course, one of the most devastating blows to American life. In a country already bombarded with problems—racial tensions, war, population explosion, the destruction of our natural environment, technology "gone mad," plus institutionalism and a shifting moral base—open and uncontrolled pornography has only served to deliver the staggering American culture another stunning blow.

This leads us to a final major factor that is aggravating the American crisis—our moral and spiritual climate. This condition has grown naturally out of our shift away from the biblical principles upon which we built our culture, as well as the ideas and philosophies proposed by the various voices "that cry in the wilderness." Lying, cheating, and all types of dishonesty in business, represent only a beginning of a flood tide of attitudes and behavior that reflect a "life style" quite different from our forefathers. This is not to suppose that early Americans were always morally upright and spiritual. As W. W. Sweet states, "We Americans have been accustomed to over-idealize our Colonial forefathers and give them, as a whole, virtues which the majority never possessed. We think of them in terms of the best rather than in terms of the average."[16]

---

16. W. W. Sweet, *Revivalism in America* (New York: Scribners, 1945), pp. 2-3.

It is true, nevertheless, that our value system has changed in America. The following circles will illustrate this shift. The circle in Figure 10 illustrates our system of cultural values in the early days of the American society. Figure 11 represents two circles nearly identical and overlapping in meaning. Here we see the circle of biblical values overlapping that of cultural values, for it is no secret that these value systems were closely aligned and related in the early days of our culture. In fact, generally speaking, these two value systems co-existed very nicely for many years.

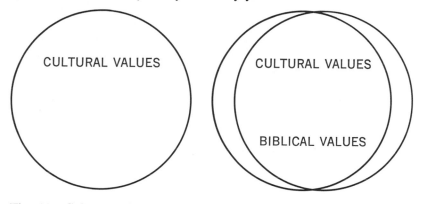

Fig. 10.　Cultural Values in the Early Days of the American Society

Fig. 11.　Cultural and Biblical Values in the Early Days of the American Society

James DeForest Murch, in describing the Protestant ethic, is actually describing these value systems very well in his penetrating volume *Teach or Perish*. As you read, it will become evident it is difficult to separate what is biblical from what was an accepted cultural way of life. For example, consider the following quotes:

> In the "game of life" there were certain accepted rules. They begin by taking God into account. His moral code must be obeyed. Respectability included going to church on Sunday and engaging in no worldly pleasures or business on God's day. Most leaders of community life had high regard for the clergy, paid their church dues, read their Bible at least occasionally, prayed, and did a little church work. Prayer before a business deal was not an uncommon practice. All the blessings of life were considered the gift of God. A rich man was considered a special mark of God's favor. There was even a Thanksgiving Day each year in which the whole community assem-

bled in some church or churches to thank God for its material growth and prosperity.

Then there was hard work. Slothfulness was considered a sin. It was believed that genius was at least half due to a full day's work. Self-denying workers seldom looked at the clock and were willing to labor sixteen hours a day if that were necessary to achieve a worthy goal.

Honor and integrity were prized possessions. It was believed that shrewdness and ambition were good, but not at the sacrifice of virtue. "A man's word was as good as his bond." A friend dependable and true, the advisor honest and fearless, the competitor just and chivalrous, were characteristic of American business at its best.[17]

Then, of course, sexual mores were written into the legal documents of the land. Adultery was unlawful, as well as homosexuality. Fornication was condemned as immoral and a violation of the law of God.

With our shift away from biblical absolutes came a new ethic— an ethic of freedom. In culture, generally, it has been classified by some as the "Freudian ethic." And more recently a concept of "situation ethics" has been introduced—the existential theologians' attempt to solve the moral dilemma. But both deny the existence of biblical absolutes and true Christian morality.

Consequently a decided shift has taken place. Figure 12 shows

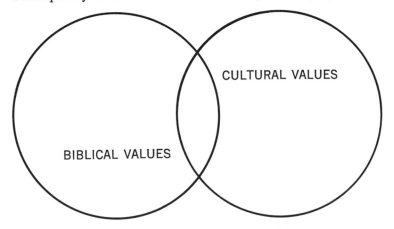

Fig. 12.   Cultural and Biblical Values in Contemporary Society

17. Murch, p. 19-20.

that the two circles that once overlapped have radically moved apart until in our contemporary culture the areas that overlap may be—in many instances—very slight.

This change in moral and spiritual values is one of the most significant tragedies in the American society. If we continue on our present course, our doom is written in the pages of the Bible as well as in the pages of secular history. "Righteousness exalts a nation, but sin is a disgrace to any people," wrote Solomon in Proverbs 14:34. So, many and varied cultural analysts remind us that there are symptoms that are startlingly similar to previous cultures, such as Greece and Rome, that caused them to crumble, disintegrate, and disappear.

Summing Up

The purpose of this chapter has been to present some of the causes that have precipitated the American crisis, and continue to aggravate that crisis.

1. We have become a victim of the natural process of institutionalization.
2. We have departed from our founding principles.
3. We have become a pluralistic society.
4. We are living in an era of unprecedented change.
5. We have experienced a communications revolution.
6. We are caught in a moral and spiritual vacuum.

The chapter to follow presents, on the basis of these observations, some implications for the twentieth century church.

19

CULTURAL IMPLICATIONS FOR THE TWENTIETH CENTURY CHURCH

Prominent Christian personalities who walk across the pages of the New Testament, *could not* and *did not* ignore cultures. Jesus Christ took into consideration cultural backgrounds, effectively demonstrated in His dealings with such people as the woman at the well, or in contrast, with Nicodemus. We see this demonstrated by the apostles, as they faced and solved the problem between the Hellenistic Jews and the native Hebrews in Jerusalem. We see it demonstrated by the church at Jerusalem, as they were confronted with the circumcision controversy. And we see it demonstrated in a most unusual way by Paul, both in his methodology and language, as he moved from the Jewish community out into the Greek culture.

The twentieth century church, too, must not ignore cultures. If we do, we are neglecting a very significant factor in formulating a philosophy of the ministry that is truly biblical, and a contemporary strategy that is relevant, practical and workable.

What then are some cultural implications for the twentieth century church?

First, and basically, the church of Jesus Christ must develop a correct perspective regarding the multiple causes of our present American crisis. We must be realistic without being pessimistic. We must also be aware of reductionistic thinking, which causes us to say that our problems are caused by "this" or "that," or "something else." We are in trouble today because of many interweaving factors; some more significant than others! But to understand our crisis means looking objectively at the total picture.

Some Christians (along with many Americans who are Christian in name only) make the mistake of believing that a return to the "good old days" would solve our American problems. We must face the fact that these days are gone forever. They no longer exist. The population explosion, developing technology and a big society have changed everything. We cannot return to a simple culture—apart from a nuclear holocaust which would simplify things fast, but not to our liking.

Some believe that if we could once again become a "Christian nation," we would be on our way back to stability. Again we must face reality. We never *were* a "Christian nation" in the true sense of the word. We were only a nation built on certain Christian principles; a nation that was soon populated by a majority who knew nothing of a "personal relationship with Jesus Christ." We can never, therefore, go back to something that never existed.

Some Christians believe that if we destroy the forces of Communism we will save America. Or if we clean up pornography we will turn the tide. All of these approaches—though some are noble and worthy objectives—are not based on realistic thinking regarding the overall problems. For Christians to exert their primary efforts in attempting to achieve these objectives, sidetracks them from more basic biblical injunctions. We must realize that apart from a very unusual, supernatural intervention by God Himself, the church cannot save America. Our deep-rooted institutionalization, our departure from our founding principles, and our pluralistic thinking have so weakened us politically, morally, and spiritually that we stand on the brink of total decadence and disintegration.

But realism must not lead to pessimistic thinking on the part of a Christian. There is much we can do to minister to the needs of humanity and to penetrate culture, just as the New Testament Christians penetrated their culture. And though it seems impossible, humanly speaking, to turn the overall tide in America, we can make a tremendous impact for Jesus Christ.

A little careful reflection makes it difficult, for those of us who have been privileged to live in the American society, to understand why God has granted us this blessing. Many Christians before us and many of our contemporaries have never experienced the religious freedom and material blessings that we enjoy. But one thing is sure! With privilege goes responsibility—the responsibility to be totally Christian in all of our relationships and activites. We must, as Jesus commanded, love the Lord with all our hearts, and all our souls, and with all our minds, and our neighbors as ourselves (Mt 22:37-39). This, of course, means both vertical and horizontal responsibilities. At the divine level we are to maintain a dynamic relationship with God, keeping ourselves untainted from this world system (1 Pe 2:11). At the human level we must love all men, both Christians and non-Christians.

Second, the church must develop a correct view of history. Life on this earth will not continue indefinitely. History is inevitably moving toward a great culmination. Eternity, for all men collectively, will eventually begin. Time as we know it will cease to exist. Most Christians, of course, "know" this "theologically," but we seem to live as if it is not true.

Many forces and factors seem to be combining and emerging in the total world environment, which point to the fulfillment of prophetic statements regarding the end of this age. The establishment of the nation of Israel is probably one of the most significant signs that could mean the soon return of Jesus Christ. And when He comes, it will just be a matter of time that "time will be no more"—and eternity will begin.

This correct view of history gives the Christian hope, no matter what happens in our society. It was a significant factor in sustaining the New Testament Christians, including the apostle Paul. From their perspective they were looking for the return of Christ, within their lifetime, to deliver them from their cultural environment, and in many instances, the persecution that existed in the first century.

The twentieth century church, then, must develop a correct philosophy of history, recognizing that when time runs out, our sojourn in space-time history will cease to exist. We will stand before Christ, to give account of what we have done with the time He has alloted us to carry out His purposes on earth. As American Christians, we will no doubt be evaluated in the light of the opportunities we have had to live in a culture that has provided us with more blessings and resources in life than any other people before us. We need to remind ourselves of the words of the Lord Jesus Christ Himself, who said while on earth, "And from everyone who has been given much shall much be required; and to whom they entrusted much, of him they will ask all the more" (Lk 12:48).

This concept leads us naturally to the next cultural implication.

Third, the church must understand clearly why God has left us on earth, and strive with His help to fulfill that purpose. Cultural problems can blur our purpose and sidetrack us onto peripheral issues.

The Bible is clear-cut at this point. We are not here *primarily* to make a living, or to build material security for ourselves and our families, both legitimate objectives. Furthermore, we are not on earth to save America from destruction, or to perpetuate the democratic system, again both noble goals. Our *primary task* is to fulfill the Great Commission of our Lord Jesus Christ, to both "make disciples" and to "teach those disciples." We are to be everlastingly busy at this task until Jesus Christ comes again.

This primary task does not mean we should not have earthly concerns: to provide for our families, both presently and in the future. It does not mean we should not be good citizens and do what we can to preserve our nation from moral and spiritual decay. Christians should be the *best citizens*. But all of these concerns must be kept in proper perspective, and must be subordinate to our ultimate purpose for being on earth. The sooner we realize—not just in our heads, but in our hearts—that we are but "aliens and strangers" on this earth (1 Pe 2:11; Heb 11:13), the better we will fulfill the purpose God has left us on earth to fulfill. We must realize, as never before, that America is *not* our real home.

Fourth, though "America is not our real home," the church must recognize it has a divine mandate to show a vital concern for our government leaders in the life of our nation. One of our primary responsibilities specified in Scripture is to pray for our national and international leaders. Paul made this clear to Timothy when he instructed him regarding the function of the New Testament church in relation to the political structure of his day. "I urge," he said, "that entreaties and prayers, petitions and thanksgivings, be made on behalf of all men, for kings and all who are in authority." But notice why we are to pray: ". . . in order that we may live a tranquil and quiet life in all godliness and dignity. This is good and acceptable in the sight of God our Savior, who desires all men to be saved and to come to the knowledge of the truth" (1 Ti 2:1-4).[1]

---

1. It is recognized that there is some problem in establishing the connection between verse 2 and verse 3. However the total context seems to point to the fact that the *salvation of all men* is directly related to *both* prayer and an environment that is conducive to dynamic Christian living and witness.

The church, as it proceeds to carry out the Great Commission, must not neglect to *pray* for our national and international leaders, with a view that they may be able to lead in such a way as to maintain a cultural environment that is conducive to living for Jesus Christ, and also conducive to sharing Him with all men.

It is also clear from Scripture that "governing authorities" and the position they hold are related to God's sovereign wishes (Ro 13:1). We must recognize this fact and fulfill our responsibility to them, even though they may be in error. This does not mean that we meekly tolerate sin and digression from the laws of God without voicing our disagreement. Assuredly, "we must obey God rather than men" (Ac 5:29), particularly when the two are in contradiction. But it also means respecting our leaders and praying for them, and recognizing their God-ordained appointments and responsibilities.

A correct view of American culture should put all Christians on their knees for the President of the United States, and his associates. Their ultimate task is seemingly insurmountable and many of their problems almost insoluble. They, like the American people, seem to be shackled by the same big institutionalized machine that rumbles on and keeps them from bringing about needed changes that could, at least to a certain extent, ameliorate the American situation. And obviously they are not unaffected by the moral and ethical degeneration that is taking place in our culture. There has probably never been a time in our history when there has been more corruption and sin in high places.

But, in addition to praying for our leaders, as Christians we must also function as good citizens. We must be aware of cultural issues and problems both in local and national elections and use all available channels to implement changes that will right what is wrong in our society.

Whatever our position and vocation in American life, whether in a government role or at an ordinary job, we must remember our primary task. We are God's witnesses in this world and we are part of the functioning body of Christ, with the responsibility to contribute to the health and welfare of that body. In so doing, the church can become a dynamic force against many of the environmental factors that are leading America away from truth and justice.

Fifth, the church must provide an atmosphere where Christians can relate to one another in a non-institutionalized environment. Unfortunately many local churches have become as institutionalized as the American structures. People who are fed up with an impersonal society often find an impersonal atmosphere in the church as well. People who are tired of being "cogs" in a secular machine find that in their church they become "cogs" in a religious machine.

The "church gathered" must realize that it can become a haven for lonely and frustrated people. Through providing a place that is a dynamic and loving community, it can counteract the plastic environment in which people live. Schaeffer comments graphically relative to this point:

> Our Christian organizations must be communities in which others see what God has revealed in the teaching of His Word. They should see that what has happened in Christ's death and reconciliation on the cross back there in space and time and history is relevant, that it is possible to have something beautiful and unusual in this world in our communication and in communities in our own generation. . . .
>
> The Christian community and the practice of that community should cut across all lines. Our churches have largely been preaching points and activity generators. Community has had little place. In the New Testament church this practiced community was not just a banner, but cut all the way down into the hard stuff of the material needs of the members of the community. . . .
>
> I want to see us treating each other like human beings, something that the humanistic student rebels desire but have been unable to produce. . . . . Every Christian community everywhere ought to be a pilot plant to show that we can have horizontal relationships with men and that this can result in a community that cares not only for Man with a capital "M," but for the individual, not only for the upper case human rights, but for the whole man and all of his needs.
>
> Unless people see in our churches not only the preaching of the truth but the practice of the truth, the practice of love and the practice of beauty; unless they see that the thing that the humanists rightly want but cannot achieve on the humanist base—human communication and human relationship—is able to be practiced in our communities, then let me say it clearly: they will not listen and they should not listen.[2]

---

2. Francis Schaeffer, *The Church at the End of the Twentieth Century*, pp. 39-40.

Sixth, the church must provide stability and security for people—something which culture is increasingly failing to do. In a day of unprecedented change, Christians can give people something to believe that is true and trustworthy.

America—as a nation—has abandoned its absolutes. It is like a ship at sea, caught in a storm without an anchor or a compass. Its crew, unfortunately, does not even fully realize that not too far away are dangerous reefs than can send it plunging to the depths.

Not so with the Bible-believing church. We may have lost our focus, we may have become institutionalized, we may not be fulfilling our primary purpose for existence. But we have not lost our anchor or compass. We have a foundation to which to return. We have a body of literature that can give us directives and a philosophy of life that allows us to look into the future realistically and with certainty. This, of course, cannot be said of the liberal church, the church that has—like America—abandoned its absolutes. Whether it represents the church that has returned to the use of "Bible words," or the old liberal who has abandoned even biblical terminology, both have left their authoritative base. Ultimately they have nothing more to offer humanity than any social organization, including the American culture itself.

Thus the evangelical church must recognize with renewed vision that we have the *only* authoritative answers to our society's deepest needs. We must realize that the pluralisms and many uncertain voices in our society today provide us with unprecedented and unparalleled opportunities for evangelism. Men everywhere are confused, but they have the potential to differentiate truth from error. The Holy Spirit is still at work in the world, enlightening the hearts of men and honoring the Word of God.

Parents—many of whom hold to absolutes "in memory only"—are experiencing tremendous insecurity regarding their children. They see their own flesh and blood floundering in the mire of relativism. Though they do not understand it completely, they see the effects of movies, literature, friends, and professors. And many inwardly (and some outwardly) are crying out for stability—something to really believe in. When they attempt to give answers to their youth, their own children point their finger and cry "hypocrite", for they see clearly that the answers their parents are giving are not based on convictions believed as well as lived.

People need what the church can provide: stability and security, something to believe and to make a part of their total life style and that squares with reality. Never has there been a more "teachable moment" than in America today. Our national crisis can be turned into a blessing—one that can bring many people into the kingdom of God.

Seventh, the church must help Christians to "live in the world" without being a "part of the world." Christians must not consciously or unconsciously adopt the aspects of the American value system that are contradictory to the Christian value system.

God has not yet called the church "out of the world" (1 Co 5:9-11). He never intended for Christians to withdraw from society and to live in a Christian community. For how else can we carry out Christ's commission to reach all nations with the good news than to be "in the world." This is one reason why we are here on earth. How unfortunate when Christians confuse "separation" with "isolation." We are not to become a part of the world—living like the world lives—but neither are we to become isolated from the world. Others need to (they must) see in us what it means to be a disciple of Jesus Christ.

Church leaders must also help Christians who live in the midst of our American culture to understand the conflicting value systems. In days gone by, when the majority of Americans held to a cultural value system that was compatible with biblical values, there was very little conflict. In the business world most men were honest. In school very few students cheated on exams. Moral and sexual mores were basically Christian. Generally speaking, Christians and non-Christians could trust one another and relate to one another harmoniously, at least at the social level.

But not so today. And the problem is not just one of being unable to trust one another. In some cases it is a problem of being able to survive financially or academically or socially. Today there are some Christian businessmen who are pitted against shrewd and dishonest individuals who walk off with all the profits because they tell bold-faced lies. In colleges and universities, there are students who receive all the top grades because they cheat on exams and plagiarize, thus putting the honest person at an extreme disadvantage. And some youths today are bypassed, or isolated socially, because they will not participate in nonbiblical practices and activities.

These conflicting value systems are separating the committed Christians from the uncommitted. Co-existence when value systems were almost identical presented very little difficulty for Christians of yesteryear. But today it is a different story. In some instances, there is a "great gulf" between the person who is a "Christian" and a person who is simply an "American." Again this is a blessing in disguise. It used to be that it was difficult to explain to people why being "born in America" was not equal to "being a Christian." But today this is no problem. Most people clearly see the difference. And again this provides us with unlimited opportunities in evangelism.

Eighth, the church must recognize, and understand and adapt to the cultural effects of the communications revolution.

John Culkin, a McLuhan interpreter, points out that "each culture develops its own balance of the senses in response to the demands of its environment. The most generalized formulation of the theory would maintain that the individual's modes of cognition and perception are influenced by the culture he is in, the language he speaks, and the media to which he is exposed. Each culture, as it were, provides its constituents with a custom-made set of goggles."[3]

The important issue facing the church today is *how* the present communications explosion in America is modifying cognition and perception, on the part of both the Christian and the non-Christian. It is already possible to conclude that the Sesame Street generation is a new breed. They are used to exciting and stimulating approaches to learning. In living color, the characters of Sesame Street have reached out and almost touched their viewers. As noted by Culkin, "in the process of delivering content the medium also works the sensorium of the consumer. . . . It takes hold of them, it jostles them, it bounces them around, it massages them. It opens and closes windows in their sensorium."[4]

For proof of this statement, Culkin asks that we "look out the window at the TV generation. They are rediscovering texture, move-

---

3. John Culkin, "A Guide to McLuhan," *Religious Teacher's Journal,* October 1969, p. 26.
4. Ibid.

ment, color, and sound as they retribalize the race." Television particularly, he says, "is a real grabber; it really massages those lazy, unused senses."[5]

Many youth who are affected by the new approaches to communication, rather than responding to high-powered verbal presentations, like to sit around and "rap." Beautifully structured and highly polished prose doesn't necessarily impress the new generation. (This, of course, could change and move in still other directions.)

Many adults, too, are tired of sitting passively while the preacher practices his rhetoric. Many want to get involved, share their own thoughts, interact, and be a part of the process of communication. In short, a new mentality has appeared that is affecting all ages.

Another factor pointing to man's loneliness and alienation in our culture, is the almost hungry response, on the part of American people, to become involved in small sensitivity groups. Feeling cut off from their fellows, they find here an opportunity to get close to people. Unfortunately, many of these groups have led to excesses. Without a moral base, some have led to extreme permissiveness and immorality.

Again the important issue is that the church must not—it cannot—overlook the cultural implications that grow out of our current communications revolution. Like Paul of old, who was faced with the challenge of a new mentality as he encountered the Greek culture, we, too, must adapt our communication approaches to reach people where they are. We cannot ignore their perceptive apparatus by proceeding to communicate in ways that once appealed to us, but no longer to the new generation. Whether we are ministering to children, youth or adults, we must adapt and change in order to communicate effectively. Our message, of course, remains unchanged; our methods and channels must be contemporary and able to reach people today.

This, of course, raises another problem! In the church we have both the old and new generation. On the one hand, the older generation (not necessarily in age) is threatened and feels insecure and uncomfortable with new communication forms; and on the other hand, the new generation is "turned off" by what appeals to the "old."

All the more reason for all members of the body of Christ to understand culture and how it affects us all. Understanding at least

---

5. Ibid.

helps create tolerance and acceptance and love for one another. It helps the church itself to exist in harmony and unity—an ingredient so basic to Christian growth as well as Christian witness.

The functioning body of Christ itself is a significant answer to the communications revolution. It has always been a "form" in itself for communicating a profound message. In a real sense, McLuhan's aphorism, "the medium is the message," applies to what God intended the body of Christ to be. It is a group of people who, as they function, create an atmosphere and environment that communicates the Christian message. To other Christians, the message is one of love and reality. To the unsaved, the unified body says that here are people who are followers of Jesus Christ, the God-man.

The church, then, can become the means that can provide what the American culture does not—an environment that radiates acceptance, security, and stability—and at a personal level. This is the challenge that faces a New Testament church in the twentieth century.

Ninth, the church must understand the cultural effects on life-style, particularly of our youth, and learn to differentiate between what is a violation of biblical principles, and what is a violation of the cultural norms we have come to accept as absolute.

One of the most tragic consequences of cultural change is that some Christians cannot emotionally tolerate a variance in life style because they have come to equate certain externalities with being biblical. For example, men's hair lengths and beards have caused unusual disturbance among some Christians. Some equate the two as being reflective of unspiritual or sinful behavior—forgetting that some of our great Christian leaders in the early 1900's looked quite similar.

It is easy to see how this false conclusion came into existence. Those who first demonstrated this "new" life style were radical youth, who also went much further in demonstrating life style characteristics that were definitely non-Christian. But many Christians—as we so often do—failed to differentiate between characteristics that violated Christian values and those that did not. We fell into the subtle trap of developing caricatures and forming generalizations based on false conclusions.

Even more tragic is a Christian who allows his prejudice toward

Christians to also include non-Christians. When believers will not tolerate having on the church premises non-Christian youth whose life-style does not measure up to certain accepted middle-class norms, we are guilty of what James specifically called it—SIN (Ja 2:9). Though he was speaking in this instance in his epistle regarding prejudice towards the poor, the principle is clear. Just because a person "looks" different does not mean he is immoral, effeminate, or as some would almost imply, less than human. But even if he should be all of these, he is a person for whom Christ died. He is a human being and he needs love and compassion.

The same problem, of course, has been evident among Christians towards blacks and other minority groups. We often look for scriptural rationalizations to support our prejudicial thinking, and like most pseudo-Christian cults, we can make the Bible prove anything we want it to. All we need do is take it out of context to support our subjective biases.

God forbid that we become guilty of failing to distinguish between biblical norms and cultural norms. In the words of Francis Schaeffer when lecturing at Dallas Theological Seminary, we evangelicals have tended to "lose our way." We have developed an "ugliness" that must be terribly repulsive to our Saviour, who died for all men because He loved them. Christian "ugliness" is the saddest kind of "ugliness," for it is demonstrated by those who should demonstrate it least.

It is unfortunate, indeed, when we who are to be the "salt of the earth" and the "light of the world" are so indoctrinated with a non-Christian value system that we no longer can feel compassion towards those who are in deepest spiritual need. May God help us all to shed our carnality and prejudice and become spiritual people—people who love *all men,* not just those we can tolerate intellectually and emotionally.

Tenth, the church must do all it can to strengthen the home, and to counteract the devastating cultural attacks upon this basic of all institutions. Family life has been hit the hardest by the American crisis. Divorce rates are increasing, while children from these broken unions are frequently the victims of an increasing adult selfishness and insensitivity, leaving many in a state of disillusionment and insecurity.

Paralleling the breakdown and abandonment of the traditional approach to home life, have come a variety of marriage experiments, such as collective marriages, trial marriages, and just plain "living together" without any legal or moral commitments. "What lies ahead for American marriage is probably as difficult to predict as what the future holds for any one of us," reports *Life* magazine.[6]

The Christian home, too, is being affected. Though divorce rates are relatively low among Christian families, our homes are still—in many ways—being split apart. Vocational demands have frequently left the family "fatherless," and financial or social pressures have "forced" mothers into a working role.

The church, too, is guilty. Unconsciously imitating an institutionalized society, we have developed forms and structures that literally keep families apart.

The greatest contribution the church can make to our decaying society, is to help build the home. Strong families build strong churches, and together strong homes and strong churces can do more than any one thing to stabilize and revitalize our American culture.

To Sum Up

There are many implications for the church that grow out of an understanding of American culture. As a starter consider these:

1. Develop a correct perspective regarding the multiple causes of our present American crisis.
2. Develop a correct view of history.
3. Understand clearly why Jesus Christ has left the church on earth, and strive with His help to fulfill that purpose.
4. Show a vital concern for government leaders and the state of the nation.
5. Provide an atmosphere in the church where Christians can relate to one another in a non-institutionalized environment.
6. Provide security and stability for people.
7. Help Christians to "live in the world," without being a "part of the world."
8. Recognize, understand, and adapt to the cultural effects of the communications revolution.
9. Understand the cultural effects on life style—particularly on our youth—and learn to differentiate between what is a violation of

---

6. "The Marriage Experiments," *Life*, April 28, 1972, p. 41.

biblical principles, and what is a violation of cultural norms we have come to accept as absolute.

10. Do everything possible to strengthen the home, and counteract the devastating cultural attacks on this basic of all institutions.

PART IV
DEVELOPING A CONTEMPORARY STRATEGY

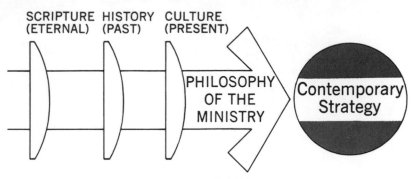

SCRIPTURE HISTORY CULTURE
(ETERNAL) (PAST) (PRESENT)

PHILOSOPHY
OF THE
MINISTRY

Contemporary
Strategy

PRINCIPLES LESSONS IMPLICATIONS

Fig. 13. A Contemporary Strategy

Thus far in our study we have looked through three lenses in order to develop a clear focus for the church in the twentieth century: the lens of Scripture, the lens of history, and the lens of culture.

The lens of Scripture has yielded dynamic New Testament *principles;* the lens of history has reflected some significant *lessons;* and the lens of culture has surfaced important *implications*.

Our task now is to develop a step-by-step contemporary strategy, that will provide a practical approach for achieving constant renewal in the twentieth century church—an approach that truly reflects a biblical philosophy of the ministry.

20

DEVELOPING PROPER PERSPECTIVE — STEP BY STEP

How can we renew our church? Or how can we launch a new church that is characterized by New Testament life and vitality?

These are questions that are being asked today by numerous concerned Christians: by pastors, ministerial students, and laymen representing all segments of church life.

The two chapters in this final section are designed to help answer these questions. They present a step-by-step plan for renewal—a strategy for developing proper perspective and a practical approach for implementing change.

At this juncture it is *very important* to remember that church renewal within the evangelical church means dealing with the "body of Christ." Each member is part of "us"—and a part of Him. To stomp on the body, to hurt the body, is to hurt ourselves and Jesus Christ, the head. Furthermore, to approach the church with brutal force and insensitivity, is to violate the very principles we believe in.

There will be those, of course, who are carnal and insensitive and inflexible. We cannot move forward for Jesus Christ without hurting someone. But this may be a necessary "hurt," and one that, in the end, will help transform that person into the image of Jesus Christ.

But the important concern before us is *how* can we approach the need for renewal, in a way that is biblical and Christlike, and help the majority to see what must be done. And then, as a body, move forward in oneness and unity to function as a New Testament church in the twentieth century.

THE LENS OF SCRIPTURE

To start a new work or to renew an established church, it is very important to begin with the perspective of the Word of God. Bible-believing Christians, particularly since they believe the Bible *is* the Word of God, are responsive to the Scriptures. It is to this Book we must turn as our authoritative base. The problem in many churches is that Christians (including both pastors and people) don't really know what the Bible teaches about the New Testament church. The principles that grow out of such a study are not clearly focused in their thinking.

You must begin, then, where we began in this study: with the *lens of Scripture.* You must start with the Great Commission and help people see *why* the church exists, both as a church "in the world" and as a "gathered community." Christians must see clearly the five important areas in the New Testament that relate to the church: evangelism, edification, church leadership, communication, and organization and administration. As they study the church's activities and the results of those activities in the book of Acts, and as they carefully consider the directives and objectives given to the church in the epistles, the New Testament principles we have discovered will also emerge in *their* thinking.

It should be noted, that, to this point, we have identified these concepts as *principles.* However, as will be shown later, they must be translated into New Testament purposes; that is, biblical objectives which need to be clearly focused and set up as targets for the twentieth century church.

These New Testament principles and purposes are summarized as follows:

PRINCIPLES AND PURPOSES OF EVANGELISM

1. Every body of believers must be responsible for its own community first.
2. Corporate evangelism is basic to personal evangelism.
3. Presenting the gospel to the unsaved is to take place primarily "in the world," not "in the church."
4. The primary target for evangelism should be adults and, consequently, whole households.
5. The church is responsible to identify those who are especially endowed by God as people who can carry the good news, in a special way, out into the community and beyond the immediate community—even to "the remotest part of the earth."

6. New believers, as soon as possible, should be integrated into the life of the church.

7. The twentieth century church must develop its own contemporary structures and approaches to evangelism, utilizing the principles and purposes just stated as biblical guidelines.

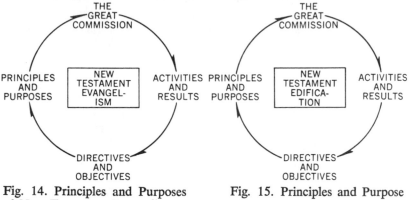

Fig. 14. Principles and Purposes of New Testament Evangelism

Fig. 15. Principles and Purpose of New Testament Edification

PRINCIPLES AND PURPOSES OF EDIFICATION

1. The local church must be kept in focus as the primary means by which edification is to take place.

2. Believers must be provided with a basic knowledge of the Word of God.

3. Believers must be provided with an in-depth knowledge of the Word of God.

4. Believers must be provided with opportunities to develop capacities that go beyond knowledge.

5. Believers must be provided with the sum total of experiences, which will help them get beyond the knowledge level—vital learning experiences with the Word, vital relational experiences with one another and with God, and vital witnessing experiences both individually and corporately.

6. All believers must be equipped for Christian service.

7. Believers must be helped to develop qualitative family life.

8. The twentieth century church must develop its own contemporary forms and structures for applying the biblical principles just outlined.

PRINCIPLES AND PURPOSES OF LEADERSHIP

1. The most important criterion for selecting church leadership is spiritual qualifications.
2. The true test of a man's qualifications for church leadership must be based on "quality"—not "quantity."
3. Multiple leadership in the church is a New Testament principle.
4. Local church leaders are to truly fulfill a pastoral and teaching role—particularly those who are the spiritual leaders of the church.
5. A spiritual leader in the church must learn to establish priorities in the ministry.
6. Specific function spelled out for New Testament leaders leaves much room for creative thinking and performance on the part of twentieth century church leaders.
7. Christians need not be restricted to certain titles and names to describe church leaders.

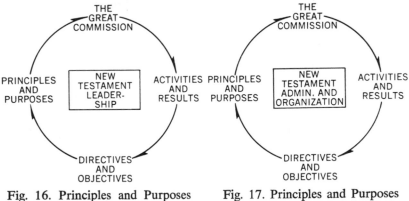

Fig. 16. Principles and Purposes of New Testament Leadership

Fig. 17. Principles and Purposes of New Testament Administration and Organization

PRINCIPLES AND PURPOSES OF ADMINISTRATION AND ORGANIZATION

Administration

1. Face the reality of problems.
2. Develop a proper perspective on the problem before reaching a concrete solution.
3. Establish priorities.

4. Delegate responsibility to qualified people.
5. Maintain a proper balance between divine and human factors.
6. Take an approach to problem solving and decision making that considers the attitudes and feelings of everyone who is involved.
7. Solve every problem creatively, under the leadership of the Holy Spirit.

Organization

1. Organize to apply New Testament principles and to reach New Testament purposes.
2. Organize to meet needs.
3. Keep organization simple.
4. Keep organization flexible.

Fig. 18. Principles and Purposes of New Testament Communication

PRINCIPLES AND PURPOSES OF COMMUNICATION

1. Christian communication is a distinctive process, including both human and divine elements.
2. Christian communication should be to all kinds and classes of people.
3. Christian communication should be carefully balanced between a ministry to groups, as well as a ministry to inidviduals.
4. Effective Christian communication must include an in-depth ministry to a select group, as well as a ministry to the larger group of Christians.
5. For communication to be qualitative it must get beyond the verbalization level.
6. In Christian communication example is foundational to verbalization.

7. Effective Christian communication doesn't just happen—it takes self-sacrifice and hard work.
8. Christians must never be restricted to certain patterns and forms in communication but be free and flexible.

THE LENS OF HISTORY

Christians today need to "look through" the lens of history. Obviously in this study it has been impossible to treat every lesson the twentieth century church can learn from history. We have attempted to open up the area by selecting one major area which relates particularly to the problems of the church today—that of institutionalism. There are many other areas in history that will also challenge our thinking. But from the study of institutionalism in history, we can isolate at least five important lessons:

1. Our greatest strength—our emphasis on teaching and learning the content of the Bible—has also helped to create some of our greatest problems. In our attempt to teach the Bible we have neglected two other vital experiences: relational experiences with God and with one another, and also the vital experience of corporate witness.
2. We have made the church a "soul-winning" station rather than a "life-building" station, thus weakening both the functioning *body* of Christ and our witness in the world.

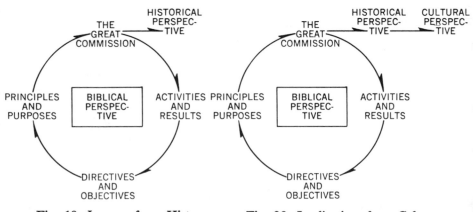

Fig. 19. Lessons from History   Fig. 20. Implications from Culture

3. We are beginning to support the institution, rather than its reason for existence. Put another way, we are more concerned *with* existence than our *cause* for existence.
4. We have emphasized correct doctrine and neglected the quality of one's life. Furthermore, the criteria for evaluating spirituality has often been based on externalities, rather than on inner spiritual qualities.
5. We have fallen into the subtle trap of allowing non-absolutes to become absolute; of making forms and structures, methods and approaches ends in themselves, rather than means to biblical ends.

The Lens of Culture

If we are to renew the church, we must also help twentieth century believers understand contemporary culture—how it affects our thinking; and how easy it is to confuse purely cultural values and biblical values. Of all the influences that shape our thinking, culture can blur it more than any other.

Culture, too, is a large subject. Consequently we have limited our study to the American culture, which in many respects is reflective of the emerging "world culture."

From this analysis we arrived at at least ten implications for the twentieth century church. They are as follows:

1. The church must develop a correct perspective regarding the multiple causes of our present American crisis.
2. The church must develop a correct view of history. We are moving on target toward the climax of history and the return of Jesus Christ.
3. The church must understand clearly why Jesus Christ has left us on earth, and strive with His help to fulfill that purpose. Culture çan blur this purpose and sidetrack us onto peripheral issues.
4. The church must show a vital concern for government leaders, giving primary attention to prayer for them, as well as living an exemplary life.
5. The church must provide an atmosphere where Christians can relate to one another in a non-institutionalized environment.
6. The church must provide security and stability for people—something which culture is increasingly failing to do.
7. The church must help Christians to "live in the world," without

being a "part of the world." Christians must not, consciously or unconsciously, adopt the aspects of the American value system that are contradictory to a Christian value system.

8. The church must recognize, understand, and adapt to the cultural effects of the communications revolution.

9. The church must understand the cultural effects on life-style—particularly of our youth—and learn to differentiate between what is a violation of biblical principles, and what is a violation of the cultural norms we have come to accept as absolute.

10. The church must do all it can to strengthen the home, and counteract the devastating cultural attacks on this basic of all institutions.

DEVELOPING A CONTEMPORARY STRATEGY

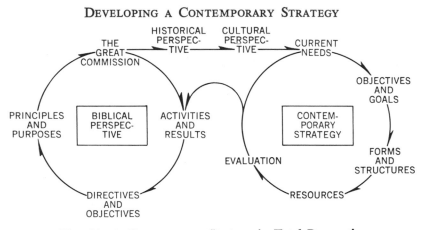

Fig. 21. A Contemporary Strategy in Total Perspective

Once Christians have a clear view of biblical principles, significant lessons from history, and the most important cultural implications, our next move in church renewal is to help them develop greater perspective by looking at the five important steps which must be taken to develop a contemporary strategy: (1) to determine current needs in their own church; (2) to formulate and set up both immediate and long-range objectives and goals; (3) to change, reshape, and develop functional forms and structures; (4) to discover and utilize all relevant and legitimate resources; and (5) to constantly evaluate to see if our total perspective is in focus biblically, historically, culturally, and functionally. This overall, on-going process and strategy can be viewed in figure 21.

DETERMINING CURRENT NEEDS

In order to determine current needs in our local church, we need to reshape each biblical principle into significant and penetrating questions, incorporating our insights from history and culture. These questions will form the criteria by which we can evaluate our present situation. This process will help us to spot strengths as well as weaknesses in our church.

The following section illustrates the kinds of questions which can be formulated:

Evangelism

1. Is our church concerned about its immediate community? Are we reaching people for Christ? Or, are we substituting a program of foreign missions and neglecting those who live within the context of our local witness?

2. Are we active "as a body" in local church evangelism? Are we providing backdrop against which individual evangelism can take place? Or do we expect individual Christians to witness in a vacuum?

3. Are we substituting the "church gathered" as the primary place to "preach the gospel," rather than a place to develop Christians and serve as a dynamic example of Christian love and unity to the world? Are we using the "church gathered" as a place where non-Christians can "come" to get saved rather than as a bridge to the world?

4. Are we reaching whole households with the gospel, concentrating first on reaching parents? Or are we substituting a program of child and youth evangelism for adult evangelism?

5. Are we discovering and recognizing those in the church who feel especially called to evangelism, and are we encouraging them in their community and worldwide witness through moral and financial support?

6. Are new believers integrated into the life of the local church as soon as possible?

7. Are we utilizing contemporary strategies and approaches to com-

munity and worldwide evangelism, that are distinctive and unique to our particular twentieth century problems in reaching people for Christ?

Edification

1. Is our local church a conducive place for edification to take place? Does it provide a warm inviting atmosphere that makes new, as well as old Christians and immature, as well as mature Christians feel comfortable and satisfied? Are we concentrating on making the local church a primary means whereby edification can take place? (Note: This does not mean the "building.") Do we exclude people or make them feel uncomfortable because of our own cultural hang-ups and prejudices? Are we differentiating between life-syles that are a violation of purely cultural values, and those that violate true Christian values?

2. Are we providing new believers with a basic knowledge of the Word of God? Are they taught basic Bible doctrine that will stabilize them in the Christian faith?

3. Are we providing believers with an in-depth knowledge of the Word of God? Are we helping them to understand and appropriate the deep truths of the Scriptures?

4. Are we helping Christians to get beyond the Bible-knowledge level to develop capacities that include wisdom, enlightenment, appreciation, and awareness and sensitivity to the Holy Spirit; a sensitivity to members of the body of Christ, and a sensitivity to the needs of *all* men? Are Christians developing the sensitivity to be able to differentiate between values that are cultural and those that are Christian?

5. Are we providing believers with the sum total of experiences that will help them get beyond the knowledge level—vital learning experiences with the Word of God, vital relational experiences with one another and with God, and vital witnessing experiences, both corporately and individually?

6. Are all believers being equipped for Christian service—both in the world and within the church?

7. Are we helping husbands and wives, fathers and mothers, and children to develop qualitative Christian family life? Are we doing all we can to unite families, to encourage families and to

provide them with the spiritual equipment to combat the negative influences of the secular and materialistic culture?

8. Are we developing contemporary church forms and structures that will enable us to be a dynamic New Testament church in the twentieth century? Do we have forms and structures that provide a sense of Christian community—an atmosphere that is in contrast to the institutionalized environment in the American culture?

Leadership

1. Are we giving primary attention to biblical qualifications in the selection of all church leadership? Do we give primary concern to their reputation, ethics, morality, temperament, habits, spiritual maturity, psychological stability, their knowledge of the Word of God, and their ability to manage their own households well? Or do we select leaders primarily on the basis of their outward abilities?

2. Do we evaluate a person's qualifications on the basis of "inner quality" rather than "outward quantity"? That is, do we look also for the inner qualities specified above, rather than only the number of people who follow and admire him?

3. Do we emphasize the mutuality of the ministry; that is, do we recognize the biblical principle of multiple leadership in the church? Or do we tend to function with a "one man" operation?

4. Do our spiritual leaders—particularly those "worthy of double honor"—function as true pastor-teachers? Or are they so burdened with administrative and organizational work that they are unable to function adequately in ministering to the needs of people, and in teaching the Word of God effectively?

5. Do our spiritual leaders, particularly, establish priorities in the ministry and give their primary attention to fulfilling their God-appointed roles—shepherding, being an example to the flock, teaching the Word of God, refuting false doctrine, and visiting and praying for the sick?

6. Do our church leaders exercise spiritual creativity in fulfilling their roles in the twentieth century church? Or are they locked in to patterns of responsibility that are purely a product of cultural development?

7. Do we put an undue emphasis on terminology and titles, rather

than on New Testament function? In other words, do we allow ourselves to get sidetracked onto peripheral issues?

Organization and Administration

ADMINISTRATION

1. Do we face problems realistically, recognizing their existence and doing something about them as soon as possible?
2. Do we develop a proper perspective upon problems before trying to arrive at concrete solutions?
3. Do we establish priorities, especially as spritual leaders in the church, determining where primary attention must be given?
4. Do the spiritual leaders in the church delegate responsibility to qualified people, especially to handle problems that will take away from their primary roles and responsiblities?
5. Do leaders in the church maintain a proper balance between divine and human factors in performing their administrative roles?
6. Do we use an approach to problem solving and decision making in our church that takes into consideration the attitudes and feelings of everyone involved?
7. Do we solve problems creatively under the leadership of the Holy Spirit? Or are we hampered by approaches that have worked in the past or that have worked for someone else?

ORGANIZATION

1. Is organization used primarily as a means to apply New Testament principles and reach New Testament purposes? Or has organization become an end in itself?
2. Do we organize to meet needs? Or do we organize just to organize?
3. Do we keep our organizational structures simple and functional?
4. Do we keep our organizational structures flexible? Or do we get locked up by structures that are outdated, outmoded, and nonfunctional?

Communication

1. Do we recognize both the divine and human elements in effective Christian communication? Do we recognize God's sovereign work through the Holy Spirit and the Word of God, and at the same time recognize the importance of human factors such as concern, good methods, and hard work?

2. Are we communicating with all kinds and classes of people, both Christians and non-Christians? Or are we demonstrating partiality and prejudice?

3. Are we carefully balancing our ministry to groups with that of a ministry to individuals?

4. Do we have an in-depth ministry to a select group of Christians, as well as a ministry to the total group of believers?

5. Are we communicating primarily with "words," or are we involving people totally in the process of learning? Are we getting beyond the verbalization level, to the level of visualization and total involvement?

6. Do we explore and practice the importance of Christian example as basic to verbal communication?

7. Are we "working hard" at Christian communication? Or do we expect it to "just happen"?

8. Are we being creative in developing and using twentieth century communication forms? Or are we restricting ourselves to forms that are a product of past culture, and are we unknowingly classifying them as biblical and absolute?

FORMULATING OBJECTIVES AND GOALS

Once we have evaluated the overall function of our local church, and isolated both strengths and weaknesses, we then need to formulate both immediate and long-range objectives and goals. This is a key step, and a step that will call for some very careful thinking. It will take time and effort, but it is, in some respects, the most important step in the whole process of renewal. When approached correctly, it can help to create unified thinking in the local body of Christ—an element which is basic to effective change and renewal.

On the other hand, if this step is not taken prayerfully, carefully, and thoroughly, all of the efforts put forth in focusing biblical principles, historical lessons, cultural implications, and current needs may achieve very little.

Because this is such an important step, the entire next chapter is given over to how this process can be carried out.

CHANGING, RESHAPING, AND DEVELOPING FUNCTIONAL FORMS AND STRUCTURES

If formulating objectives and goals is the most *important* step in the process of renewal, then changing, reshaping, and developing functional forms and structures is the most *difficult*. It is at this point that we begin to tamper with tradition, and emotion. Forms and structures represent our way of doing things. And they have provided us with a great deal of security. We know what is going to happen next; that is, how things are going to be done because of our forms and structures.

But if certain forms and structures are no longer or even halfway achieving New Testament purposes because they are no longer functional, they *must* be changed. If they are not, we are failing to be New Testament. We have allowed ourselves to become chained to non-absolutes. We are resisting the Holy Spirit. We are in bondage to ourselves. We are carnal.

If you have proceeded carefully to this point—and particularly if you have helped people clearly focus New Testament principles—most will begin to see the difference between absolutes and non-absolutes. The Holy Spirit Himself will use the Word of God to clear away fuzzy thinking and to renew vision.

This does not mean there will not be those who will *resist* change. This is natural among all people, whether Christian or non-Christian. Management studies show that about ten percent of a group of people in an organization are *innovators*—people willing to try most any new form or structure or idea. About eighty percent are *conservative*—people who are hesitant to change, until they have all the facts and have their feet firmly planted on projections that seem to be completely feasible. Only about ten percent are *inhibitors*—people who are against any kind of change, whether they have the facts or not.[1]

If we approach a body of believers with biblical, historical, and cultural facts, theoretically ninety percent will be ready to change when they see God's plan clearly. And hopefully, since we have the authoritative Word of God and the Holy Spirit on our side, we can reduce the number to less than ten percent who resist just to "resist." In other words, people who are Christians *should* shatter the world's statistical norms.

---

1. Lawrence O. Richards, *A New Face for the Church* (Grand Rapids: Zondervan, 1970), pp. 42-43.

DISCOVERING AND UTILIZING RESOURCES

We live in a technological age that has provided the church with unusual resources. They should never, of course, be thought of as being more important than the spiritual resources available to the church; that is, the Word of God, prayer and the Holy Spirit, and the dynamic of the body of Christ itself. But to ignore the human resources available in the twentieth century is to be less than spiritually alert.

Jesus Christ used the resources available in His day. Whether it was a well, the wind, a sower, a child, or a temple, all were used to communicate His eternal message. Paul used Greek logic, various literary styles, parchments, ships, and a messenger service. Limited, yes, but he used them all to carry out the Great Commission.

Today the church needs to use every relevant and legitimate means to reach the same New Testament objectives that captured the minds and hearts of our biblical forefathers. Literature, cassettes, videotape, films—whatever! We need to consider new methods, new approaches, new ideas to communicate the eternal and never-changing message. The communications revolution in our culture has set the stage for a communications revolution in the church.

This is not to say that preaching is no longer relevant or necessary. But what we need to do is "preach" in new and more creative ways. The Bible does not tell us *how* to preach; it just tells us "to preach" and gives us a variety of illustrations as to the way it was done. So it is with teaching. If we are to keep up with the Sesame Street generation, we cannot sit idly by and continue to perform in the same old way. Many will not listen to us. Their boredom will "win out." What's more, some will become "drop outs," especially if the problem is not counteracted by the home. At the same time we may become guilty of sitting back and complaining about the unresponsive and spiritually hardened generation.

We live in a different world. Man's cognitive and perceptive abilities have changed. He thinks faster, knows more, and asks more questions; and in many instances is more confused. But his heart is the same! It still cries out for understanding, sympathy, support and security. And what he needs is what the church of Jesus Christ

can give. Our challenge is to use every resource available to meet
his needs.

EVALUATING

The word *evaluation* is a threatening word, but it is a biblical
word. In the King James Version, Paul exhorted the Corinthians to
"prove" themselves (2 Co 13:5): to put themselves to the test,
examine themselves, scrutinize themselves. To the Galatians, he
wrote, "Let every man prove his own work" (Gal 6:4); and he admonished the Thessalonians to "prove all things" (1 Th 5:21).
Paul also practiced this concept in his own ministry. He sent Timothy back to Thessalonica to evaluate the state of the church—to see
how they were (1 Th 3:5). He was constantly anxious to get reports
from various sources, as to what was happening in all the churches,
regarding their problems, their needs, their concerns, and their
progress.

Several things should be noted regarding the process of evaluation.

First, it should be constant. As illustrated in figure 21, it applies
to every aspect of the process of developing a biblical philosophy
of the ministry. We must constantly search the Word of God to see
if we have clearly focused biblical principles. We must constantly re-
consider history in the light of contemporary culture. We must
constantly determine current needs against the backdrop of biblical
principles, historical lessons, and cultural implications. We must
constantly refocus our objectives and goals, particularly in the light of
biblical purposes. We must constantly evaluate our forms and structures to see if they are appropriately applying biblcal principles and
reaching New Testament goals and objectives. We must constantly
look for resources to help us be a New Testament church in the
twentieth century. And finally we must evaluate, evaluate, evaluate!

Second, evaluation should be carried out by the whole body of
Christ. It is only as *all* are involved in this process that *all* will want
to change. This is why it is important to help each member of the
body to know what *is* and what *is not* a New Testament principle;
what *is* and *is not* a biblical norm or absolute; what *is* and what *is not*
cultural. When every member of the body of Christ is involved in the
process, it also provides assurance that we are arriving at a correct
perspective on our problems. It is dangerous for one individual to

evaluate alone. All of us are, to a certain extent, in bondage to subjective feelings. We need the body of Christ and its many members to help correct any incorrect perceptions.

Third, though evaluation is threatening, it is ultimately rewarding. We are afraid of evaluation, because we are afraid we will discover that we have done something wrong, and that reflects on us personally.

But let's face reality! Not one of us is perfect. We all make mistakes. This is why we need the "body." When all are involved, all are "to blame" when we make mistakes. "Together" we must evaluate; and "together" we must plan; and "together" we will become what God wants us to become.

Summing Up

To renew your church step by step:

1. Help the church to focus biblical principles and purposes by looking through the lens of Scripture.
2. Help the church focus lessons of history by looking through the lens of history.
3. Help the church focus implications from culture by looking through the lens of culture.
4. Help the church determine its current needs in the light of biblical, historical and cultural perspective.
5. Help the church formulate immediate and long-range objectives and goals.
6. Help the church develop contemporary forms and structures.
7. Help the church discover and utilize relevent resources.
8. Help the church use this step-by-step process to constantly evaluate and to "prove themselves."

21

FORMULATING OBJECTIVES, GOALS, AND STANDARDS

It was emphasized in the previous chapter that formulating objectives, goals and standards was one of the most important steps in bringing about renewal in the church. Because this is true, this final chapter is designed as a "model" for goal setting. How can this be done?

DEFINITION OF TERMS

First we must define our terms.

A *purpose* is a broad statement of an aspiration. It describes the general direction we want to go. This is why the principles which have emerged in our study of the New Testament church are identified as *purposes* as well as *principles*. In each instance, they are broad, scriptural statements that apply to evangelism, edification, leadership, communication, organization and administration.[1]

An *objective* is a more specific statement of an aspiration, which, if attained, will produce progress toward fulfilling each scriptural purpose. There are usually two or more objectives for each purpose.

The *goal* is a still more specific statement of what is to be accomplished to produce progress toward an objective. There are usually two or more goals for each objective.

A *performance standard* is a measurement by which performance can be evaluated. Standards can be expressed in terms which are relative to a *purpose* or an *objective* or a *goal*. There are usually two or more standards for each goal.

---

1. Dr. John Alexander, President of Inter-Varsity Christian Fellowship, has in many respects set the pace in goal setting among evangelical leaders. It is from his book, *Managing Our Work* (Downers Grove, Ill.: Inter-Varsity, 1972, that the basic definitions and model are taken (pp. 15, 22-23). The specific adaptation to the work of the church has been made on the basis of the material discussed in these chapters.

The Basic Model

On the basis of these definitions, the following model is set up to illustrate how a biblical principle can be translated into a purpose, and how objectives, goals and standards can be formulated for a local church. A principle of New Testament evangelism is used to illustrate this process.

Purposes

Purposes should be the same for every Bible-believing church. Since they are based on biblical principles, they are supracultural.

Objectives

Objectives vary from church to church, community to community, and culture to culture. They are based upon current needs and concerns within a particular church. There are usually two or more objectives for each purpose.

Example A

One of the purposes of New Testament evangelism is *to give primary attention to reaching our own community with the gospel.*

Examples Under A

1. To educate people relative to this important New Testament principle.
2. To motivate people relative to this important New Testament principle.

Goals

Goals are specific statements of steps to be taken if objectives are to be achieved. There usually are two or more goals for each objective.

Standards

Standards are specific statements of conditions to be met if each goal is to be reached. There are usually two or more standards for each goal.

Examples Under A-1

(a) To expose people to this concept of community evangelism through biblical teaching on the subject.
(b) To expose people to this concept by sharing with them what other churches are doing to reach their communities.

Examples Under A-1-a

(i) The whole congregation is exposed to this concept at least once a year through a sermon.
(ii) A group of selected people will explore this concept in a small group training session once a year.

An Expanded Model

This model includes all of the New Testament principles which have emerged in our study of the first century church. They have been translated into purposes; and in the first section on evangelism, two purposes have been developed to illustrate what a "certain" church *might* do to formulate objectives, goals, and standards to carry out these two purposes. Hereafter, only the purposes are listed under each section, with the exception of the partial development of purpose A in the area of edification. This process of development should be carried out for each purpose, including at least two objectives, two goals under each objective, and two standards under each goal. It should be realized, however, that some situations may call for more than two statements under each category, and some may call for less than two. Each individual church should complete this task in view of their own particular current needs. In developing each section, it will help to rethink the material covered previously in this study.

Evangelism

Purpose A. To give primary attention to reaching our own community with the gospel

    Objective 1. To *educate* people relative to this important New Testament principle

        Goal a). To expose people to this concept of community evangelism through biblical teaching on the subject

            Standard (1). The whole congregation is exposed to this concept at least once a year through a sermon.

            Standard (2). A smaller group of people explores this concept in the Bible in a small group training session once a year.

        Goal b). To expose people to this concept by sharing with them what other churches are doing to reach their own communities

            Standard (1). A film on the subject will be shown during a special evening session to the whole congregation to launch this emphasis.

Standard (2). Each member of the local body is encouraged to read one book on the subject by means of the church bulletin. A list of books appears once a month.

Objective 2. To *motivate* people relative to this important New Testament principle

Goal a). To bring in guest laymen from other churches to share how God is using them to reach their community for Christ

Standard (1). One Sunday is designated every two months when laymen from other churches are invited to come in and share in a morning service.

Standard (2). One Sunday is designated every two months when laymen from other churches are invited to come and share in an evening service.

Goal b). To provide opportunity for people to share with others how God is using them to reach their neighbors, friends, and business associates for Christ

Standard (1). Opportunity is given every Sunday evening for people to share their witnessing experiences.

Standard (2). People are regularly encouraged to share prayer needs with other members of the body, regarding unsaved neighbors, friends, and business associates.

Purpose B. To emphasize that corporate evangelism is basic to personal evangelism

Objective 1. To explain what corporate evangelism is

Goal a). To expose people to this concept through biblical teaching

Standard (1). The whole congregation is exposed to this concept through a sermon.

Standard (2). This concept is explored by means of a small group Bible study in a four-part series in each adult Sunday school class, following the introductory sermon on this subject.

Goal b). To demonstrate how this concept works

Standard (1).   A dramatic presentation is made one Sunday evening to show how corporate evangelism opens up opportunities for individual witness.

Standard (2).   People are encouraged each Sunday evening to share opportunities that have come to them for Christian witness because of the functioning body of Christ.

Objective 2. To explain that we must devise ways and means to expose unsaved people to the functioning body of Christ

Goal a)   To encourage people to invite unsaved people to share in a special church function that demonstrates the functioning body

Standard (1).   A special church function is planned once a month that is conducive for inviting unsaved friends to see the body of Christ function in love and unity.

Standard (2).   A regular body-life service is planned once a week in which any non-Christian may see the body of Christ functioning in love and unity.

Goal b). To encourage people as families to invite their neighbors for dinner or a picnic, in order to demonstrate the functioning body of Christ at the family level

Standard (1).   People are regularly encouraged to share experiences with other believers as to what they are doing to build bridges to unsaved neighbors.

Standard (2).   Whenever a person comes to know Christ through seeing individual families function in love and unity, that person is invited to share his testimony with the total church family in a church service.

Purpose C. To follow the New Testament example of reaching people for Christ "outside the church"; that is, apart from structuring a regular church service as an evangelistic meeting

Purpose D. To reach whole households for Christ, beginning with fathers and mothers

Purpose E. To identify those in the church who are specifically called to evangelism, and to provide both moral and financial support so they can function effectively.

Purpose F. To integrate new believers into the life of the church as soon as possible

Purpose G. To develop contemporary strategies and approaches to reach New Testament purposes

Edification

Purpose A. To develop a local church that can, indeed, serve as a primary means by which effective edification can take place for all twentieth century believers, young and old, and Christians from all walks of life

Objective 1. To expose all believers in the church to this concept

Goal a). To expose, first of all, the spiritual leaders in the church to this concept

Standard (1). This concept will be discussed in a series of luncheons, with key spiritual leaders in the church suggesting a series of Bible studies with the whole board.

Standard (2). This concept will then be developed in a series of Bible studies with the spiritual leaders of the church, assuming that this will be supported by these leaders.

Goal b). To specifically expose the whole congregation to this concept after the spiritual leaders have been exposed

Standard (1).

Standard (2).

Objective 2. To expose all believers in the church to Christians who do not live in the same cultural situation as we do

Goal a).
   Standard (1).
   Standard (2).
Goal b).
   Standard (1).
   Standard (2).

Purpose B. To provide new believers with a knowledge of the basic doctrines of the Christian faith.

Purpose C. To provide all believers with an in-depth knowledge of the Scriptures

Purpose D. To help believers to develop capacities that go beyond the knowledge level

Purpose E. To provide all leaders with balanced New Testament experiences

Purpose F. To equip all believers for Christian service

Purpose G. To help parents develop qualitative family life

Purpose H. To develop contemporary forms and structures in the church that will serve as the best means for reaching these purposes, objectives and goals

Leadership

Purpose A. To select all leaders in the church on the basis of New Testament qualifications

Purpose B. To evaluate an individual's qualifications for church leadership by means of quality—not quantity

Purpose C. To develop a church that is characterized by multiple leadership and mutuality of the ministry

Purpose D. To make sure spiritual leaders in the church are truly functioning in a pastoral and teaching role

Purpose E. To assist spiritual leaders, particularly, to establish priorities in the ministry

Purpose F. To make sure spiritual leaders in the church are performing creatively within the broad job description outlined in Scripture.

Purpose G. To devise titles and names for church leadership that are best suited to our community and culture

Organization and Administration

ADMINISTRATION

Purpose A. To face all problems immediately and realistically

Purpose B. To develop a proper perspective on all problems, before seeking a concrete solution

Purpose C. To establish priorities

Purpose D. To delegate responsibility to qualified people

Purpose E. To practice an approach to problem solving and decision making that considers the attitudes and feelings of everyone involved

Purpose F. To solve every problem creatively under the leadership of the Holy Spirit

ORGANIZATION

Purpose A. To devise organizational structures that will carry out New Testament principles and reach New Testament purposes

Purpose B. To organize on the basis of needs

Purpose C. To keep organization simple

Purpose D. To keep organization flexible

Communication

Purpose A. To maintain a proper balance between divine and human factors in communication

Purpose B. To communicate with all kinds and classes of people

Purpose C. To maintain a proper balance between a ministry to groups and to individuals

Purpose D. To maintain a proper balance between a ministry in-depth to a small group of Christians and a general ministry to all Christians

Purpose E. To get beyond the verbalization level in communication

Purpose F. To make sure Christian example is basic to verbal communication

Purpose G. To put forth the necessary effort to attain good Christian communication

Purpose H. To use and develop twentieth century patterns and forms in communication

SUMMING UP

Formulating objectives, goals and standards on the basis of New Testament purposes is the most important step a local church can take to bring about spiritual renewal. When this process is carried out properly—and as a body—the necessary forms and structures and the utilization of relevant resources will follow naturally.

This does not mean that every individual will cease to be threatened by change, but it does mean that "together" the body of Christ will carry out the Great Commission of our Lord Jesus Christ more effectively. On some occasions it will mean new churches must be established; for some churches have become so institutionalized and some individuals have departed so far from the Word of God, that even the Scriptures mean very little in their lives. But when Christians believe the Word of God and are committed to it, they are hardened indeed if they do not respond to the Holy Spirit as He exposes them to its teachings regarding the New Testament church.

A PRAYER

O God give us perspective! Help us to see clearly the principles in Your Word which will give us direction for our churches. Help us to see clearly the lessons from history we should learn—lessons that will keep us from repeating the errors of our forefathers; and lessons that will help us to do again, but even better, what they did right. Help us to understand our contemporary culture, and not to be in bondage to it nor totally separated from it, but to use it as a bridge to a troubled humanity. Help us not to get locked in to non-absolutes and keep us from getting sidetracked onto peripheral issues. Above all, help us to fulfill the great purpose for which You left us here on earth—to "make disciples" of all nations and to be a functioning part of a dynamic body of New Testament believers.

"Now to Him who is able to do exceeding abundantly beyond all that we ask or think, according to the power that works within us, to Him be the glory in the church and in Christ Jesus to all generations forever and ever. Amen" (Eph 3:20-21).

Appendix A
AN OPPORTUNITY TO MAKE YOUR OWN INDUCTIVE STUDY

The commission given by Jesus Christ in Matthew 28:19-20 has been separated into two basic tasks: *evangelism* (why the church exists in the world) and *edification* (why the "church gathered" exists). Evangelism involves *going* and *making disciples,* and edification involves *baptizing* them and *teaching* them.

These two tasks have been used to develop two columns, which include Scriptures, to illustrate the way in which these tasks were carried out. The book of Acts has been used as a basic source for this information, and the epistles have been correlated with the basic flow of events which appear in Acts.

You will note, however, that though the basic purpose of the epistles was edification and hence their total content could appear in column two, they also include material that is illustrative of, and particularly pertinent to, the tasks in both columns. Therefore selected scripture verses from the epistles appear in both columns.

For an exciting study, work through the Scriptures which have been compiled for you in this appendix. As you study, you will note that a pattern emerges in relationship to the way in which the Great Commission was carried out. (See model chart "Why Does the Church Exist?")

In column one (the evangelism column) you will see *activities* and *results* in the book of Acts. As you move into the epistles in the same column, you will see *directives* and *objectives.*

WHY DOES THE CHURCH EXIST?

	EVANGELISM — Going—Make Disciples (Why the Church Exists in the World)		EDIFICATION — Baptizing—Teaching Them (Why the Church Exists as a Gathered Community)	
	Activities and Directives	Results and Objectives	Activities and Directives	Results and Objectives
ACTS	Declaring Speaking Proclaiming Preaching Testifying Etc.	Many believed The Word of God kept on spreading Some were persuaded Etc.	Baptizing Teaching Encouraging Strengthening Reporting Etc.	Were of one mind Were of one heart and soul Were being built up Etc.
EPISTLES	Love your neighbor as yourself Keep your behavior excellent among the Gentiles	So that . . . they may glorify God in the day of visitation	Encourage one another Build up one another We admonish and teach every man	That we may present every man complete in Christ

In column two (the edification column) you will see the same pattern emerge: that is, activities and results in the book of Acts and directives and objectives in the epistles. (Again see the model which will help clarify this pattern.

Now for your specific assignment!

1. Use a color code to identify: red—activities; blue—results; black—directives; green—objectives. 2. Carefully study your findings. What do you see? Use the following questions to prod your thinking:

REGARDING EVANGELISM

a. What kind of evangelism activities did Christians engage in in the book of Acts?

b. What were the results of these activities?

c. What evangelism directives are given by the writers of the epistles?

d. What objectives are to be achieved as a result of carrying out these directives?

REGARDING EDIFICATION

a. What kind of edification activities did Christians engage in in the book of Acts?

b. What were the results of these activities?

c. What edification directives are given by the writers of the epistles?

d. What objectives are to be achieved as a result of carrying out these directives?

3. Now back off from your study and answer these two questions:

a. As a result of your study what would be principles of evangelism for a New Testament church in the last quarter of the twentieth century?

b. As a result of your study, what would be principles of edification for a New Testament church in the last quarter of the twentieth century?

SELECTED SCRIPTURE VERSES

Go, therefore and make disciples of all the nations, baptizing them in the name of the Father and the Son and the Holy Spirit, teaching them to observe all that I commanded you; and lo, I am with you always, even to the end of the age." Matthew 28:19-20

WHY DOES THE CHURCH EXIST IN THE WORLD? EVANGELISM GOING— MAKE DISCIPLES	WHY DOES THE "CHURCH GATHERED" EXIST? EDIFICATION BAPTIZING THEM— TEACHING THEM
Acts 1:8. But you shall receive power when the Holy Spirit has come upon you; and you shall be My witnesses both in Jerusalem, and in all Judea and Samaria, and even to the remotest part of the earth.	
Acts 2:14. But Peter, taking his stand with the eleven, raised his voice and declared to them: "Men of Judea, and all you who live in Jerusalem, let this be known to you, and give heed to my words."	**Acts 2:41-42.** So then, those who had received his word were baptized; and there were added that day about three thousand souls. And they were continually devoting themselves to the apostles' teaching and to fellowship, and to the breaking of bread and to prayer.

Acts 2:46-47. And day by day continuing with one mind in the temple, and breaking bread from house to house, they were taking their meals together with gladness and sincerity of heart, praising God, and having favor with all the people. And the Lord was adding to their number day by day those who were being saved.

Acts 4:1-2, 4. And as they were speaking to the people, the priests and the captain of the temple guard, and the Sadducees, came upon them, being greatly disturbed because they were teaching the people and proclaiming in Jesus the resurrection from the dead. . . . But many of those who had heard the message believed; and the number of the men came to be about five thousand.	

Acts 4:31. And when they had prayed, the place where they had gathered together was shaken, and they were all filled with the Holy Spirit, and began to speak the word of God with boldness.

Acts 5:12-14. And at the hands of the apostles many signs and wonders were taking place among the people; and they were all with one accord in Solomon's portico. But none of the rest dared to associate with them; however, the people held them in high esteem. And all the more believers in the Lord, multitudes of men and women, were constantly added to their number.

Acts 5:19-21a. But an angel of the Lord during the night opened the gates of the prison, and taking them out he said, "Go your way, stand and speak to the people in the temple the whole message of this Life." And upon hearing this, they entered into the temple about daybreak, and began to teach.

Acts 5:25. But someone came and reported to them, "Behold, the men whom you put in prison are standing in the temple and teaching the people!"

Acts 5:27-28. And when they had brought them, they stood them before the Council. And the high priest questioned them, saying, "We gave you strict orders not to continue teaching in

Acts 4:32. And the congregation of those who believed were of one heart and soul; and not one of them claimed that anything belonging to him was his own; but all things were common property to them.

this name, and behold, you have filled Jerusalem with your teaching, and intend to bring this man's blood upon us."

Acts 5:42. And every day, in the temple, from house to house, they kept right on teaching and preaching Jesus as the Christ.

Acts 6:4, 7. "But we will devote ourselves to prayer, and to the ministry of the word.". . . . And the word of God kept on spreading; and the number of the disciples continued to increase greatly in Jerusalem, and a great many of the priests were becoming obedient to the faith.

Acts 8:1b, 4. And on that day a great persecution arose against the church in Jerusalem; and they were all scattered throughout the regions of Judea and Samaria, except the apostles. . . . Therefore, those who had been scattered went about preaching the word.

Acts 8:5. And Philip went down to the city of Samaria and began proclaiming Christ to them.

Acts 8:25. And so, when they [Peter and John] had solemnly testified and spoken the word of the Lord, they started back to Jerusalem, and were preaching the gospel to many villages of the Samaritans.

Acts 8:35. And Philip opened his mouth, and beginning from this Scripture he preached Jesus to him.

Acts 8:12. But when they believed Philip preaching the good news about the kingdom of God and the name of Jesus Christ, they were being baptized, men and women alike.

Acts 8:36, 38. And as they went along the road they came to some water; and the eunuch said, "Look! Water! What prevents me from being baptized?"

. . . And he ordered the chariot to stop; and they both went down into the water, Philip as well as the eunuch; and he baptized him.

Acts 9:20. And immediately he [Paul] began to proclaim Jesus in the synagogues, saying, "He is the Son of God."

Acts 9:31. So the church throughout all Judea and Galilee and Samaria enjoyed peace, being built up; and, going on in the fear of the Lord and in the comfort of the Holy Spirit, it continued to increase.

Acts 10:42-43. "And He ordered us to preach to the people, and solemnly to testify that this is the One who has been appointed by God as Judge of the living and the dead. Of Him all the prophets bear witness that through His name every one who believes in Him has received forgiveness of sins."

Acts 11:19-21. So then those who were scattered because of the persecution that arose in connection with Stephen made their way to Phoenicia and Cyprus and Antioch, speaking the word to no one except to Jews alone. But there were some of them, men of Cyprus and Cyrene, who came to Antioch and began speaking to the Greeks also, preaching the Lord Jesus. And the hand of the Lord was with them, and a large number who believed turned to the Lord.

Acts 11:22-26. And the news about them reached the ears of the church at Jerusalem, and they sent Barnabas off to Antioch. Then when he had come and witnessed the grace of God, he rejoiced and began to encourage them all with resolute heart to remain true to the Lord; for he was a good man, and full of the Holy Spirit and of faith. And considerable numbers were brought to the Lord. And he left for Tarsus to look for Saul; and when he had found him, he brought him to Antioch. And it came about that for an entire year they met with the church, and taught considerable numbers; and the disciples were first called Christians in Antioch.

Acts 12:24. But the word of the Lord continued to grow and to be multiplied.

Acts 13:5a. And when t h e y reached Salamis, they began to proclaim the word of God in the synagogues of the Jews.

Acts 13:13-16, 42-44. Now Paul and his companions put out to sea from Paphos and came to Perga in Pamphylia; and John left them and returned to Jerusalem. But going on from Perga, they arrived in Pisidian Antioch, and on the Sabbath day they went into the synagogue and sat down. And after the reading of the Law and the Prophets the synagogue officials sent to them, saying, "Brethren, if you have any word of exhortation for the people, say it." And Paul stood up, and motioning with his hand, he said, "Men of Israel, and you who fear God, listen. . . ." And as Paul and Barnabas were going out, the people kept begging that these things might be spoken to them the next Sabbath. Now when the meeting of the synagogue had broken up, many of the Jews and of the God-fearing proselytes followed Paul and Barnabas, who, speaking to them, were urging them to continue in the grace of God. And the next Sabbath nearly the whole city assembled to hear the word of God.

Acts 13:45-49. But when the Jews saw the crowds, they were filled with jealousy, and began contradicting the things spoken by Paul, and were blaspheming. And Paul and Barnabas spoke out boldly and said, "It was necessary that the word of God should be spoken to you first; since you repudiate it, and judge yourselves unworthy of eternal life, behold, we are turning to the Gentiles. For thus the Lord has commanded us, 'I HAVE PLACED YOU AS A LIGHT FOR THE GENTILES, THAT YOU SHOULD BRING SALVATION TO THE END OF THE EARTH.' " And when the Gentiles heard this, they began rejoicing and glorifying the word of the Lord; and as many as had been appointed to eternal life believed. And the word of the Lord was being spread through the whole region.

Acts 14:1. And it came about that in Iconium they entered the synagogue of the Jews together, and spoke in such a manner that a great multitude believed, both of Jews and of Greeks.

Acts 14:5-7. And when an attempt was made by both the Gentiles and the Jews with their rulers, to mistreat and to stone them, they became aware of it and fled to the cities of Lycao-

THE EPISTLE OF JAMES

James 3:1-2. Let not many of you become teachers, my brethren, knowing that as such we shall incur a stricter judgment. For we all stumble in many ways. If any one does not stumble in what he says, he is a perfect man, able to bridle the whole body as well.

nia, Lystra and Derbe, and the surrounding region; and there they continued to preach the gospel.

Acts 14:19-21a. But Jews came from Antioch and Iconium, and having won over the multitudes, they stoned Paul and dragged him out of the city, supposing him to be dead. But while the disciples stood around him, he arose and entered the city. And the next day he went away with Barnabas to Derbe. And after they had preached the gospel to that city and had made many disciples. . . .

Acts 14:25. And when they had spoken the word in Perga, they went down to Attalia; . . .

Acts 14:21b-23. They returned to Lystra and to Iconium and to Antioch, strengthening the souls of the disciples, encouraging them to continue in the faith, and saying, "Through many tribulations we must enter the kingdom of God." And when they had appointed elders for them in every church, having prayed with fasting, they commended them to the Lord in whom they had believed.

Acts 14:26-28. And from there they sailed to Antioch, from which they had been commended to the grace of God for the work that they had accomplished. And when they had arrived and gathered the church together, they began to report all things that God had done with them and how He had opened a door of faith to the Gentiles. And they spent a long time with the disciples.

Acts 15:2-4. And when Paul and Barnabas had great dissension and debate with them, the brethren determined that Paul and Barnabas and certain others of them, should go up to Jerusalem to the apostles and elders concerning this issue.

Therefore, being sent on their way by the church, they were passing through both Phoenicia and Samaria, describing in detail the conversion of the Gentiles, and were bringing great joy to all the brethren. And when they arrived at Jerusalem, they were received by the church and the apostles and the elders, and they reported all that God had done with them.

Galatians 6:10a. So then, while we have opportunity, let us do good to all men.

THE EPISTLE TO THE GALATIANS
Acts 15:22-23a, 30-32. Then it seemed good to the apostles and elders, with the whole church, to choose men from among them to send to Antioch with Paul and Barnabas—J u d a s called Barsabbas, and Silas, leading men among the brethren, and they sent this letter by them, . . . So, when they were sent away, they went down to Antioch; and having gathered the congregation together, they delivered the letter. And when they had read it, they rejoiced because of its encouragement. And Judas and Silas, also being prophets themselves, encouraged and strengthened the brethren with a lengthy message.

Acts 15:35. But Paul and Barnabas stayed in Antioch, teaching and preaching with many others also the word of the Lord.

Acts 15:36, 40-41. And after some days Paul said to Barnabas, "Let us return and visit the brethren in every city in which we proclaimed the word of the Lord, and see how they are." . . . But Paul chose Silas and departed, being committed by the brethren to the grace of the

Lord. And he was traveling through Syria and Cilicia, strengthening the churches.

Acts 16:4-5a. Now while they were passing through the cities, they were delivering the decrees, which had been decided upon by the apostles and elders who were in Jerusalem, for them to observe. So the churches were being strengthened in the faith.

Acts 16:5b. And were increasing in number daily.

Acts 16:10. And when he had seen the vision, immediately we sought to go into Macedonia, concluding that God had called us to preach the gospel to them.

Acts 16:13. And on the Sabbath day we went outside the gate to a river side, where we were supposing that there would be a place of prayer; and we sat down and began speaking to the women who had assembled.

Acts 16:31-32. And they said, "Believe in the Lord Jesus, and you shall be saved, you and your household." And they spoke the word of the Lord to him together with all who were in his house.

Acts 16:33-34, 40. And he took them that very hour of the night and washed their wounds, and immediately he was baptized, he and all his household. And he brought them into his house and set food before them, and rejoiced greatly, having believed in God with his whole household. . . . And they went out of the prison and entered the house of Lydia, and when they saw the brethren, they encouraged them and departed.

Acts 17:2-4. And according to Paul's custom, he went to them, and for three Sabbaths reasoned with them from the Scriptures, explaining and giving evidence that the Christ had to suffer and rise again from the dead, and saying, "This Jesus whom I am proclaiming to you is the Christ." And some of them were persuaded and joined Paul and Silas, along with a great multitude of the God-fearing Greeks and a number of the leading women.

1 Thessalonians 1:5-10. For our gospel did not come to you in word only, but also in power and in the Holy Spirit and with full conviction; just as you know what kind of men we proved to be among you for your sake. You also became imitators of us and of the Lord, having received the word in much tribulation with the joy of the Holy Spirit, so that you became an example to all the believers in Macedonia and in Achaia. For the word of the Lord has sounded forth from you, not only in Macedonia and Achaia, but also in every place your faith toward God has gone forth, so that we have no need to say anything. For they themselves report about us what kind of a reception we had with you, and how you turned to God from idols to serve a living and true God, and to wait for His

THE THESSALONIAN EPISTLES
(Written from Corinth)

1 Thessalonians 2:7-12. But we proved to be gentle among you, as a nursing mother tenderly cares for her own children. Having thus a fond affection for you, we were well pleased to impart to you not only the gospel but also our own lives, because you had become very dear to us. For you recall, brethren, our labor and hardship, how working night and day so as not to be a burden to any of you, we proclaimed to you the gospel of God. You are witnesses, and so is God, how devoutly and uprightly and blamelessly we behaved toward you believers; just as you know how we were exhorting and encouraging and imploring each one of you as a father would his own children, so that you may walk in a manner worthy of God who calls you into His own kingdom and glory.

1 Thessalonians 3:1-5. Therefore when we could endure it no longer, we thought it best to be left behind at Athens alone; and we sent Timothy, our brother and God's fellow-worker in the gospel of Christ, to strengthen and encourage you as to your faith; so that no man may be disturbed by these afflictions; for you yourselves know that we have been destined for this. For indeed when

Son from heaven, whom He raised from the dead, that is Jesus, who delivers us from the wrath to come.

2 Thessalonians 3:1. Finally, brethren, pray for us that the word of the Lord may spread rapidly and be glorified, just as it did also with you.

we were with you, we kept telling you in advance that we were going to suffer affliction; and so it came to pass, as you know. For this reason, when I could endure it no longer, I also sent to find out about your faith, for fear that the tempter might have tempted you, and our labor should be in vain.

1 Thessalonians 3:10-13. As we night and day keep praying most earnestly that we may see your face, and may complete what is lacking in your faith? Now may our God and Father Himself and Jesus our Lord direct our way to you; and may the Lord cause you to increase and abound in love for one another, and for all men, just as we also do for you; so that He may establish your hearts unblamable in holiness before our God and Father at the coming of our Lord Jesus with all His saints.

1 Thessalonians 5:11. Therefore encourage one another, and build up one another, just as you also are doing.

1 Thessalonians 5:14-15. And we urge you, brethren, admonish the unruly, encourage the fainthearted, help the weak, be patient with all men. See that no one repays another with evil for evil, but always seek after that which is good for one another and for all men.

Acts 17:10-12. And the brethren immediately sent Paul and Silas away by night to Berea; and when they arrived, they went into the synagogue of the Jews. Now these were more noble-minded than those in Thessalonica, for they received the word with great eagerness, examining the Scriptures daily, to see whether these things were so. Many of them therefore believed, along with a number of prominent Greek women and men.

Acts 17:16-17. Now while Paul was waiting for them at Athens, his spirit was being provoked within him as he was beholding the city full of idols. So he was reasoning in the synagogue with the Jews and the God-fearing Gentiles, and in the market place every day with those who happened to be present.

Acts 17: 22-31. (Paul's sermon in Athens)

Acts 17:34. But some men joined him and believed, among whom also was Dionysius the Areopagite and a woman named Damaris and others with them.

Acts 18:4-5. And [in Corinth] he was reasoning in the synagogue every Sabbath and trying to persuade Jews and Greeks. But when Silas and Timothy came down from Macedonia, Paul began devoting himself completely to the word, solemnly testifying to the Jews that Jesus was the Christ.

Acts 18:8-11. And Crispus, the leader of the synagogue, believed in the Lord with all his household, and many of the Corinthians when they heard were believing and being baptized. And the Lord said to Paul in the night by a vision, "Do not be afraid any longer, but go on speaking and do not be silent; for I am with you, and no man will attack you in order to harm you, for I have many people in this city." And he settled there a year and six months, teaching the word of God among them.

THE CORINTHIAN EPISTLES
(Written from Ephesus and Macedonia)

1 Corinthians 1:17. For Christ did not send me to baptize, but to preach the gospel, not in cleverness of speech, that the cross of Christ should not be made void.

1 Corinthians 1:21-24. For since in the wisdom of God the world through its wisdom did not come to know God, God was well pleased through the foolishness of the message preached to save those who believe. For indeed Jews ask for signs, and Greeks search for wisdom; but we preach Christ crucified, to Jews a stumbling block, and to Gentiles foolishness, but to those who are the called, both Jews and Greeks, Christ the power of God and the wisdom of God.

1 Corinthians 2:1-5. And when I came to you, brethren, I did not come with superiority of speech or of wisdom, proclaiming to you the testimony of God. For I determined to know nothing among you except Jesus Christ, and Him crucified. And

1 Corinthians 1:10. Now I exhort you, brethren, by the name of our Lord Jesus Christ, that you all agree, and there be no divisions among you, but you be made complete in the same mind and in the same judgment.

1 Corinthians 4:17. For this reason I have sent to you Timothy, who is my beloved and faithful child in the Lord, and he will remind you of my ways which are in Christ, just as I teach everywhere in every church.

I was with you in weakness and in fear and in much trembling. And my message and my preaching were not in persuasive words of wisdom, but in demonstration of the Spirit and of power, that your faith should not rest on the wisdom of men, but on the power of God.

1 Corinthians 5:9-10. I wrote you in my letter not to associate with immoral people; I did not at all mean with the immoral people of this world, or with the covetous and swindlers, or with idolaters; for then you would have to go out of the world.

1 Corinthians 9:16. For if I preach the gospel, I have nothing to boast of, for I am under compulsion; for woe is me if I do not preach the gospel.

1 Corinthians 11:26. For as often as you eat this bread and drink the cup, you proclaim the Lord's death until He comes.

1 Corinthians 14:23-25 If therefore the whole church should assemble together and all speak in tongues, and ungifted men or unbelievers enter, will they not say that you are mad? But if all prophesy, and an unbeliever or an ungifted man enters, he is convicted by all, he is called to account by all; the secrets of his heart are disclosed; and so he will fall on his face and worship God, declaring that God is certainly among you.

1 Corinthians 15:58. Therefore, my beloved brethren, be steadfast, immovable, always abounding in the work of the Lord, knowing that your toil is not in vain in the Lord.

2 Corinthians 1:19. For the Son of God, Christ Jesus, who was preached among you by us,— by me and Silvanus and Timothy—was not yes and no, but is yes in Him.

2 Corinthians 3:2-3. You are our letter, written in our hearts, known and read by all men; being manifested that you are a letter of Christ, cared for by us, written not with ink, but with the Spirit of the living God, not on tablets of stone, but on tablets of human hearts.

2 Corinthians 4:5. For we do not preach ourselves but Christ Jesus as Lord, and ourselves as your bond-servants for Jesus' sake.

2 Corinthians 5:18-20. Now all these things are from God, who reconciled us to Himself through Christ, and gave us the ministry of reconciliation, namely, that God was in Christ reconciling the world to Himself, not counting their trespasses against them, and He has committed to us the word of reconciliation. Therefore, we are ambassadors for Christ, as though God were entreating through us; we beg you on behalf of Christ, be reconciled to God.

Acts 18:19-21. And they came to Ephesus, and he left them there. Now he himself entered the synagogue and reasoned with the Jews. And when they asked him to stay for a longer time, he did not consent, but taking leave of them and saying, "I will return to you again if God wills," he set sail from Ephesus.

Acts 18:22-23. And when he had landed at Caesarea, he went up and greeted the church, and went down to Antioch. And having spent some time there, he departed and passed successively through the Galatian region and Phrygia, strengthening all the disciples.

Acts 18:24-28. Now a certain Jew named Apollos, an Alexandrian by birth, an eloquent man, came to Ephesus; and he was mighty in the Scriptures. This man had been instructed in the way of the Lord; and being fervent in spirit, he was speaking and teaching accurately the things concerning Jesus, being acquainted only with the baptism of John; and he began to speak out boldly in the synagogue. But when Priscilla and Aquila heard him, they took him aside and explained to him the way of God more accurately. And when he wanted to go across to Achaia, the brethren encouraged him and wrote to the disciples to welcome him; and when he had arrived, he helped greatly those who had believed through grace; for he powerfully refuted the Jews in public, demonstrating by the Scriptures that Jesus was the Christ.

Acts 19:1-7. And it came about that while Apollos was at Corinth, Paul having passed through the upper country came to Ephesus, and found some disciples, and he said to them, "Did you receive the Holy Spirit when you believed?" And they said to him, "No, we have not even heard whether there is a Holy Spirit." And he said, "Into what then were you baptized?" And they said, "Into John's baptism." And Paul said, "John baptized with the baptism of repentence, telling the people to believe in Him who was coming after him, that is, in Jesus." And when they heard this, they were baptized in the name of the Lord Jesus. And when Paul had laid his hands upon them, the Holy Spirit came on them, and they began speaking with tongues and prophesying. And there were in all about twelve men.

Acts 19:8. And he entered the synagogue and continued speaking out boldly for three months, reasoning and persuading them about the kingdom of God.

Acts 19:9. But when some were becoming hardened and disobedient, speaking evil of the Way before the multitude, he withdrew from them and took away the disciples, reasoning daily in the school of Tyrannus.

Acts 19:10, 20. And this took place for two years, so that all who lived in Asia heard the word of the Lord, both Jews and Greeks. . . . So the word of the Lord was growing mightily and prevailing.

Acts 19:23; 20:1-2. And about that time there arose no small disturbance concerning the Way. . . . And after the uproar had ceased, Paul sent for the disciples and when he had exhorted them and taken his leave of them, he departed to go to Macedonia. And when he had gone through those districts and had given them much exhortation, he came to Greece.

THE EPISTLE TO THE ROMANS

Romans 1:8. First, I thank my God through Jesus Christ for you all, because your faith is being proclaimed throughout the whole world.

Romans 1:9-13. For God, whom I serve in my spirit in the preaching of the gospel of His Son, is my witness as to how unceasingly I make mention of you, always in my prayers making request, if perhaps now at last by the will of God I may succeed in coming to you. For I long to see you in order that I may impart some spiritual gift to you, that you may be established; that is, that I may be encouraged together with you while among you, each of us by the other's faith, both yours and mine. And I do not want you to be unaware, brethren, that often I have planned to come to you (and have been prevented thus far) in order that I might obtain some fruit among you also, even as among the rest of the Gentiles.

Romans 1:14-15. I am under obligation both to Greeks and to barbarians, both to the wise and to the foolish. Thus, for my part, I am eager to preach the gospel to you also who are in Rome.

Romans 13:8-10. Owe nothing to anyone except to love one another; for he who loves his neighbor has fulfilled the law. For this, YOU SHALL NOT COMMIT ADULTERY, YOU SHALL NOT

MURDER, YOU SHALL NOT
STEAL, YOU SHALL NOT COVET,"
and if there is any other commandment, it is summed up in
this saying, "YOU SHALL LOVE
YOUR NEIGHBOR AS YOURSELF."
Love does no wrong to a neighbor; love therefore is the fulfillment of the law.

Romans 16:25-27. Now to Him who is able to establish you according to my gospel and the preaching of Jesus Christ, according
to the revelation of the mystery which has been kept secret for
long ages past, but now is manifested, and by the Scriptures of the
prophets, according to the commandment of the eternal God, has
been made known to all the nations, leading to obedience of faith;
to the only wise God, through Jesus Christ, to whom be the glory
forever. Amen.

Acts 20:6-7. And we sailed from
Philippi after the days of Un-
leavened Bread, and came to
them at Troas within five days;
and there we stayed seven days.
And on the first day of the
week, when we were gathered
together to break bread, Paul began talking to them, intending
to depart the next day, and he
prolonged his message until
midnight.

Acts 20:17-21. And from Miletus he sent to Ephesus and
called to him the elders of the
church. And when they had
come to him, he said to them,
"You yourselves know, from the
first day that I set foot in Asia,
how I was with you the whole
time, serving the Lord with all
humility and with tears and with

Acts 20:22-24. And now, behold, bound in spirit, I am on my way to Jerusalem, not knowing what will happen to me there, except that the Holy Spirit solemnly testifies to me in every city, saying that bonds and afflictions await me. But I do not consider my life of any account as dear to myself, in order that I may finish my course, and the ministry which I received from the Lord Jesus, to testify solemnly of the gospel of the grace of God.

trials which came upon me through the plots of the Jews; how I did not shrink from declaring to you anything that was profitable, and teaching you publicly and from house to house, solemnly testifying to both Jews and Greeks of repentence toward God and faith in our Lord Jesus Christ.

Acts 20:25-35. And now, behold, I know that you all, among whom I went about preaching the kingdom, will see my face no more. Therefore I testify to you this day, that I am innocent of the blood of all men. For I did not shrink from declaring to you the whole purpose of God. Be on guard for yourselves and for all the flock, among which the Holy Spirit has made you overseers, to shepherd the church of God which He purchased with His own blood. I know that after my departure savage wolves will come in among you, not sparing the flock; and from among your own selves men will arise, speaking perverse things, to draw away the disciples after them. Therefore be on the alert, remembering that night and day for a period of three years I did not cease to admonish each one with tears. And now I commend you to God and to the word of His grace, which is able to build you up and to give you the inheritance among all those who are sanctified. I have coveted no one's silver or gold or clothes. You yourselves know that these hands ministered to my own needs and to the men who were with me. In every thing I showed you that by working hard in this manner you must help the weak and remember the words of the Lord Jesus, that He Himself said, "It is more blessed to give than to receive."

Acts 22. (Paul's testimony in Jerusalem)

Acts 23. (Paul's testimony before the Council)

Acts 24. (Paul's testimony before Felix)

Acts 25. (Paul's testimony before Festus)

Acts 26. (Paul's testimony before Agrippa)

Acts 27. (Paul sails to Rome)

Acts 28:23-24. And when they had set a day for him, they came to him at his lodging in large numbers; and he was explaining to them by solemnly testifying about the kingdom of God, and trying to persuade them concerning Jesus, from both the Law of Moses and from the Prophets, from morning until evening. And some were being persuaded by the things spoken, but others would not believe.

THE PRISON EPISTLES

PHILEMON
EPHESIANS

Ephesians 1:15-19a; 3:14-19. For this reason I too, having heard of the faith in the Lord Jesus which exists among you, and your love for all the saints, do not cease giving thanks for you, while making mention of you in my prayers; that the God of our Lord Jesus Christ, the Father of glory, may give to you a spirit of wisdom and of

Acts 28:30-31. And he stayed two full years in his own rented quarters, and was welcoming all who came to him, preaching the kingdom of God, and teaching concerning the Lord Jesus Christ with all openness, unhindered.

Ephesians 3:8-9. To me, the very least of all saints, this grace was given, to preach to the Gentiles the unfathomable riches of Christ, and to bring to light what is the administration of the mystery which for ages has been hidden in God, who created all things.

revelation in the knowledge of Him. I pray that the eyes of your heart may be enlightened, so that you may know what is the hope of His calling, what are the riches of the glory of His inheritance in the saints, and what is the surpassing greatness of His power toward us who believe. . . . For this reason, I bow my knees before the Father, from whom every family in heaven and on earth derives its name, that He would grant you, according to the riches of His glory, to be strengthened with power through His Spirit in the inner man; so that Christ may dwell in your hearts through faith; and that you, being rooted and grounded in love, may be able to comprehend with all the saints what is the breadth and length and height and depth, and to know the love of Christ which surpasses knowledge, that you may be filled up to all the fulness of God.

Ephesians 2:19-22. So then you are no longer strangers and aliens, but you are fellow-citizens with the saints, and are of God's household, having been built upon the foundation of the apostles and prophets, Christ Jesus Himself being the cornerstone, in whom the whole building, being fitted together is growing into a holy temple in the Lord; in whom you also are being built together into a dwelling of God in the Spirit.

Ephesians 4:11-16. And He gave some as apostles, and some as prophets, and some as evangelists, and some as pastors and teachers, for the equipping of the saints for the work of service, to the building up of the body of Christ; until we all attain to the unity of the faith, and of the knowledge of the Son of God, to a mature man, to the measure of the stature which belongs to the fulness of Christ. As a result, we are no longer to be children, tossed here and there by waves, and carried about by every wind of doctrine, by the trickery of men, by craftiness in deceitful scheming; but speaking the truth in love, we are to grow up in all aspects into Him, who is the head, even Christ, from whom the whole body, being fitted and held together by that which every joint supplies, according to the proper working of each individual part, causes the growth of the body for the building up of itself in love.

Ephesians 6:1-4. Children, obey your parents in the Lord, for this is right. Honor your father and mother (which is the first commandment with a promise), that it may be well with you, and that you may live long on the earth. And, fathers, do not provoke your children to anger; but bring them up in the discipline and instruction of the Lord.

COLOSSIANS

Colossians 1:9-12. For this reason also, since the day we heard of it, we have not ceased to pray for you and to ask that you may be filled with the knowledge of His will in all spiritual wisdom and understanding, so that you may walk in a manner worthy of the Lord, to please Him in all respects, bearing fruit in every good work and increasing in the knowledge of God; strengthened with all power, according to His glorious might, for the attaining of all steadfastness and patience, joyously giving thanks to the Father, who has qualified us to share in the inheritance of the saints in light.

Colossians 1:25-29. Of this church I was made a minister according to the stewardship from God bestowed on me for your benefit, that I might fully carry out the preaching of the word of God, that is, the mystery which has been hidden from the past ages and generations; but has now been manifested to His saints, to whom God willed to make known what is the riches of the glory of this mystery among the Gentiles, which is Christ in you, the hope of glory. And we proclaim Him, admonishing every man and teaching every man with all wisdom that we may present every man complete in Christ.

Colossians 4:5-6. Conduct yourselves with wisdom toward outsiders, making the most of the opportunity. Let your speech always be with grace, seasoned, as it were, with salt, so that you may know how you should respond to each person.

And for this purpose also I labor, striving according to His power, which mightily works within me.

Colossians 2:2-5. That their hearts may be encouraged, having been knit together in love, and attaining to all the wealth that comes from the full assurance of understanding, resulting in a true knowledge of God's mystery, that is, Christ Himself, in whom are hidden all the treasures of wisdom and knowledge. I say this in order that no one may delude you with persuasive argument. For even though I am absent in body, nevertheless I am with you in spirit, rejoicing to see your good discipline and the stability of your faith in Christ.

Colossians 3:16. Let the word of Christ richly dwell within you; with all wisdom teaching and admonishing one another with psalms and hymns and spiritual songs, singing with thankfulness in your hearts to God.

Colossians 3:18-23. Wives, be subject to your husbands, as is fitting in the Lord. Husbands, love your wives, and do not be embittered against them. Children, be obedient to your parents in all things, for this is well pleasing to the Lord. Fathers, do not exasperate your children, that they may not lose heart. Slaves, in all things obey those who are your masters on earth, not with external service, as those who merely please men, but with sincerity of heart, fearing the Lord. Whatever you do, do your work heartily, as for the Lord rather than for men.

PHILIPPIANS

Philippians 1:12-14. Now I want you to know, brethren, that my circumstances have turned out for the greater progress of the gospel, so that my imprisonment in the cause of Christ has become well-known throughout the whole praetorian guard and to everyone else, and that most of the brethren, trusting in the Lord because of my imprisonment, have far more courage to speak the word of God without fear.

Philippians 1:27-28. Only conduct yourselves in a manner worthy of the gospel of Christ; so that whether I come and see you or remain absent, I may hear of you that you are standing firm in one spirit, with one mind striving together for the faith of the gospel; in no way alarmed by your opponents—which is a sign of destruction for them, but of salvation for you, and that too, from God.

Philippians 2:1-4. If therefore there is any encouragement in Christ, if there is any consolation of love, if there is any fellowship of the Spirit, if any affection and compassion, make my joy complete by being of the same mind, maintaining the same love, united in spirit, intent on one purpose. Do nothing from selfishness or empty conceit, but with humility of mind let each of you regard one anther as more important than himself; do not merely look out for your own personal interests, but also for the interests of others.

Philippians 2:19-24. But I hope in the Lord Jesus to send Timothy to you shortly, so that I also may be encouraged when I learn of your condition. For I have no one else of kindred spirit who will genuinely be concerned for your welfare. For they all seek after their own interests, not those of Christ Jesus. But you know of his proven worth that he served with me in the furtherance of the gospel like a child serving his father. Therefore I hope to send him immediately, as soon as I see how things go with me; and I trust in the Lord that I myself also shall be coming shortly.

Philippians 4:9. The things you have learned and received and heard and seen in me, practice these things; and the God of peace shall be with you.

THE PASTORAL EPISTLES

1 TIMOTHY

1 Timothy 2:1-7. First of all, then, I urge that entreaties and prayers, petitions and thanksgivings, be made on behalf of all men, for kings and all who are in authority, in order that we may lead a tranquil and quiet life in all godliness and dignity. This is good and acceptable in the sight of God our

1 Timothy 1:3-7. As I urged you upon my departure from Macedonia, remain on at Ephesus, in order that you may instruct certain men not to teach strange doctrines, nor to pay attention to myths and endless genealogies, which give rise to mere speculation rather than furthering God's provision which is by

Saviour, who desires all men to be saved and to come to the knowledge of the truth. For there is one God, and one mediator also between God and men, the man Christ Jesus, who gave Himself a ransom for all, the testimony borne at the proper time. And for this I was appointed a preacher and an apostle (I am telling the truth, I am not lying) as a teacher of the Gentiles in faith and truth.

faith. But the goal of our instruction is love from a pure heart and a good conscience and a sincere faith. For some men, straying from these things, have turned aside to fruitless discussion, wanting to be teachers of the Law, even though they do not understand either what they are saying or the matters about which they make confident assertions.

1 Timothy 4:11-16. Prescribe and teach these things. Let no one look down on your youthfulness, but rather in speech, conduct, love, faith and purity, show yourself an example of those who believe. Until I come, give attention to the public reading of Scripture, to exhortation and teaching. Do not neglect the spiritual gift within you, which was bestowed upon you through prophetic utterance with the laying on of hands by the presbytery. Take pains with these things; be absorbed in them, so that your progress may be evident to all. Pay close attention to yourself and to your teaching; persevere in these things; for as you do this you will insure salvation both for yourself and for those who hear you.

1 Timothy 5:17. Let the elders who rule well be considered worthy of double honor, especially those who work hard at preaching and teaching.

1 Timothy 6:1-2. Let all who are under the yoke as slaves regard their own masters as worthy of all honor so that the name of God and our doctrine may not be spoken against.

And let those who have believers as their masters not be disrespectful to them because they are brethren, but let them serve them all the more, because those who partake of the benefit are believers and beloved. Teach and preach these principles.

2 TIMOTHY

2 Timothy 1:6-11. And for this reason I remind you to kindle afresh the gift of God which is in you through the laying on of my hands. For God has not given us a spirit of timidity, but of power and love and discipline. Therefore do not be ashamed of the testimony of our Lord, or of me His prisoner; but join with me in suffering for the gospel according to the power of God; who has saved us, and called us with a holy calling, not according to our works, but according to His own purpose and grace which was granted us in Christ Jesus from all eternity, but now has been revealed by the appearing of our Savior Christ Jesus, who abolished death, and brought life and immortality to light through the gospel, for which I was appointed a preacher and an apostle and a teacher.

2 **Timothy 2:2.** And the things which you have heard from me in the presence of many witnesses, these entrust to faithful men, who will be able to teach others also.

2 **Timothy 3:14-17.** You, however, continue in the things you have learned and become convinced of, knowing from whom you have learned them; and that from childhood you have known the sacred writings which are able to give you the wisdom that leads to salvation through faith which is in Christ Jesus. All Scripture is inspired by God and profitable for teaching, for reproof, for correction, for training in righteousness; that the man of God may be adequate, equipped for every good work.

2 **Timothy 4:4-5.** And will turn away their ears from the truth, and will turn aside to myths. But you, be sober in all things, endure hardship, do the work of an evangelist, fulfill your ministry.

2 **Timothy 4:1-2.** I solemnly charge you in the presence of God and of Christ Jesus, who is to judge the living and the dead, and by His appearing and His kingdom: preach the word; be ready in season and out of season; reprove, rebuke, exhort, with great patience and instruction.

TITUS

Titus 1:5. For this reason I left you in Crete, that you might set in order what remains, and appoint elders in every city as I directed you. . . .

Titus 2:1-15. But as for you, speak the things which are fitting for sound doctrine. Older

men are to be temperate, dignified, sensible, sound in faith, in
love, in perseverance. Older
women likewise are to be rever-
ent in their behavior, not malicious gossips, nor enslaved to
much wine, teaching what is
good, that they may encourage
the young women to love their
husbands, to love their children,
to be sensible, pure, workers at
home, kind, being subject to
their own husbands, that the
word of God may not be dis-
honored. Likewise urge the
young men to be sensible; in
all things show yourself to be
an example of good deeds, with
purity in doctrine, dignified,
sound in speech which is beyond reproach, in order that
the opponent may be put to
shame, having nothing bad to
say about us. Urge bondslaves
to be subject to their own masters in everything, to be well
pleasing, not argumentative, not
pilfering, but showing all good
faith that they may adorn the
doctrine of God our Savior in
every respect. For the grace of
God has appeared, bringing salvation to all men, instructing us
to deny ungodliness and world-
ly desires and to live sensibly,
righteously and godly in the
present age, looking for the
blessed hope and the appearing
of the glory of our great God
and Savior, Christ Jesus; who
gave Himself for us, that He
might redeem us from every

lawless deed and purify for Himself a people for His own possession, zealous for good deeds. These things speak and exhort and reprove with all authority. Let no one disregard you.

ADDITIONAL EPISTLES
HEBREWS, PETER, JOHN

Hebrews 3:12-14. Take care, brethren, lest there should be in any one of you an evil, unbelieving heart, in falling away from the living God. But encourage one another day after day, as long as it is still called "Today," lest any one of you be hardened by the deceitfulness of sin. For we have become partakers of Christ, if we hold fast the beginning of our assurance firm until the end. . . .

Hebrews 5:12-14. For though by this time you ought to be teachers, you have need again for some one to teach you the elementary principles of the oracles of God, and you have come to need milk and not solid food. For every one who partakes only of milk is not accustomed to the word of righteousness, for he is a babe. But solid food is for the mature, who because of practice have their senses trained to discern good and evil.

Hebrews 6:1. Therefore leaving the elementary teaching about the Christ, let us press on to maturity, not laying again a foundation of repentance from dead works and of faith toward God.

Hebrews 10:24-25. And let us consider how to stimulate one another to love and good deeds, not forsaking our own assembling together, as is the habit of some, but encouraging one another; and all the more, as you see the day drawing near.

1 PETER

1 Peter 2:1-5. Therefore, putting aside all malice and all guile and hypocrisy and envy and all slander, like newborn babes, long for the pure milk of the word, that by it you may grow in respect to salvation, if you have tasted the kindness of the Lord. And coming to Him as to a living stone, rejected by men, but choice and precious in the sight of God, you also, as living stones, are being built up as a spiritual house for a holy priesthood, to offer up spiritual sacrifices acceptable to God through Jesus Christ.

1 Peter 4:10-11. As each one has received a special gift, employ it in serving one another, as good stewards of the manifold grace of God. Whoever speaks, let him speak, as it were, the utterances of God; whoever serves, let him do so as by the strength which God supplies; so that in all things God may be glorified through Jesus Christ,

1 Peter 2:12. Keep your behavior excellent among the Gentiles, so that in the thing in which they slander you as evildoers, they may on account of your good deeds, as they observe them, glorify God in the day of visitation.

1 Peter 2:18. Servants, be submissive to your masters with all respect, not only to those who are good and gentle, but also to those who are unreasonable.

1 Peter 3:1-2. In the same way, you wives, be submissive to your own husbands so that even if any one of them are disobedient to the word they may be won without a word by the behavior of their wives, as they observe your chaste and respectful behavior.

1 Peter 3:15. But sanctify Christ as Lord in your hearts, always being ready to make a defense to every one who asks you to give an account for the hope that is in you, yet with gentleness and reverence.

to whom belongs the glory and dominion forever and ever. Amen.

1 Peter 5:1-3. Therefore, I exhort the elders among you, as your fellow-elder and witness of the sufferings of Christ, and a partaker also of the glory that is to be revealed, shepherd the flock of God among you, not under compulsion, but voluntarily, according to the will of God; and not for sordid gain, but with eagerness; not yet as lording it over those allotted to your charge, but proving to be examples to the flock.

1 JOHN

1 John 1:1-4. What was from the beginning, what we have heard, what we have seen with our eyes, what we beheld and our hands handled, concerning the Word of life—and the life was manifested, and we have seen and bear witness and proclaim to you the eternal life, which was with the Father and was manifested to us—

what we have seen and heard we proclaim to you also, that you also may have fellowship with us; and indeed our fellowship is with the Father, and with His Son Jesus Christ. And these things we write, so that our joy may be made complete.

Appendix B
ACTIVITIES AND DIRECTIVES—
RESULTS AND OBJECTIVES

This compilation of activities and directives with results and objectives is made from the book of Acts and the epistles. Section 1 relates to evangelism, and Section 2 relates to edification.

EVANGELISM	
ACTIVITY AND DIRECTIVES	RESULTS AND OBJECTIVES
Acts	
Declaring Speaking Teaching Proclaiming Preaching Testifying Witnessing Exhorting Praising Reasoning Refuting Explaining Demonstrating Giving evidence Persuading	They had favor with all the people (2:47). Many believed (4:4). The people held them in high esteem (5:13). The Word of God kept on spreading (6:7). The number of the disciples continued to increase greatly (6:7). Many of the priests were becoming obedient to the faith (6:7). The multitudes were giving attention to what was said (8:6). They spoke in tongues (10:45). A large number turned to the Lord (11:21). The people kept begging that these things might be spoken to them the next sabbath (13:42).

Nearly the whole city (Pisidian Antioch) assembled to hear the Word of God (13:44).

They made disciples (14:21).

Some were persuaded (17:4).

Received the Word with great eagerness, and examined the Scriptures daily to see whether these things were so (17:11).

Epistles

For our gospel did not come to you in word only, but also in power and in the Holy Spirit and with full conviction. . . .

You also became imitators of us and the Lord, having received the word in much tribulation with the joy of the Holy Spirit (1 Th 1:5-6).

For the word of the Lord hath sounded forth from you, . . . in every place your faith toward God has gone. . . .

For they themselves report . . . how you turned to God from idols to serve a living and true God (1 Th 1:8-9).

Make it your ambition to lead a quiet life and attend to your own business and work with your own hands, . . .

so that you may behave properly toward outsiders and not be in any need (1 Th 4:11-12).

that the word of the Lord may spread rapidly and be glorified (2 Th 3:1).

Paul for us [Paul, Silas, Timothy]

Whether, then, you eat or drink or whatever you do, do all to the glory of God. Give no offense either to Jews or to Greeks or to the church of God; just as I also please all men in all things, not seeking my own profit, but the profit of the many,

that they may be saved (1 Co 10:31-33).

Prophesy. . . .

He is convicted by all, he is called to account by all; the secrets of his heart are disclosed; . . . so he will fall on his face and worship God, declaring that God is among you (1 Co 14:24-25).

You are our letter, . . .
I thank my God through Jesus Christ for you all, . . .

known and read by all men (2 Co 3:2).

Love your neighbor as yourself (Ro 13:9).

because your faith is being proclaimed throughout the whole world (Ro 1:8).

Pray on my behalf, . . .

that utterance may be given to me in the opening of my mouth, to make known with boldness the mystery of the gospel (Eph 6:19).

Conduct yourselves with wisdom toward outsiders, making the most of the opportunity (Col 4:5).
Let your speech always be with grace, seasoned, as it were, with salt,

so that you may know how you should respond to each person (Col 4:6).

Conduct yourselves with wisdom worthy of the gospel . . .

so that . . . you are standing firm in one spirit, with one mind striving together for the faith

[Make] entreaties and prayers, petitions and thanksgiving. . . on behalf of all men, . . .

in order that we may lead a tranquil and quiet life in all godliness and dignity (1 Ti 2:1-2).

of the gospel; in no way alarmed by your opponents (Phil 1:27-28).

Regard [unsaved] masters as worthy of all honor,

so that the name of God and our doctrine may not be spoken against (1 Ti 6:1).

From childhood you have known the sacred writings

which are able to give you the wisdom that leads to salvation through faith which is in Christ Jesus (2 Ti 3:15).

Do the work of an evangelist (2 Ti 4:5).

Keep your behavior excellent among the Gentiles,

so that . . . they may . . . glorify God in the day of visitation (1 Pe 2:12).

Be submissive to your masters (1 Pe 2:18).

Be submissive to your [unsaved] husbands

so . . . they may be won without a word by the behavior of their wives (1 Pe 3:1-2).

[Be] ready to make a defense to every one who asks you to give an account for the hope that is in you (1 Pe 3:15).
Keep a good conscience

so that . . . those who revile your good behavior . . . may be put to shame (1 Pe 3:16).

EDIFICATION	
ACTIVITY AND DIRECTIVES	RESULTS AND OBJECTIVES
Acts	
Baptizing Teaching Fellowshipping Breaking Bread Praying Praising God Encouraging Strengthening Reporting Describing Dissenting Debating Writing Imploring Exhorting Establishing Admonishing	Were of one mind (2:46) Taking their meals together with gladness and sincerity of heart (2:46) Were of one heart and soul (4:32) Enjoyed peace (9:31) Were being built up (9:31) Brought great joy to all the brethren (15:3) Rejoiced because of its (the letters) encouragement (15:31) The churches were being strengthened in the faith (15:32) The word of the Lord was growing mightily and prevailing (19:20)
Epistles	
We were exhorting and encouraging and imploring each one of you, . . .	so that you may walk in a manner worthy of the God who calls you (1 Th 2:11-12).
We . . . keep praying . . . that we may see your face,	and may complete what is lacking in your faith (1 Th 3:10).
May the Lord cause you	to increase and abound in love for one another, and for all men (1 Th 3:12).
We request and exhort you in [the name of Jesus Christ] that, as you received from us instruction as to how you ought to to walk and please God, . . .	that you may excel still more (1 Th 4:1).

You yourselves are taught by God to love one another. . . .

But we urge you, brethren, to excel still more (1 Th 4:9-10).

Encourage one another (1 Th 5:11).

Build up one another (1 Th 5:11).

Admonish the unruly (1 Th 5:14).

Encourage the fainthearted (1 Th 5:14).
Help the weak (1 Th 5:14).
Seek after that which is good for one another (1 Th 5:15).
To this end also we pray for you always that our God may count you worthy of your calling, and fulfill every desire for goodness and the work of faith with power; . . .

in order that the name of our Lord Jesus may be glorified in you, and you in Him (2 Th 1:11-12).

All agree . . . [avoid divisions], . . .

be made complete in the same mind, (1 Co 1:10)

I have sent to you Timothy . . .

and he will remind you of my ways which are in Christ, just as I teach everywhere in every church (1 Co 4:17).

Be imitators of me, just as I . . . am of Christ (1 Co 11:1).

Seek to abound for the edification of the church (1 Co 14:12).

When you assemble, each one has a psalm, has a teaching, has a revelation, has a tongue, has an interpretation.

Let all things be done for edification (1 Co 14:26).

Always [abound] in the work of the Lord (1 Co15:58).

This we also pray for,

        that you be made complete (2 Co 13:9).

Rejoice, be made complete, be comforted, be like-minded, live in peace;

        and the God of love and peace shall be with you (2 Co 13:11).

I long to see you . . .

        that I may impart some spiritual gift to you (Ro 1:11).

Accept one another, just as Christ also accepted us (Ro 15:7).

I urge you . . . to present your bodies a living and holy sacrifice. . . . And do not be conformed to this world, but be transformed by the renewing of your mind,

        that you may prove what the will of God is, that which is good and acceptable and perfect (Ro 12:1-2).

Let us pursue the things

        which make for peace and the building up of one another (Ro 14:19).

Now we who are strong ought to bear the weaknessess of those without strength (Ro 15:1).

Now may the God who gives perseverance . . .

        grant you to be of the same mind with one another according to Christ Jesus (Ro 15:5).

Now may the God of hope

        fill you with all joy and peace in believing, that you may abound in hope by the power of the Holy Spirit (Ro 15:13).

[I] do not cease giving thanks for you, while making mention of you in my prayers;

that . . . God . . . may give to you a spirit of wisdom and of revelation in the knowledge of Him (Eph 1:16-17) that the eyes of your heart may be enlightened . . .

that you may know what is the hope of His calling (Eph 1:18).

that you may know . . . what are the riches of the glory of His inheritance in the saints (Eph 1:18).

[that you may know] what is the surpassing greatness of His power toward us who believe (Eph 1:19).

[that you may] be strengthened with power through His Spirit in the inner man (Eph 3:16).

that Christ may dwell in your hearts through faith (Eph 3:17).

[that you] may be able to comprehend . . . the breadth and length and height and depth, and to know the love of Christ which surpasses knowledge (Eph 3:18-19).

that you may be filled up to all the fulness of God (Eph 3:19).

[Apostles, prophets, evangelists, pastors, and teachers are given]

for the equipping of the saints for the work of service . . .

until we all attain to the unity of the faith, and of the knowledge of the Son of God, to a mature man,

[that] we are no longer . . . children, tossed here and there; . . .

[that] the whole body [be] held

Children, obey your parents (Eph 6:1).

Honor your father and mother . . . ,

together by that which every joint supplies, . . .

for the building up of itself in love (Eph 4:11-16).

that it may be well with you (Eph 6:2-3).

Fathers, do not provoke your children to anger; but bring them up in the discipline and instruction of the Lord (Eph 6:4). Do not exasperate your children,

We pray for you,

that they may not lose heart (Col 3:21).

that you may walk in a manner worthy of the Lord.

[that . . . you may] please Him in all respects,

. . . bearing fruit in every good work (Col 1:9-10).

We . . . [admonish] and [teach] every man . . .

that we may present every man complete in Christ (Col 1:28).

As you therefore have received Christ Jesus the Lord,

so walk in Him, having been firmly rooted and now being built up in Him and established in your faith, just as you were instructed, and overflowing with gratitude (Col 2:6-7).

In Him

you have been made complete (Col 2:10).

[Hold] fast to the Head, from whom the entire body, being supplied and held together by the joints and ligaments,

grows with a growth which is from God (Col 2:19).

And beyond all these things put on love,

which is the perfect bond of unity (Col 3:14).

Teaching and admonishing one another with psalms and hymns and spiritual songs (Col 3:16).

Wives, be subject to your husbands (Col 3:18).

Husbands, love your wives (Col 3:19).

Whatever you do, do your work heartily, as for the Lord rather than for men (Col 3:23).

Make my joy complete by being of the same mind, maintaining the same love, united in spirit (Phil 2:2).

[Be] intent on one purpose. Do nothing from selfishness or empty conceit, but with humility of mind let each of you regard one another as more important than himself (Phil 2:2-3).

I [Paul] press on toward the goal for the prize of the upward call of God in Christ Jesus (Phil 3:14).

The things you have learned and received and heard and seen in me, practice these things (Phil 4:9).

The goal of our instruction is love from a pure heart and a good conscience and a sincere faith (1 Ti 1:5).

Prescribe and teach these things. . . . Give attention to the public reading of Scripture, to exhortation and teaching (1 Ti 4:11, 13).

[Appoint elders] (1 Ti 5:17).

[do] not be disrespectful to [believing masters] (1 Ti 6:2).

And the things which you have heard from me in the presence of many witnesses, these entrust to faithful men, who will be able to teach others also (2 Ti 2:2).

All Scripture is inspired by God and profitable for teaching, for reproof, for correction, for training in righteousness; that the man of God may be adequate, equipped for every good work (2 Ti 3:16-17).

Preach the word; be ready in season and out of season; reprove, rebuke, exhort (2 Ti 4:2).
Set in order what remains (Titus 1:5).
Speak the things which are fitting for sound doctrine (Titus 2:1).

Leav[e] the elementary teaching about the Christ,
Now the God of peace . . . press on to maturity (Heb 6:1).
equip you in every good thing to do His will (Heb 13:20-21).

Long for the pure milk of the word, that by it you may grow in respect to salvation (1 Pe 2:2).

Submit yourselves for the Lord's sake to every human institution: whether to a king as the one in authority; or to governers as sent by him for the punishment of evildoers and the praise of those who do right.
For such is the will of God that by doing right you may silence the ignorance of foolish men (1 Pe 2:13-15).

Shepherd the flock of God (1 Pe 5:2).
These things we write, . . . that your joy may be made complete (1 Jn 1:4).

Contend earnestly for the faith (Jude 1:3).
Keep yourselves in the love of God (Jude 1:21).

SELECTED BIBLIOGRAPHY

These books have been selected for the following reasons:
1. As of the date of publication of *Sharpening the Focus of the Church,* they are relatively current and contemporary.
2. They all speak to the problems of the church in the twentieth century.
3. Though they are all basically evangelical, they represent a variety of viewpoints—both theologically and in their suggestions for correcting the ills of the church.
4. They all can be used to stimulate discussion and interaction.

You will not (as I do not) agree with everything that is said. But you cannot ignore the concerns expressed by the various authors.

NOTE: No attempt has been made to list in the bibliography the many resources used in writing this book, such as commentaries, exegetical works, dictionaries, historical works, and articles and books analyzing contemporary culture.

Girard, Robert C. *Brethren, Hang Loose.* Grand Rapids: Zondervan, 1972.
Halverson, Richard C. *How I Changed My Thinking About the Church.* Grand Rapids: Zondervan, 1972.
Haney, David. *Renew My Church.* Grand Rapids: Zondervan, 1972.
Henley, Gary. *The Quiet Revolution.* Carol Stream, Ill. Creation House, 1970.
Kuen, Alfred F. *I Will Build My Church.* Chicago: Moody, 1971.
Larson, Bruce & Osborne, Ralph. *The Emerging Church.* Waco, Tex.: Word, 1970.
Mains, David R. *Full Circle.* Waco, Tex.: Word, 1971.
Patterson, Bob E. *The Stirring Giant.* Waco, Tex.: Word, 1971.
Peters, George W. *Saturation Evangelism.* Grand Rapids: Zondervan, 1970.
Richards, Lawrence O. *A New Face for the Church.* Grand Rapids: Zondervan, 1970.
Schaeffer, Francis A. *The Church at the End of the 20th Century.* Downers Grove, Ill.: Inter-Varsity, 1970.
———. *The Church Before the Watching World.* Downers Grove, Ill.: Inter-Varsity, 1971.
Stedman, Ray C. *Body Life.* Glendale, Calif.: Gospel Light, 1972.

INDEX